my vocabulary did this to me

wesleyan poetry

my vocabulary did this to me

The Collected Poetry of
JACK SPICER

Edited by Peter Gizzi and Kevin Killian

Wesleyan University Press Middletown, Connecticut

Published by Wesleyan University Press
Middletown, CT 06459
www.wesleyan.edu/wespress
© 2008 by the Estate of Jack Spicer
Introduction © 2008 by Peter Gizzi and Kevin Killian
Printed in the United States of America
5 4 3 2 1

Library of Congress Cataloging in Publication Data

Spicer, Jack.
My vocabulary did this to me : the collected poetry of Jack Spicer /
edited by Peter Gizzi and Kevin Killian.
    p.   cm. — (Wesleyan poetry)
Includes bibliographical references and index.
ISBN 978–0-8195–6887–8 (cloth : alk. paper)
I. Gizzi, Peter. II. Killian, Kevin. III. Title.
PS3569.P47M9 2008
811'.54—dc22   2008024997

FRONTISPIECE ILLUSTRATION: Jack Spicer at the 6 Gallery
opening in San Francisco, 1954. Photo © Robert Berg.

This project is supported in part by an award from the National
Endowment for the Arts

NATIONAL
ENDOWMENT
FOR THE ARTS
A great nation
deserves great art.

Wesleyan University Press is a member of the
Green Press Initiative. The paper used in this book
meets their minimum requirement for recycled paper.

CONTENTS

II. (1956–1965)

SAN FRANCISCO (1956–1965)

ACKNOWLEDGMENTS

Many helped us in the years during which we edited this book. First of all, we would like to thank Robin Blaser, who shepherded these materials for forty years and whose edition of Spicer's *Collected Books* (1975) was a landmark volume. Blaser's kindness is legendary, but it's real. The late Donald Allen, Spicer's friend and editor, answered a hundred questions with patience. The present volume builds on the work he did in the 1957 "San Francisco Scene" issue of *Evergreen Review*, in his anthology *The New American Poetry*, and in *One Night Stand*, the volume of Spicer's shorter poems he published in 1980. To the painter Fran Herndon, we owe the survival of *The Holy Grail* manuscript, as well as the "Fix" sequence known as *Golem*, and the files of *J*, the magazine she and Spicer edited in 1959. Lewis Ellingham established chronologies, elucidated texts, sought out informants, shared his knowledge intimate and arcane, kept the flame alive—an invaluable resource in every conceivable way.

A special thanks to Anthony Bliss and Tanya Hollis of the Bancroft Library; without their generosity and vision this book could not have come to pass. At the Bancroft we owe thanks all around, and especially to Bonnie Bearden, Steven Black, Bonnie Hardwick, Jocelyn Saidenberg, Teresa Salazar, Dean Smith, and Susan Snyder. At the Special Collections and Rare Books Department of Simon Fraser University Library in Burnaby, British Columbia, we were fortunate in working with the late Charles Watts and with his successor, Tony Power. Robert Bertholf and Michael Basinski showed us many kindnesses at the Lockwood Library at SUNY Buffalo.

Thanks to Aaron Kunin for his work transcribing and inputting manuscript material newly discovered at the Bancroft in the summer of 2004. Similar help came from a crew of artists and poets including Brandon Brown, Simon Evans, Kelly Holt, David Hull, Charles Legere, Jason Morris, John Sakkis, and Logan Ryan Smith.

Many others—too many to name here—aided us with information about Spicer's life and work, alerted us to potential leads, provided cultural context for this material, made comments on the text, put us up while we were away from home on this quest, published our preliminary findings, and/or answered questions cheerfully over the past ten years. Beyond those already mentioned, we would like to thank Christopher Alexander, Joshua Beckman, Dan Bouchard, George Bowering, the late Jess Collins, the late Robert Creeley, Clark Coolidge, Beverly Dahlen, Michael Davidson, Richard Deming, Steve Dickison, Nathaniel Dorsky, Ernesto Edwards, Steve Evans, Thomas Evans, the late Landis Everson, David Farwell, Dora FitzGerald, Nemi Frost, Jack Gilbert, John Granger, George Herms, Susan Howe, Andrew Hoyem, Lisa Jarnot, Kent Jones, Daniel Katz, Joanne Kyger, Nathaniel Mackey, Michael McClure, Ben Mazer, W. S. Merwin, Alvin William Moore, Jennifer Moxley, Barbara Nicholls, Miriam Nichols, Geoffrey O'Brien, Michael Ondaatje, John Palattella, Ariel Parkinson, Kristin Prevallet, Peter and Meredith Quartermain, Tom Raworth, Adrienne Rich, Jim Roberts, Jennifer Scappettone, Don Share, Ron Silliman, Rod Smith, Matthew Stadler, George Stanley, Ellen Tallman, Glenn Todd, John Emil Vincent, Tom Vogler and Mary-Kay Gamel, Christopher Wagstaff, Anne Waldman, Rosmarie Waldrop, Emily Warn, and Scott Watson.

For their assistance in final manuscript and galley preparation we thank Sean Casey, Matthew Gagnon, Jay Johnson, Aaron Kunin, Steve Zultanski, and especially Lori Shine and Elizabeth Willis for their crucial work.

Thanks also to the folks at Wesleyan University Press and University Press of New England, but primarily to Suzanna Tamminen, Director and Editor-in-Chief at Wesleyan, for her good will, vision, and ongoing commitment to publishing Spicer's work.

Since we began working on this collection, a number of poems have appeared in the following publications, sometimes in altered form: *The Chicago Review,* "They Murdered You: An Elegy on the Death of Kenneth Rexroth"; *Eleven Eleven,* "IInd Phase of the Moon," "IIIrd Phase of the Moon," "IVth Phase of the Moon"; *Fulcrum,* "Imagine Lucifer . . ."; *Golden Handcuffs Review,* "Map Poems"; *Harper's,* "The city of Boston . . ."; *Jubilat,* "Letters to James Alexander"; *The Massachusetts Review,* "Homosexuality," "A Portrait of the Artist as a Young Landscape," "The city of Boston . . ."; *The Nation,* "Two Poems for the Nation"; *Nest,* "For Steve Jonas Who Is in Jail for Defrauding a Book Club," "A Birthday Poem for Jim (and James) Alexander"; *The Poker,* "The city of Boston . . ."; and *Poetry,* "Any fool can get into an ocean . . . ," "A Second Train Song for Gary," "Imagine Lucifer . . . ," "A Poem for Dada Day at The Place, April 1, 1958," and "Five Poems from 'Helen: A Revision.'" Our thanks to the editors involved.

And more than we can say, thanks to Dodie Bellamy and Elizabeth Willis.

INTRODUCTION

In 1965, when Jack Spicer wrote "get those words out of your mouth and into your heart," he voiced an imperative to both poet and reader addressing the perilous honesty that the lived life of the poem demands. This admonition is startling coming from a poet who claimed that his poems originated outside himself, who insisted that a poet was no more than a radio transmitting messages; a poet who professed an almost monkish practice of dictation, from "Martians" no less, who rejected what he called "the big lie of the personal"; and yet in the process he created one of the most indelible and enduring voices in American poetry. This voice, and its appeal, are all the more notable since Spicer was never fully embraced within either the official culture or counter-culture of his period. Still, in the past forty years, Spicer has had a broad and lasting effect on a diverse range of writers nationally and internationally; his impact on contemporary writing will undoubtedly be felt for generations to come.

Born John Lester Spicer on January 30, 1925, in Los Angeles, Jack Spicer was the elder of two sons. His parents, Dorothy Clause and John Lovely Spicer, were Midwesterners who met and married in Hollywood and ran a small hotel business. He attended Fairfax High School and, when ill health gave him 4-F draft status, he worked variously as a private detective, a defense worker, and an extra in Hollywood studio films.[1] Spicer spent two years at the University of Redlands in San Bernardino before transferring north to the Berkeley campus of the University of California in 1945. He had started writing poetry at fourteen, and at Berkeley he summarized his poetic influences for his professor, Josephine Miles. His parents, he told her, had been ("though naively and uncritically") fond of the early Imagists—Amy Lowell, Carl Sandburg, H.D., Pound—and had, he claimed, taught him to recite Vachel Lindsay's "The Chinese Nightingale" (1917) by the time he was three:

"How, how," he said. "Friend Chang," I said,
"San Francisco sleeps as the dead—
Ended license, lust and play:
Why do you iron the night away?
Your big clock speaks with a deadly sound,
With a tick and a wail till dawn comes round.
While the monster shadows glower and creep,
What can be better for man than sleep?"[2]

He knew the nonsense verse of Lewis Carroll and Edward Lear "from childhood up"—all his life he was to remain devoted to so-called children's literature—and at fourteen he discovered the Uranian mysteries of Oscar Wilde and A. E. Housman. Rimbaud and Dickinson, he wrote, "burst upon me like a bombshell when I was fifteen." The astonishments kept coming: by the time he was twenty-one he knew the masters of modern jazz as well as he knew the new romanticisms of T. S. Eliot, Dylan Thomas, and Stefan George. Nights spent listening to Billie Holiday and Art Tatum on Central Avenue or the Sunset Strip fueled Spicer's intimations of an international modernism centered in California, and gave heft to his 1949 manifesto, "The Poet and Poetry," in which he avowed, "We must become singers, become entertainers. [. . .] There is more of Orpheus in Sophie Tucker than in R. P. Blackmur; we have more to learn from George M. Cohan than from John Crowe Ransom."[3]

Spicer spent five years at UC Berkeley, receiving his B.A. in 1947 and his M.A. in 1950. He studied Old Norse, Anglo-Saxon, and German to prepare for a career in linguistics, and took a course or two in playwriting, adapting Hawthorne's *Young Goodman Brown* and Mary Butts's modernist grail hunt *Armed with Madness* to the stage. While taking classes with the German medievalist Ernst Kantorowicz and the poet Josephine Miles, Spicer quickly met other gay male poets, including Robin Blaser, Robert Duncan, and Landis Everson. Spicer would later cite his birth year as 1946, the year he met Blaser and Duncan; out of the intense fraternity of these bookish young men was born the "Berkeley Renaissance," as they sometimes called it, half in irony, half sincerely.

His poetry of this period is, by turns, elegiac, lyrical, modernist, and intensely homoerotic. Spicer's best-known poems of the Berkeley period became the first "Imaginary Elegies," which gained him fame when they appeared, years later, in Donald Allen's influential anthology *The New American Poetry* (1960). "When I praise the sun or any bronze god derived from it," he wrote in the first elegy, "Don't think I wouldn't rather praise the very tall blond boy / Who ate all of my potato-chips at the Red Lizard. / It's just that I won't see him when I open my eyes / And I will see the sun."[4]

A self-proclaimed anarchist, Spicer found his academic career stalled after he refused to sign the Loyalty Oath of 1950, a provision of the Sloan-Levering Act that required all California state employees (even graduate teaching assistants at Berkeley) to swear loyalty to the United States.[5] As a result, Spicer left Berkeley with an M.A. and spent much of 1950–1952 teaching at the University of Minnesota. During this time, he made his first trip to the East Coast to attend the Language Society of America conference in New York, and with David Reed, his mentor at Berkeley, published a scholarly article in linguistics.

He returned to Berkeley in 1952 and continued work on a Ph.D. he was never to finish. The early fifties were a period of retrenchment and experiment for Spicer. His production slowed, and he seemed more committed to a protracted examination of the "miracle" of the Berkeley period than to what was happening at the moment. This period of stasis ended abruptly in the spring of 1953 when, confounded by injustice and homophobia, Spicer plunged headlong into political activism with the Mattachine Society, an early gay liberation organization with headquarters in Los Angeles and chapters in Oakland, San Francisco, and Berkeley. Organizing, overseeing committees, writing white papers and mission statements on a statewide basis, serving as a delegate to a constitutional convention: all this gave him an insider's view of politics as they are lived. His fervor eventually alienated the backroom "captains" who had thought they could keep him in line, and a conservative backlash forced his resignation by the end of the year. Abruptly he moved to San Francisco where a new job awaited him as a lecturer in humanities at the California School of Fine Arts (now the San Francisco Art Institute). Here he began intimate association with visual artists, a group with whom he had had little previous contact. At the time San Francisco was undergoing a surge of vital, experimental painting and art practice, and CSFA was at the heart of it. Among Spicer's students (he was only twenty-eight, in fact younger than some of them) were an up-and-coming generation of brilliant artists from all disciplines. With five of them he founded his own avant-garde emporium, the influential "6" Gallery on Fillmore Street which became the site for the now famous first reading of Ginsberg's *Howl* and the official kick-off of the Beat Generation.[6]

Having spent two years perfecting a full-length drama, *Troilus,* Spicer once again left San Francisco during the summer of 1955 to make a career in New York City. It was the age of Poets' Theater; in New York and in Boston experimental poets were finding audiences by taking to the stage. Established modernists like T. S. Eliot, Dylan Thomas, and Archibald MacLeish were seeing their work on Broadway, some of them even winning Pulitzer Prizes. With the aid of a Berkeley friend, the painter John Button, Spicer encountered the poets of the New York School and their circle, among them Frank O'Hara, Barbara Guest, John Ashbery, James Schuyler, and Joe LeSueur.[7] Not finding suitable work and unhappy, Spicer wrote his friend Allen Joyce: "Like most primitive cultures, New York has no feeling for nonsense. Wit is as far as they can go. That is what I miss the most, other than you, and what is slowly pulling my identity apart. No one speaks Martian, no one insults people arbitrarily, there is, to put it simply and leave it, no violence of the mind and of the heart, no one screams in the elevator."[8] Within months, Spicer left New York for Boston. While Robin Blaser worked at Harvard's Widener Library, he helped Spicer secure a position on the staff of the Rare Book Room at the Boston Public Library, though this position lasted less than a year in 1955–56.

During this period Spicer found camaraderie with the Boston poets John Wieners, Joe Dunn, and Stephen Jonas. And it was here that he wrote the provocative "Unvert Manifesto" and "Song for Bird and Myself" in which he compares himself to the dead Charlie Parker as an outsider to the increasingly professionalized jazz and, by implication, poetry scenes. It was in Boston that, he said, he learned from Jonas to write from his anger. His interest in theater and his turbulent inner life came together to produce a more performative sense of poetic voice on the page.

In reviewing the then-new three-volume Johnson edition of the poems of Emily Dickinson for the *Boston Public Library Quarterly,* Spicer wrote a meticulous essay in which he points out the problem of distinguishing between Dickinson's poems and letters.[9] The significance of this finding would manifest itself dramatically a year later in his own poetry, *After Lorca* (1957) and *Admonitions* (1958). In these works he developed his notion of "correspondence" and included letters as part of the overall scaffolding of the book. It is within these letters that he developed his concept of composition by book—by which he meant not a collection of poems but a community of poems that "echo and re-echo against each other" to "create resonances." As Spicer put it: "[Poems] cannot live alone any more than we can." This is why he called his earlier single poems "one night stands."

Ultimately, Spicer's unhappy year on the East Coast solidified his allegiance to the American West and his identity as a California poet. When he returned to San Francisco, he worked once again as a lecturer at San Francisco State University in 1957, where he taught his famous Poetry as Magic workshop, which attracted Helen Adam, Robert Duncan, Jack Gilbert, George Stanley, and others. Afterwards he worked as a researcher in linguistics at UC Berkeley.

A new writing practice began, first with the imitations and translations of *After Lorca* which, he claimed, had been "dictated" to him, if not by García Lorca, then by a mysterious unknown force he sometimes characterized as "Martians." This conceit he borrowed from his poetic predecessor W. B. Yeats, whose experiments in automatic writing fascinated Spicer, and from the French poet Jean Cocteau, whose 1950 film *Orphée* explores the notion of a poetry given from beyond the grave. These poems rarely came singly; with Robert Duncan, Spicer conceived of and developed the "serial poem": a book-length progression of short poems that function together as a single movement. In his lectures, Spicer quoted Blaser's description of the serial poem as akin to being in a dark house, where you throw a light on in a room, then turn it off, and enter the next room, where you turn on a light, and so on. This movement from room to room in an architectural structure makes sense if you think of "stanza" as coming from the Italian for "small room." As his poetry moves from dark room to dark room, each flash of illumination leaves an afterimage on the imagination, and the lines of the poem become artifacts of an ongoing engagement with larger forces.[10] In San Francisco Spicer began teaching, and young poets flocked to him. He wanted to develop a magic school of writing, a *kreis* modeled on the *Georgekreis,* the mystic cult of poetry and love organized by the modernist German poet Stefan George to preserve the memory of a dead boyfriend.

In the last nine years of his short life, Jack Spicer saw to press seven books of poetry (and left behind at least ten more), establishing a poetic tradition on the West Coast that ran parallel, yet counter, to the contemporaneous Beat movement—parallel, yet counter, to the poetry of the New York School poets as well. His anarchist convictions led him to refuse copyright on his poetry since he believed that he was in no sense its owner, and its creator in only the most tenuous sense. Spicer's own students came to include many of the finest poets, both gay and straight, working in San Francisco. He founded the magazine, *J,* in 1959, to publish their writing, alongside his own, and in 1964 oversaw another monthly journal, Stan Persky's *Open Space.* What he had learned from the internal struggles of the Mattachine was to gain control of the means of production, so the presses that issued his work were all local and, insofar as possible, under his thumb. For Spicer the local became paramount, a seedbed of honest and vital work.

In 1965 he gave four important lectures shortly before his death from alcoholism at the age of forty. His legendary last words were "My vocabulary did this to me."

★

There is a contradiction between the life and the legend of Jack Spicer, the work and what we want it to say. When we look to him for company, his poems respond with "loneliness is necessary for pure poetry." When we want to believe that poetry matters, we're told "no one listens to poetry." When we read for solace, a sense of location and connection, we find instead "blackness alive with itself at the sides of our fires. . . . A simple hole running from one thing to another." His poem *The Holy Grail,* from which these lines are taken, is not so much about the grail as about that fire.

There is a deep humanity and humor in Spicer's voice, a desperate push to apprehend what is "real." In his poems "you'll smell the oldest smells—the smell of salt, of urine, and of sleep." You'll find "white and aimless signals," "the death that young men hope for." Here is a striving for a somatic poetry that allows so much to invade the edges of its song that we hardly know where it ends and we begin. His poems combine austerity and vulnerability to unfurl a loneliness that is unflinching. The paradox in his work, which can sometimes be mistaken for cynicism, is honest and wry.

Politically rebellious, Spicer despised the left-wing pieties that, he thought, were turning postwar poetry into a culture of complaint and "self-expression." The urgency of his desire to disrupt convention occasionally led him into some extreme choices of style and content that jar and disturb. Spicer's father had been a Wobbly, and Spicer carried with him his father's book of labor anthems, but the Left had let him—and all gay men—down severely, and the traces of his disappointment are evident in his writing. Early on, he saw a kinship, a solidarity, between homosexuals and other oppressed groups internationally. The narrator of an unfinished Berkeley story observes a gay "tea dance," and compares the boys dancing with each other to figures in a "minstrel show."

> Somebody tells me that these people are human. That's silly. They are not human they are homosexual. Jews are not human either, nor Negroes, nor cripples. No one is human that doesn't feel human. None of us here feel human.[11]

The terms he has chosen here are intentionally provocative, drawing his readers into a crisis of ethical judgment in order to determine for themselves the truth value of the paradigms he presents—and more importantly, where his readers stand in relation to his provocation. In such passages, Spicer carries over into the poetry something of the sociological reality of his time—using the raw terms with which one's humanity might be judged by a governing body. Note that two of these categories (homosexuality and disability) disqualify one for military service, and that the status of all oppressed groups was certainly part of his consciousness during the conservative 1950s, when ad hominem attacks were common and names were named before congressional committees like HUAC. His 4-F status (deemed unfit for military service), his status as an unattractive gay man, his resistance to many of the conventions of his period, and his abject loneliness, conspire at times to take the form of self-loathing. What remains is a raw, unedited, contaminating voice, using outrageous tropes of hate speech to provoke or shock the "genteel reader" into an unsettled reality. In some of his poems, and in his proto-serial work, "The Unvert Manifesto and the Diary of Oliver Charming," Spicer conflated a Trumanesque "plain speaking" with his lifelong drive to approach the abyss and view it head on, and that's when his writing embraces the repulsive, as satiric tropes of racism, misogyny and self-loathing attach themselves to the underside of the work. A streak of abjection animates Spicer's poetry, as his dissatisfaction with his own body sometimes flips over into ugly projection.

And yet Spicer remains one of our great poets of love and heartache. His love poetry is rueful, tender, colloquial, anguished. It's as though he felt that if he could just write well enough, the poem would become "almost a bedroom." He may also be characterized as a late devotional poet who wrote from a mix of doubt, irreverence, and belief. He is an erudite poet, with a knowledge of linguistics, Latin, German, Spanish, French, Old Norse, and Old English, but one who also delighted in organizing and presiding over "Blabbermouth Night," an event in which poets were encouraged to speak in tongues and to babble and were judged on the duration and invention of their noises. He was deeply committed to the depth and authenticity of sound. He worked on a linguistic project that mapped slight changes in vowel sounds from town to town in northern California, a project that would profoundly inform his later poetry, in particular *Language* and *Book of Magazine Verse*. He hosted Harry Smith on the first radio show devoted to folk music at KPFA in the late '40s, where he also troubled the folk movement's quest for the authentic and original by presenting his own fake versions of songs he claimed his friends had just heard down on the pier.

Spicer delighted in provocative and incongruous combinations. His statements are mercurial, and his lines refuse to be pinned down into a single register. His poems repeatedly disrupt even their own procedures by jamming the frequencies of meaning they set up. They make use of his life-long fascination with games and systems: bridge, baseball, chess, pinball, computers, magic, religion, politics, and linguistics. Like a grail search, what Spicer's work ultimately accomplishes is not so much a declared goal but the gathering of a community for a potentially endless adventure in reading. Even though he's a dissembler—using misunderstanding, misdirection, puns, or counter-logic—his poems don't leave us with a lack of meaning but rather an excess of meaning, with figures echoing and bumping against each other. The "Camelot presidency" becomes a grail circle; the Tin Woodman's heart is made of silicon. His poetry engages in conversations with other texts, both high and low, often invoking works that have already been widely retold and transformed and are thus already "corrupt": *The Odyssey,* grail legend, bible stories, *Alice in Wonderland,* the Oz books, the legend of Billy the Kid, nursery rhymes, and the evening news—the H bomb, the deaths of J.F.K. and Marilyn Monroe, even the Beatles's U.S. tour.

Spicer's outrageous literary debut exemplifies the gamesmanship, macabre humor, and sheer brilliance of his work. *After Lorca* was published in 1957 by White Rabbit, a small San Francisco press edited by Joe Dunn, the young Boston poet who had gone west. In the 1950s one of the most established venues for a first book was the Yale Younger Poets Series. In that decade, W. H. Auden was the judge, selecting work and writing introductions to books by Adrienne Rich, W. S. Merwin, John

Ashbery, James Wright, John Hollander, and James Dickey. For his own book, Spicer adapted the format of the established older poet vetting the emerging poet, turning to Federico García Lorca to introduce him even if the martyred Lorca had to do so from the grave. Understandably put out, Lorca begins: "Frankly I was quite surprised when Mr. Spicer asked me to write an introduction for this volume." And thus begins Spicer's provocative poetics of engaging the dead in his literary practice.

Lorca is perhaps the only major international gay poet he could propose to rival Auden's endorsement. But as a reluctant interlocutor whose cultural capital is surely compromised by the fact that he is dead, Lorca supplies, in many ways, the opposite of an Auden introduction. His approval is unlikely to help the poet get reviewed, find an agent, get a second book taken, or even get a job. But his position offers unique connections to the underworld for an orphic poet, and he provides both the perfect vehicle for unrequited love and the perfect emblem of literary inheritance and tradition.

After Lorca is ostensibly composed of translations of Lorca's work, the faithfulness of which even Lorca questions. There are also nearly a dozen original Spicer poems masquerading as translations, combined with six now-famous programmatic letters to Lorca in which Spicer articulates his poetics and his sense of personal woe with respect to poetry, love, and his contemporaries. With these letters, translations, and fake translations, Spicer established a unique correspondence with literary tradition, one that would further evolve into a resonant intertextual practice of assemblage.

His debut had an element of punk youthfulness, but in that stroke he revealed himself as a traditionalist as much as an innovator. The first letter to Lorca describes tradition as "generations of different poets in different countries patiently telling the same story, writing the same poem. . . ." Rather than distinguishing himself as a uniquely promising younger writer, the letter places Spicer within the context of poets as a class of workers who are all engaged in the same basic project. In this way, the correspondence between Keats's negative capability, Rimbaud's systematic derangement of the senses, Yeats's vision, Rilke's angelic orders, Lorca's duende, Pound's personae, Eliot's sense of tradition, and Moore's imaginary gardens can "build a whole new universe"—albeit a universe in which things do not fit seamlessly together. As he puts it, "Things do not connect, they correspond." Later, in his "A Textbook of Poetry," we find:

> It does not have to fit together. Like the pieces of a totally unfinished jigsaw puzzle my grandmother left in the bedroom when she died in the living room. The pieces of the poetry or of this love.

For Spicer, reading and writing are repeatedly associated with a loss of boundaries. Spicer makes what the film critic Manny Farber has called "termite art," an art that eats its own borders.[12] As the poem just quoted continues, this aesthetic is literalized: "As if my grandmother had chewed on her jigsaw puzzle before she died. / / Not as a gesture of contempt for the scattered nature of reality. Not because the pieces would not fit in time. But because this would be the only way to cause an alliance between the dead and the living."

As his last letter to Lorca suggests, the mingling of poets in the sheets of a book is the mingling of lovers, but this union suggests an eros beyond sex, through which their textual bodies become as indistinguishable as bodies decaying together in the earth, gradually recombined into the same substance—in effect, made new: "the pieces of the poetry or of this love." Surely no poet was more aware of this blurring of the here and the hereafter than Jack Spicer, who aptly characterized the haunted nature of poetry this way: "The ghosts the poems were written for are the ghosts of the poems. We have it second-hand. They cannot hear the noise they have been making." Indeed, Spicer left behind an achieved body of work whose afterlife continues to astonish, admonish, and haunt his readers.

Peter Gizzi and Kevin Killian

Notes

1. For more on Spicer's early years see his biography: *Poet Be Like God: Jack Spicer and the San Francisco Renaissance* by Lewis Ellingham and Kevin Killian (Wesleyan U P, 1998).

2. In response to a questionnaire for Robert Duncan's workshop at San Francisco State in 1958, Spicer named Lindsay as one of his major influences, along with Yeats, Lorca, Pound, Cocteau, his teacher Josephine Miles, his contemporaries Duncan and Blaser, Untermeyer's anthology, Dada, The English Department, and his favorite bar of the period, The Place. He left one space designated "to be found."

3. "The Poet and Poetry," reprinted in *The House That Jack Built: The Collected Lectures of Jack Spicer,* ed. Peter Gizzi (Wesleyan U P: 1998).

4. In her brief omnibus review of *The New American Poetry,* Marianne Moore praises Spicer's elegies: "Jack Spicer is not indifferent to T. S. Eliot and is not hackneyed, his specialty being the firefly flash of insight, lightening with dry detachment . . . the accents suiting the sense." Given Moore's affection for Eliot and his work, and Eliot's high literary standing in the period, this was high praise (*Complete Prose* [New York: Viking, 1986]: 536).

5. Spicer's petition against the oath was found in his handwriting in one of his Berkeley notebooks. He was 24 at the time:

> We, the Research Assistants and Teaching Assistants of the University of California, wish to register our protest against the new loyalty oath for the following reasons.
>
> (1) The testing of a University faculty by oath is a stupid and insulting procedure. If this oath is to have the effect of eliminating Communists from the faculty, we might as logically eliminate murderers from the faculty by forcing every faculty member to sign an oath saying that he has never committed murder,
>
> (2) That such an oath is more dangerous to the liberties of the community than any number of active Communists should be obvious to any student of history. Liberty and democracy are more often overthrown by fear than by stealth. Only countries such as Russia or Spain have institutions so weak and unhealthy that they must be protected by terror.
>
> (3) Oaths and other forms of blackmail are destructive to the free working of man's intellect. Since the early Middle Ages universities have

zealously guarded their intellectual freedom and have made use of its power to help create the world we know today. The oath that Galileo was forced by the Inquisition to swear is but a distant cousin to the oath we are asked to swear today, but both represent the struggle of the blind and powerful against the minds of free men.

We, who will inherit the branches of learning that one thousand years of free universities have helped to generate, are not Communists and dislike the oath for the same reason we dislike Communism. Both breed stupidity and indignity; both threaten our personal and intellectual freedom. (Jack Spicer Papers 2004/209, The Bancroft Library)

For a discussion of the impact of Spicer's non-signing of the Oath, see *Poet Be Like God: Jack Spicer and the San Francisco Renaissance*.

6. The other members of the 6 Gallery were: Wally Hedrick, Hayward King, Deborah Remington, John Allen Ryan, and David Simpson. When Ginsberg and Whalen and others read on October 7, 1955, Spicer was living briefly in New York City.

7. In a letter from 1989 Schuyler remembered Spicer this way: "When he was in New York in the early 50s he hung out at a Village bar, the San Remo, which went through a gay phase, and I never met anyone else quite so morose and grouchy. And that's what I find when I try to read him. But my friend the painter John Button said that the poetry was very good, when you stopped reading it *that* way" (*Just the Thing: Selected Letters of James Schuyler*, ed. William Corbett [New York: Turtle Point 2004]: 450).

8. Spicer's letters to Allen Joyce, edited by Bruce Boone, *Sulfur* 10: 142.

9. "The Poems of Emily Dickinson," reprinted in *The House That Jack Built: The Collected Lectures of Jack Spicer*.

10. For Spicer, both the lines of the poem and the serial structure of the poem are dictated. For a fuller discussion of dictation and seriality see Lectures 1 and 2 and the Afterword in *The House That Jack Built: The Collected Lectures of Jack Spicer*.

11. From a Berkeley notebook (Jack Spicer Papers 2004/209, The Bancroft Library).

12. See "White Elephant Art vs. Termite Art" in *Negative Space* (New York: Praeger, 1971).

ABOUT THIS EDITION

A poet's life work comes into print culture for many reasons and in many different formats and presentations; that is to say, no poet's work comes to a final state in a uniform way, nor without the rich life of textual work and its attendant discourse.

The majority of the work collected here consists of poetry from Spicer's two posthumous collections, which have served his readers for the past twenty-five years. The primary of these, *The Collected Books of Jack Spicer* (Los Angeles: Black Sparrow, 1975), was edited by Robin Blaser in the decade after Spicer's death. He adhered as much as possible to his friend's strictures on seriality, collecting in this volume the poems Spicer published in his individual books (*After Lorca, Billy the Kid, Lament for the Makers, The Heads of the Town Up to the Aether, The Holy Grail*, and *Language*) along with unpublished and posthumously published books (*Admonitions, A Book of Music, Fifteen False Propositions Against God, Apollo Sends Seven Nursery Rhymes to James Alexander, A Red Wheelbarrow*, and *Book of Magazine Verse*). That edition also included Blaser's groundbreaking study of his friend's revelatory poetics entitled "The Practice of Outside," now reprinted in *The Fire: The Collected Essays of Robin Blaser* (Berkeley: University of California Press, 2006).

A second collection of Spicer's work, *One Night Stand & Other Poems* (San Francisco: Grey Fox, 1980) was edited by Donald Allen and includes a lengthy introduction by Robert Duncan. In 1957, after avowing serial poetry and composition by book, Spicer famously disowned his earlier single poems as "one night stands." Allen's aptly titled posthumous edition essentially offers the prequel to Spicer's mature work, and many of the individual poems collected therein reveal Spicer's poetics in the making. Though Spicer claimed to have abandoned the single poem for good in *Admonitions*, strictly speaking he was "printing the legend," as he continued to write and publish such poems through the end of his career.

Unlike most poets, Spicer restricted the distribution of his publications to his immediate surround, the San Francisco Bay Area, and this choice is an aspect of the work that must be kept in mind as it moves into a new context. Spicer's regionalism derived from a deep love of California and from his visionary belief in a magic circle begun at Berkeley with Blaser, Duncan, and others in his youth, though perhaps later it also functioned as a kind of armor to protect him from repeated rejection from commercial publishing venues. In his lifetime, Spicer's published books were released in small editions of 500 to 1000 copies or even fewer by small local presses, primarily Joe Dunn's—later Graham Mackintosh's—White Rabbit Press, along with Duncan and Jess [Collins]'s Enkidu Surrogate, and David Haselwood and Andrew Hoyem's Auerhahn Society.

The present volume builds from all of these previous out-of-print publications, retaining Spicer's own delineation between early and mature work, and uses them to provide the copytext for many of the poems within this volume. We have corrected obvious typographical errors in these earlier volumes but retained Spicer's idiosyncratic orthography. As Blaser notes in the *Collected Books:* "All spellings or 'misspellings' are intentional—'le damoiselle cacheresse' (*Holy Grail*), for example. After *Heads of the Town,* Jack seemed not to care for such corrections from the manuscript to the printed edition." Given Spicer's interest in folk transmission, his refusal of copyright, his insistence on the local, and his disregard of conventions of many kinds, his orthography cannot be separated from other aesthetic choices in the work.

We also include manuscript poems and fugitive works retrieved from notebooks. After Spicer's untimely death, the contents of his apartment were packed into boxes. Blaser stored these effects along with his own archive until he and Holt V. Spicer donated them to UC Berkeley's Bancroft Library in 2004. The contents of these boxes became, in effect, a time capsule, containing Spicer's prescriptions, paperback books, unopened mail, student papers, a calling card, art work, and other miscellany along with notebooks and manuscript pages. Certain works that had been considered incomplete or unfinished—"The Diary of Oliver Charming," for instance—were pieced together from notebooks. Other serial works emerged as well: *Helen: A Revision* and a work in progress we've titled *Map Poems*, for example. We have also retrieved single poems written throughout his writing life, including "Homosexuality," "Any fool can get into an ocean . . . ," "A Second Train Song for Gary," "Éternuement," "Birdland, California," "They Murdered You" (a premature elegy on the death of Kenneth Rexroth), and the heartbreaking "Dignity is a part of a man . . . ," among others. While these "new" works were unpublished during Spicer's lifetime, they make an important addition to our understanding of Spicer's life work. Also among them is the unfinished manuscript letter to Lorca about sound, to which Spicer refers in the fifth letter of *After Lorca*. Although it remained unfinished, this document, retrieved directly from Spicer's *After Lorca* notebook (and printed in our notes on the poems), is a compelling supplement to the finished series as it considers and complicates the two dueling aspects of the poem: how does it look and how does it sound?

Another series collected here, the *Letters to James Alexander*, functions both as correspondence and as a serial poem; on occasion, Spicer read from the series of letters at poetry readings. Given Spicer's interest in the blurring of letters and poems in *After Lorca* and elsewhere, this work offers another significant manifestation of his poetics of "correspondence."

The poems in this edition are arranged as precisely as possible by date of composition. Though both Blaser and Allen arranged their editions in roughly chronological order, new findings have emerged within the Spicer archive that alter the story considerably and, for the most part, a thorough picture of Spicer's writing career can be established. We have established the chronology of Spicer's writing in two ways. Most importantly, the notebooks (dozens of them in the Spicer papers at UC Berkeley) show when and in what order all the major works were composed, along with most of the shorter pieces. Through the evidence of these notebooks we can see that *Lament for the Makers*, which precedes *The Heads of the Town Up to the Aether* in Blaser's edition, actually succeeded it, as did *A Red Wheelbarrow*. When notebooks were not available (and some seem to be missing, especially from Spicer's early years at Berkeley and in Minnesota), we came to depend on a selection of aides-mémoire Spicer made for himself for various reasons. In one he names the man (or woman, but usually a man) who inspired each of his poems. In another he attempts to establish a series of different "periods" into which his early work might be placed. Several lists reveal that he, like other poets before and since, made a table of contents for the "selected poems" of his dreams even before he had published his first book. Using these methods, and following comments in his letters which date the poems more precisely, we have come up with a consistent, sometimes surprising timeline.

While the first part of this edition, 1945–1956, doesn't include every poem he wrote at this time, our aim has been to make a judicious selection of single poems from *One Night Stand* and from notebooks and manuscripts in order to provide something more than an adequate sense of Spicer's first decade of writing. Therefore this edition is not a "complete" but a "collected" poems. The poems we chose not to include from this period are poems that we deemed to be largely student work, imitations, or formal exercises. These works are not without interest, and many of them will subsequently appear along with Spicer's plays in a companion volume of uncollected work.

The second part of this book gathers a more complete picture of the second half of Spicer's writing life. It includes all the poems from the *Collected Books* as well as several fugitive series that have been uncovered and pieced together in the decades following the Black Sparrow edition (*Helen: A Revision, Map Poems,* and *Golem,* among others).[1] The dates that appear on the half-title pages of each of his "books" are dates of composition, not publication. The notes at the back of this volume provide brief publication information.

It is our aim in this volume to present a comprehensive edition of Spicer's work from 1945 to 1965 and to establish a fair text of his major poems, creating, in effect, his first collected poems to function as a standard reading edition. In gathering texts from Spicer's unwieldy archive we have sought to show the continuities as well as the evolutionary leaps within his writing practice. While the poetry gathered here represents a mere twenty-year period, it has all the features of a full and productive life work.

Note

1. Poems Spicer clearly didn't intend for publication, such as "An Exercise" (which appeared posthumously in *Boundary 2*), will appear along with other works in a second volume.

I (1945–1956)

BERKELEY RENAISSANCE   (1945–1950)

BERKELEY IN TIME OF PLAGUE

Plague took us and the land from under us,
Rose like a boil, enclosing us within.
We waited and the blue skies writhed awhile
Becoming black with death.

Plague took us and the chairs from under us,
Stepped cautiously while entering the room
(We were discussing Yeats); it paused awhile
Then smiled and made us die.

Plague took us, laughed and reproportioned us,
Swelled us to dizzy, unaccustomed size.
We died prodigiously; it hurt awhile
But left a certain quiet in our eyes.

A GIRL'S SONG

Song changes and his unburnt hair
Upon my altar changes;
We have, good strangers, many vaults
To keep the time in, but the songs are mine,
The seals are wax, and both will leak
From heat.
A bird in time is worth of two in any bush.
You can melt brush like wax; and birds in time
Can sing.
They call me bird-girl, parrot girl and worth
The time of any bird; my vault a cage,
My cage a song, my song a seal,
And I can steal an unburnt lock of hair
To weave a window there.

HOMOSEXUALITY

Roses that wear roses
Enjoy mirrors.
Roses that wear roses must enjoy
The flowers they are worn by.
Roses that wear roses are dying
With a mirror behind them.
None of us are younger but the roses
Are dying.
Men and women have weddings and funerals
Are conceived and destroyed in a formal
Procession.
Roses die upon a bed of roses
With mirrors weeping at them.

A PORTRAIT OF THE ARTIST AS A YOUNG LANDSCAPE

Watch sunset fall upon that beach like others did. The waves
Curved and unspent like cautious scythes, like evening harvesters.
Feel sorrow for the land like others did. Each eating tide,
Each sigh of surf, each sunset-dinner, pulls the earth-crop, falls
A little fuller; makes the sand grain fall
A little shorter, leaner. Leaves the earth
A breathless future harvest.
I watch, as others watched, but cannot stand
Where others stood; for only water now
Stands once where Arnold stood, or Lear or Sappho stood.
Retreating shore (each day has new withdrawals)
Breaks in feeble song—it sings and all abandoned history is spread,
A tidal panic for that conqueror.

I. The Indian Ocean: Rimbaud

I watched and saw a sailor floating in that sea
And melt before he drowned.
Asleep and fragrant as that sleep, he seemed
To draw the sun within his flesh and melt. He seemed
To draw the fire from that angel and to melt. Now he is dead.
To melt is not to drown but is enough
To shear the body of its flesh; the sea
Is meant for drowning, but when God is short
Of waters for his purpose then the sea
Becomes a pool of fire; angels ride
Astride their flamy waves
Pale as desire
Terrible angel, out of that fire
Out of the beach-bones, melted like butter
Out of the blazing waves, the hot tide
Terrible angel, sea-monster
Terrible fish-like angel, fire breather
Source of the burning ocean.

II. The Atlantic Ocean: Hart Crane

But I watch slowly, see the sand-grains fall
A little riper, fuller; watch the ocean fall
From sunset dinner. Watch the angel leave
His fire-pleasure.
                Deep in the mind there is an ocean
I would fall within it, find my sources in it. Yield to tide
And find my sources in it. Aching fathoms fall
And rest within it.
                Deep in the mind there is an ocean and below,
The ocean-ripened sand-grains and the lands it took,
The statues, and the boundaries and the ghosts.
Street-lights and pleasant images, refractions; great

Currents of pleasant indirection.
The statue of Diana in the railroad station
The elaborating, the intense, the chocolate monsters.
Under the ocean there are crushing tides, intense
And convoluted stuffings for a dream.
Deep in the mind there is an ocean and below,
A first and fishly paradise.

It is the deep-end of dreaming. There are stacks
Of broken sailors, sweet and harvested; the tacks
Do not decay; they do not bleach with daylight; they remain
Like grain in harvest.
                              But there is little human there, the face
Of statues, nothing colder than that face; it is the end
An Easter Island end of dreaming; paradise
And always afternoon.
                              But he is dead
Untroubled swarms of bees pursue their pleasures, lax and
        drowsy; steal
Sweet honey from a drunken sailor's bones.
                              But he is dead
And nothing human there can chafe his flesh;
Only the fertile sea can chafe his flesh; it is the end,
An island end of dreaming.
Harvesting angel, out of these pleasures
Out of the kelp-fields and the sea-brambles
Tide-weaver, hunter and planter,
Harvesting angel, paradise-keeper
Harvesting dolphin-angel, coffin-lover
Keep safe his sleeping bones.

III. The Pacific Ocean

But there are times the sea puts on its rouges, looks
A doom-bedraggled whore with eight diseases; seems
To cruise her ancient beaches and demand
An answer to her question—"Will you sleep?"
An answer from the living—"Will you sleep?"
"No no my girl, my dooming ocean, no
It won't do," I answer, "it won't do.
Who, girl, would drown, if all the fragrant ocean, girl,
Would be his bride and bed?
                                        Though he is dead
And though he sleep with you, your cheapness is not dead
And you are old and deep and cold and like a cheap hotel
Of sleepless corridors and whisperings.
No, I can spare your charm, my harpy ocean, spare your charm
And grunt and turn away.—No, it won't do."
This world, it will not end, it will not end;
It would look well in ashes, but it will not end. (Though he is dead.)
Dr. Johnson stamped his goutish leg upon that ocean; proved
That rocks are rocklike as the sea's a sea
Of real appearance. If the mind's a sea
And rocks are feathers in it, do not say
The sea's a feathered creature. She may fly,
The mind, I mean, may fly, but cannot spin,
The Doctor's lithic stumbling block would break her shin.
How shall I answer the whorish sea?
Sir, says the doctor, leave it all to me.
How shall I visit him where he is dead?
Sir, says the doctor, I shall go instead.
The gloomy whore is chastened and he goes.
The sun becomes a nest of singing birds and he is gone
The painted sea is gone.

Gout-ridden angel, out of these terrors,
Out of the mind's infidelity and the heart's horror
Deliver my natural body.
Gout-ridden angel, slayer of oceans
Gout-ridden common-angel, keeper of virtue
Deliver my natural body.

For it was I who died
With every tide.
I am the land.
I was the sea.
Each grain of sand
With us will be
If we are dead.

AN APOCALYPSE FOR THREE VOICES

> Lactantius writing on the Apocalypse says:
> "Qui autem ab inferis suscitabantur praeerunt
> viventibus velut judices—*They, moreover, shall
> be raised from the depths that they shall stand
> above the living as judges.*"

I dreamt the ocean died, gave up its dead.
The last spasmatic tides, the final waves
Were crowded with escaping ghosts; the tides
Were choked and strangled with the weight of flesh
And falling bone. And soon the homeward floating ceased.
The dead awoke. Once they had mouths and said,
"When all we dead awaken," they awoke.
When all we dead—

                    (but I have talked to the king of the rats
                    and I have walked with the king of
                            the rats
                    and I have bowed to the king of the rats
                    and the king of the rats has said to me—

When all we dead—
                    (but I have talked to the king of the swans
                    and I have walked with the king of
                            the swans
                    and I have bowed to the king of the swans
                    and the king of the swans has said to me—

Awaken.

The Sunday Chronicle presents the dream
In slightly different order; Angel-Face
Is chased through eight cartoons by Nemesis,
By Demon Richard Tracy; each disgrace
Each new escape, is hinted out and found
And Angel-Face is cornered, caught, and drowned.
He will arise in every Sunday Chronicle
Refaced, pursued, reburied in the lake
Till Tracy roots his ever drowning heart
Into the crossroads with a phallic stake.

Or say I turn the records in a great
Electric station, our reception famed
As far as May or Babylon and back again.
My great turntable is inevitable; it whirls
Around, around, a convoluting day
A night of static sleeplessness; it plays
Requested favorites, universal things,
And millions listen, hear some tenor sing,
It's a long, long way
From Babylon in May

To this November.
But listen to the chorus
                    When we dead—
Those flat and tuneless voices
                    When we dead—
The aching chord is broken
                    When we dead awaken
                    We will do the singing.
                    We will do the singing.
Their flat electric voices
Fill the sky
And Angel-Face has floated from his grave
Again to die.

Angel-Face hires lawyers from the firm
Of Ratface, Swanface, and Beelzebub.
Mr. Ratface, well-known Persian lawyer, takes the case
Faces the court, asks manslaughter on Tracy,
Slander on my station,
Death on me for treason.
Judge Swanface tries the case without a word
And orders Juryman Beelzebub
To give me death. The juror says,
"I sentence you to drown three times
When we dead
                    (The king of rats has bowed to me)
When we dead
                    (The king of the swans has bowed to me)
When we dead
                    (The king of the world has bowed to me)
Awaken and the living die.

ONE NIGHT STAND

Listen, you silk-hearted bastard,
I said in the bar last night,
You wear those dream clothes
Like a swan out of water.
Listen, you wool-feathered bastard,
My name, just for the record, is Leda.
I can remember pretending
That your red silk tie is a real heart
That your raw wool suit is real flesh
That you could float beside me with a swan's touch
Of casual satisfaction.
But not the swan's blood.
Waking tomorrow, I remember only
Somebody's feathers and his wrinkled heart
Draped loosely in my bed.

AN ANSWER TO JAIME DE ANGULO

If asked whether I am goyim,
Whether I am an enemy to your people,
I would reply that I am of a somewhat older people.
My people (the gay, who are neither Jew nor goyim)
Were caught in your Lord God Jehovah's first pogrom
Out at Sodom.

No one was very indignant about it.
Looking backwards at us is hard on neutrals (ask Mrs. Lot someday)
You may say it was all inhospitality to angels.
You may say we're all guilty; well, show us
An angel pacing down Hollywood, wings folded,
And try us.

A LECTURE IN PRACTICAL AESTHETICS

Entering the room
Mr. Stevens on an early Sunday morning
Wore sailor-whites and helmet.
He had brought a couple with him and they danced like bears
He had brought a bottle with him and the vapors rose
From helmet, naked bottle, couple
Haloed him and wakened us.

But Mr. Stevens, listen, sight and sense are dull
And heavier than vapor and they cling
And weigh with meaning.
To floors and bottoms of the sea, horizon them
You are an island of our sea, Mr. Stevens, perhaps rare
Certainly covered with upgrowing vegetation.
You may consist of dancing animals. The bear,
Mr. Stevens, may be your emblem,
Rampant on a white field or panting in plurals above the
        floor and the ocean,
And you a bearish Demiurge, Mr. Stevens, licking vapor
Into the shape of your island. Fiercely insular.
Out of sense and sight, Mr. Stevens, you may unambiguously
        dance
Buoying the helmet and the couple,
The bottle and the dance itself—
But consider, Mr. Stevens, though imperceptible,
We are also alive. It is not right that you should merely touch us.
Besides, Mr. Stevens, any island in our sea
Needs a geographer.

A geographer, Mr. Stevens, tastes islands
Finds in this macro-cannibalism his own microcosm.
To form a conceit, Mr. Stevens, in finding you

He chews upon his flesh. Chews it, Mr. Stevens,
Like Donne down to the very bone.
An island, Mr. Stevens, should be above such discoveries,
Available but slightly mythological.
Our resulting map will be misleading.
Though it be drawn, Mr. Stevens,
With the blood and flesh of both superimposed
As ink on paper, it will be no picture, no tourist postcard
Of the best of your contours reflected on water.
It will be a map, Mr. Stevens, a county stiffened into symbols
And that's poetry too, Mr. Stevens, and I'm a geographer.

DIALOGUE BETWEEN INTELLECT AND PASSION

"Passion is alien to intellect
As hot black doves are alien to trees
On which they do not rest—
All are alone.
Of passion and of intellect
Suspect
Neither bird nor tree
Of vicious privacy—
Nothing is intimate.
Doves without rest
Must blackly test
Each branch with every claw they lack
And trees alone
Are tough as thrones
With too much sovereignty."

"Above your branches every hot black dove
Protests his love

And gathers in great swarms
As darkness comes.
They wait
Until the darkness make
Them dream-birds black
As needles and as ultimate.
As you branch blanketed in royalty
Each lacking claw, bird-real,
Will find its rest
Throughout your naked branches,
Make you feel
Birds in the bed
Locking their claws against
Your privacy."

A NIGHT IN FOUR PARTS (Second Version)

Part I: Going to Sleep

While the heart twists
On a cold bed
Without sleep,
Under the hot light
Of an angry moon
A cat leaps.
The cat prowls
Into cold places,
But the heart stays
Where the blood is.

Part II: Light Sleeping

Down in the world
Where the cat prowls,
Heart's manikin,
His climbing doll
Prepares for love:
Spawns eye, spawns mouth,
Spawns throat, spawns genitals.
Heart is so monstrous naked that the world recoils,
Shakes like a ladder,
Spits like a cat,
Disappears.

Part III: Wet Dream

Downward it plunges through the walls of flesh,
Heart falls
Through lake and cavern under sleep
Deep like an Orpheus
A beating mandolin
Plucking the plectrum of the moon upon its strings,
It sings, it sings, it sings.
It sings, "Restore, restore, Eurydice to life.
        Oh, take the husband and return the wife."
It sings still deeper, conjures by its spell
Eurydice, the alley cat of Hell.
        "Meow, meow, Eurydice's not dead.
        Oh, find a cross-eyed tomcat for my bed."
Too late, it was too late he fell.
The sounds of singing and the sounds of Hell
Become a swarm of angry orange flies
And naked Orpheus, moon-shriveled, dies
And rises leaving lost Eurydice.
His heart falling upward towards humanity
Howling and half-awake.

Part IV: Waking

Heart wakes
Twists like a cat on hot bricks
Beating off sunlight.
Now the heart slinks back to the blood
And the day starts.
Then the blood asks,
"Who was that lover
That thrashed you around last night?"
And the heart can't answer.

ORPHEUS IN HELL

When he first brought his music into hell
He was absurdly confident. Even over the noise of the
    shapeless fires
And the jukebox groaning of the damned
Some of them would hear him. In the upper world
He had forced the stones to listen.
It wasn't quite the same. And the people he remembered
Weren't quite the same either. He began looking at faces
Wondering if all of hell were without music.
He tried an old song but pain
Was screaming on the jukebox and the bright fire
Was pelting away the faces and he heard a voice saying,
    "Orpheus!"
        He was at the entrance again
And a little three-headed dog was barking at him.
Later he would remember all those dead voices
And call them Eurydice.

ORPHEUS AFTER EURYDICE

Then I, a singer and hunter, fished
In streams too deep for love.
A god grew there, a god grew there,
A wet and weblike god grew there.
Mella, mella peto
In medio flumine.
His flesh is honey and his bones are made
Of brown, brown sugar and he is a god.
He is a god.
I know he is a god.
Mella, mella peto
In medio flumine.
Drink wine, I sang, drink cold red wine.
Grow liquid, spread yourself.
O bruise yourself, intoxicate yourself,
Dilute yourself.
You want to web the rivers of the world.
You want to glue the tides together with yourself.
You look so innocent—
Water wouldn't melt in your mouth.
I looked and saw him weep a honey tear.
I, Orpheus, had raised a water god
That wept a honey tear.
Mella, mella peto
In medio flumine.

ORPHEUS' SONG TO APOLLO

You, Apollo, have yoked your horse
To the wrong sun.
You have picked the wrong flower.
Breaking a branch of impossible
Green-stemmed hyacinth
You have found thorns and postulated a rose.
Sometimes we were almost like lovers
(As the sun almost touches the earth at sunset)
But,
At touch,
The horse leapt like an ox
Into another orbit of roses, roses.
Perhaps,
If the moon were made of cold green cheese,
I could call you Diana.
Perhaps,
If a knife could peel that rosy rind,
It would find you virgin as a star.
Too hot to move.
Nevertheless,
This is almost goodbye.
You,
Fool Apollo,
Stick
Your extra roses somewhere where they'll keep.
I like your aspiration
But the sky's too deep
For fornication.

TROY POEM

We,
Occasioned by the eye,
To look
And looking down
Saw that your city was not Troy.

Oh,
Merry Greeks,
We bear our fathers on our backs
And burdened thus
We kiss your city.

Neither
At foot or eye
Do we taste
Ruined Troy
Which was our mother.

Oh,
Merry Greeks,
When you embrace us
We, bending, thus
Pray against you:

"Rise
From our absent city
Tough as smoke—
Oh,
Flesh of Hector,
Rescue us."

"We find the body difficult to speak . . ."

We find the body difficult to speak,
The face too hard to hear through,
We find that eyes in kissing stammer
And that heaving groins
Babble like idiots.
Sex is an ache of mouth. The
Squeak our bodies make
When they rub mouths against each other
Trying to talk.
Like silent little children we embrace,
Aching together.
And love is emptiness of ear. As cure
We put a face against our ear
And listen to it as we would a shell,
Soothed by its roar.
We find the body difficult, and speak
Across its wall like strangers.

"They are selling the midnight papers . . ."

Every street has alleys and within the alleys
There are criminals and policemen.
I said, "Tonight
The moon is like a dead gangster."
I heard him giggle like a hound. "The moon,"
He said, "is spooky. We should lie upon our backs
And howl."
And so we walked, uneasy, wondering
If there were justice anywhere
Within this midnight city,

Or how, without a hat, one could distinguish
A vice-squad member from a glass of beer,
Or whether if one met them walking hand in hand
One could tell Bugsy Siegel from Virginia Woolf.
They are selling the midnight papers,
The moon is wearing brass knuckles.

"Any fool can get into an ocean . . ."

Any fool can get into an ocean
But it takes a Goddess
To get out of one.
What's true of oceans is true, of course,
Of labyrinths and poems. When you start swimming
Through riptide of rhythms and the metaphor's seaweed
You need to be a good swimmer or a born Goddess
To get back out of them
Look at the sea otters bobbing wildly
Out in the middle of the poem
They look so eager and peaceful playing out there where the water
    hardly moves
You might get out through all the waves and rocks
Into the middle of the poem to touch them
But when you've tried the blessed water long
Enough to want to start backward
That's when the fun starts
Unless you're a poet or an otter or something supernatural
You'll drown, dear. You'll drown
Any Greek can get you into a labyrinth
But it takes a hero to get out of one
What's true of labyrinths is true of course
Of love and memory. When you start remembering.

THE SCROLLWORK ON THE CASKET

To walk down the streets with a dead man or to hold conversation with him over coffee in a public restaurant would be hopelessly eccentric. To entertain a corpse in private, to worry him in the privacy of one's room or in the cramped and more frightening privacy of a short story is an eccentricity more easily forgivable.

A short story is narrower than a room in a cheap hotel; it is narrower than the wombs through which we descended. It does violence to any large dead man to force him within it. To fit him (even his body) into the casket of a few paragraphs, he must be twisted and contorted; his stiff arms, his extended legs must be hacked or broken. A rigor mortis operates within the memory; his image stiffens and resists in every inch. One must maim him to fit him in.

Then, when success is achieved and the sweating author has managed to get shut his casket of paragraphs, hammering on it in a perfect fury to keep the body from bursting out, what then? He has a casket, a small regular box with a corpse inside it, and he can sell it on the market where such boxes are sold—and it has been safer, it has been less eccentric and altogether more profitable than walking down the streets with a dead man ever could have been.

There are some complaints from the customers, however. These caskets all look alike. They are brown or gray or purple (almost never black), the customers complain that they don't look very much like people.

The customers are right. The outside of the casket is made up mostly of the writer, his descriptions, his feelings, his fancies, his regrets—little or nothing about the corpse on the inside. Nothing but a few spoken words. But it is those words, only them, which give the third dimension to the story, show that there is space inside the casket. For this reason whenever I read a short story I skip through the narrative paragraphs and concentrate on the dialogue. (That is the scrollwork on the casket.)

"Whenever I read a short story," Ken said, looking up from his coffee, "I skip through the narrative paragraphs and concentrate on the dialogue." He paused for a moment. "And that's the scrollwork on the casket," he added parenthetically.

It is Ken, of course, who is dead. It is his casket I hammer now. Obviously there is something hallucinatory in the hammering of caskets. Whenever I hammer a nail into the outside of the casket, I can hear someone, on the inside, also hammering a nail. That's the trouble with this burial business; it's hard to know who's on the inside and who's on the outside, whether the living bury the dead or the dead bury the living.

"The dead bury the living," Ken said. He pulled his coat tightly around his shoulders and walked a few yards ahead of me. "The dead never return to the living; it is the living that return to the dead. People search out the ghosts they find." He walked silently ahead of me for a while and then stopped. He leaned against a heavy box and looked at me with something like pity. "I think I'm going to be sick," he said.

I think I'm going to be sick.

THE DANCING APE

The dancing ape is whirling round the beds
Of all the coupled animals; they, sleeping there
In warmth of sex, ignore his fur and fuss
And feel no terror in his gait of loneliness.
Quaint though the dancer is, his furry fists
Are locked like lightning over all their heads.
His legs are thrashing out in discontent
As if they were the lightning's strict embodiment.
But let the dancing stop, the apish face go shut in sleep,
The hands unclench, the trembling legs go loose—
And let some curious animal bend and touch that face
With nuzzling mouth, would not the storm break—
And that ape kiss?

IMAGINARY ELEGIES

For Robin Blaser

All the philosophy a man needs is in Berkeley.
—W. B. Yeats

I.

Poetry, almost blind like a camera
Is alive in sight only for a second. Click,
Snap goes the eyelid of the eye before movement
Almost as the word happens.
One would not choose to blink and go blind
After the instant. One would not choose
To see the continuous Platonic pattern of birds flying
Long after the stream of birds had dropped or had nested.
Lucky for us that there are visible things like oceans
Which are always around,
Continuous, disciplined adjuncts
To the moment of sight.
Sight
But not so sweet
As we have seen.
When I praise the sun or any bronze god derived from it
Don't think I wouldn't rather praise the very tall blond boy
Who ate all of my potato-chips at the Red Lizard.
It's just that I won't see him when I open my eyes
And I will see the sun.
Things like the sun are always there when the eyes are open
Insistent as breath.
                    One can only worship
These cold eternals for their support of
What is absolutely temporary.
But not so sweet.

The temporary tempts poetry
Tempts photographs, tempts eyes.
I conjure up
From photographs
The birds
The boy
The room in which I began to write this poem
All
My eye has seen or ever could have seen
I love
I love—The eyelid clicks
I see
Cold poetry
At the edge of their image.
It is as if we conjure the dead and they speak only
Through our own damned trumpets, through our damned medium:
"I am little Eva, a Negro princess from sunny heaven."
The voice sounds blond and tall.
"I am Aunt Minnie. Love is sweet as moonlight here in heaven."
The voice sounds blond and tall.
"I'm Barnacle Bill. I sank with the Titanic. I rose in salty heaven."
The voice sounds blond, sounds tall, sounds blond and tall.
"Goodbye from us in spiritland, from sweet Platonic spiritland.
You can't see us in spiritland, and we can't see at all."

II.

God must have a big eye to see everything
That we have lost or forgotten. Men used to say
That all lost objects stay upon the moon
Untouched by any other eye but God's.
The moon is God's big yellow eye remembering
What we have lost or never thought. That's why
The moon looks raw and ghostly in the dark.

It is the camera shots of every instant in the world
Laid bare in terrible yellow cold.
It is the objects we never saw.
It is the dodos flying through the snow
That flew from Baffinland to Greenland's tip
And did not even see themselves.
The moon is meant for lovers. Lovers lose
Themselves in others. Do not see themselves.
The moon does. The moon does.
The moon is not a yellow camera. It perceives
What wasn't, what undoes, what will not happen.
It's not a sharp and clicking eye of glass and hood. Just old,
Slow infinite exposure of
The negative that cannot happen.
Fear God's old eye for being shot with ice
Instead of blood. Fear its inhuman mirror blankness
Luring lovers.
Fear God's moon for hexing, sticking pins
In forgotten dolls. Fear it for wolves.
For witches, magic, lunacy, for parlor tricks.
The poet builds a castle on the moon
Made of dead skin and glass. Here marvelous machines
Stamp Chinese fortune cookies full of love.

                                        Tarot cards
Make love to other Tarot cards. Here agony
Is just imagination's sister bitch.
This is the sun-tormented castle which
Reflects the sun. Da dada da.
The castle sings.
Da. I don't remember what I lost. Dada.
The song. Da. The hippogriffs were singing.
Da dada. The boy. His horns
Were wet with song. Dada.
I don't remember. Da. Forgotten.

Da. Dada. Hell. Old butterface
Who always eats her lovers.

Hell somehow exists in the distance
Between the remembered and the forgotten.
Hell somehow exists in the distance
Between what happened and what never happened
Between the moon and the earth of the instant
Between the poem and God's yellow eye.
Look through the window at the real moon.
See the sky surrounded. Bruised with rays.
But look now, in this room, see the moon-children
Wolf, bear, and otter, dragon, dove.
Look now, in this room, see the moon-children
Flying, crawling, swimming, burning
Vacant with beauty.
Hear them whisper.

III.

God's other eye is good and gold. So bright
The shine blinds. His eye is accurate. His eye
Observes the goodness of the light it shines
Then, pouncing like a cat, devours
Each golden trace of light
It saw and shined.
Cat feeds on mouse. God feeds on God. God's goodness is
A black and blinding cannibal with sunny teeth
That only eats itself.
Deny the light
God's golden eye is brazen. It is clanging brass
Of good intention.
It is noisy burning clanging brass.

Light is a carrion crow
Cawing and swooping. Cawing and swooping.
Then, then there is a sudden stop.
The day changes.
There is an innocent old sun quite cold in cloud.
The ache of sunshine stops.
God is gone. God is gone.
Nothing was quite as good.
It's getting late. Put on your coat.
It's getting dark. It's getting cold.
Most things happen in twilight
When the sun goes down and the moon hasn't come
And the earth dances.
Most things happen in twilight
When neither eye is open
And the earth dances.
Most things happen in twilight
When the earth dances
And God is blind as a gigantic bat.
The boys above the swimming pool receive the sun.
Their groins are pressed against the warm cement.
They look as if they dream. As if their bodies dream.
Rescue their bodies from the poisoned sun,
Shelter the dreamers. They're like lobsters now
Hot red and private as they dream.
They dream about themselves.
They dream of dreams about themselves.
They dream they dream of dreams about themselves.
Splash them with twilight like a wet bat.
Unbind the dreamers.
                        Poet,
Be like God.

PSYCHOANALYSIS: AN ELEGY

What are you thinking about?

I am thinking of an early summer.
I am thinking of wet hills in the rain
Pouring water. Shedding it
Down empty acres of oak and manzanita
Down to the old green brush tangled in the sun,
Greasewood, sage, and spring mustard.
Or the hot wind coming down from Santa Ana
Driving the hills crazy,
A fast wind with a bit of dust in it
Bruising everything and making the seed sweet.
Or down in the city where the peach trees
Are awkward as young horses,
And there are kites caught on the wires
Up above the street lamps,
And the storm drains are all choked with dead branches.

What are you thinking?

I think that I would like to write a poem that is slow as a summer
As slow getting started
As 4th of July somewhere around the middle of the second stanza
After a lot of unusual rain
California seems long in the summer.
I would like to write a poem as long as California
And as slow as a summer.
Do you get me, Doctor? It would have to be as slow
As the very tip of summer.
As slow as the summer seems
On a hot day drinking beer outside Riverside

Or standing in the middle of a white-hot road
Between Bakersfield and Hell
Waiting for Santa Claus.

What are you thinking now?

I'm thinking that she is very much like California.
When she is still her dress is like a roadmap. Highways
Traveling up and down her skin
Long empty highways
With the moon chasing jackrabbits across them
On hot summer nights.
I am thinking that her body could be California
And I a rich Eastern tourist
Lost somewhere between Hell and Texas
Looking at a map of a long, wet, dancing California
That I have never seen.
Send me some penny picture-postcards, lady,
Send them.
One of each breast photographed looking
Like curious national monuments,
One of your body sweeping like a three-lane highway
Twenty-seven miles from a night's lodging
In the world's oldest hotel.

What are you thinking?

I am thinking of how many times this poem
Will be repeated. How many summers
Will torture California
Until the damned maps burn

Until the mad cartographer
Falls to the ground and possesses
The sweet thick earth from which he has been hiding.

What are you thinking now?

I am thinking that a poem could go on forever.

MINNESOTA POEMS   (1950–1952)

MINNEAPOLIS: INDIAN SUMMER

What did the Indians do
In a hot Indian October?
Did the same things, I suppose,
Saw the birds flying,
Gathered the last corn.
The same things . . .
Saw the birds flying,
Followed their muddy river
Looking the last time
For a warm face
To kiss in the winter.
The same things . . .
Their muddy river still muddy.
The woods choked with red leaves . . .
Under a sun bright like a broken promise
Watched the birds flying.
And dirty October
Moved like their river
With a heat that frightened the birds away.

WATCHING A TV BOXING MATCH IN OCTOBER

The boxers show an equilibrium
Unmatched this autumn. In the air outside
Winds swirl around the big October moon
While men and boxers seek a place to hide.
Within the focus of a crowded screen
The boxers face each other. They pretend
That man can counterpunch real enemies.
They hit each other til the very end.

One wins and they embrace there while the wind
Grows louder and the screen begins to fade.
Then all the men and boxers bind their wounds
Behind an empty screen, and are afraid.

PORTRAIT OF AN ARTIST

Ovid among the Thracians soon received
A willing smile from those who baked his bread;
Walked country highways thinking of the dead;
Was nodded at by strangers as he grieved.

Not at Colonus, speaking sacred words
But cunning, exile, silence—country things.
As winter came he watched familiar birds
Fly southwards toward the sea on little wings.

SONNET FOR THE BEGINNING OF WINTER

A kind of numbness fills your heart and mine,
A gap where things and people once had been.
We fell unloved, like frozen fields of snow
Upon which not a track has broken through.
The robin and the thrush have taken wing.
The sparrow stays. He sings a dismal song
And eats the seed uncovered in the snow.
An ugly bird, call him the heart's agony.

His songs of disbelief will fill our hearts
As long as winter lasts, as long as we
Are distant partners of this agony
Too far apart to keep each other warm.
So let our hearts lie dead like fields of snow
Unloved, untouched until the distant spring
Grows closer and the gentle birds return
And fill the empty air, and sing.

ON READING LAST YEAR'S LOVE POEMS

The heart's a sprinting thing and hammers fast.
The word is slow and rigid in its pace.
But, if they part once, they must meet at last
As when the rabbit and the tortoise race.
Words follow heartbeats, arrogant and slow
As if they had forever in their load,
As if the race were won, as if they go
To meet a dying rabbit on the road.
Then, step by step, the words become their own.
The turtle creeps ahead to win the prize.
But, ah, the sweeter touch, the quicker boon
Is lost forever when the rabbit dies.

ORPHEUS IN ATHENS

The boy had never seen an honest man.
He looked among us every night he said.
He eyed each stranger like Diogenes
And took him with his lantern into bed.

He'd probe the stranger's body with that light
Search every corner of his flesh and bone
But truth was never there. He'd spend the night
Then leave him and resume his search alone.
I tried to tell him there was some mistake
That truth's a virtue only strangers lack.
But when he turned to face me with a kiss
I closed my lying heart against his lips.

TRAIN SONG FOR GARY

The trains move quietly upon
The tracks outside like animals
I hear them every night.

And sometimes I can almost see
Their glittering unhurried eyes
Move out of sight.

I think that on the day I leave
This town of quiet houses they
Will sound their horns.

I think that then that burning herd
Will turn and follow me towards you
Like unicorns.

A SECOND TRAIN SONG FOR GARY

When the trains come into strange cities
The citizens come out to meet the strangers.
> I love you, Jack, he said
> I love you, Jack, he said
> At another station.

When passengers come in from strange cities
The citizens come out to help the strangers.
> I love you too, I said
> I love you too, I said
> From another station.

The citizens are kind to passing strangers
And nourish them and kiss their lips in kindness.
> I walk the unbelieving streets
> I walk the unbelieving streets
> In a strange city.

At night in cold new beds the welcomed strangers
Achieve in memory the city's promise.
> I wake in love with you
> I wake in love with you
> At last year's station.

Then say goodbye to citizens and city
Admit this much—that they were kind to strangers.
> I leave my love with you
> I leave my love with you
> In this strange city.

BERKELEY / SAN FRANCISCO (1952–1955)

A POSTSCRIPT TO THE BERKELEY RENAISSANCE

What have I lost? When shall I start to sing
A loud and idiotic song that makes
The heart rise frightened into poetry
Like birds disturbed?

I was a singer once. I sang that song.
I saw the thousands of bewildered birds
Breaking their cover into poetry
Up from the heart.

What have I lost? We lived in forests then,
Naked as jaybirds in the ever-real,
Eating our toasted buns and catching flies,
And sometimes angels, with our hooting tongues.

I was a singer once. In distant trees
We made the forests ring with sacred noise
Of gods and bears and swans and sodomy,
And no one but a bird could hear our voice.

What have I lost? The trees were full of birds.
We sat there drinking at the sour wine
In gallon bottles. Shouting song
Until the hunters came.

I was a singer once, bird-ignorant.
Time with a gun said, "Stop,
Find other forests. Teach the innocent."
God got another and a third
Birdlimed in Eloquence.

What have I lost? At night my hooting tongue,
Naked of feathers and of softening years,
Sings through the mirror at me like a whippoorwill
And then I cannot sleep.

"I was a singer once," it sings.
"I sing the song that every captured tongue
Sang once when free and wants again to sing.
But I can sing no song I have not sung."

What have I lost? Spook singer, hold your tongue.
I sing a newer song no ghost-bird sings.
My tongue is sharpened on the iron's edge.
Canaries need no trees. They have their cage.

A POEM FOR DADA DAY AT THE PLACE, APRIL 1, 1955

Darling,
The difference between Dada and barbarism
Is the difference between an abortion and a wet dream.
An abortion
Is a conscious sacrifice of the past, the painting of a mustache
On Mona Lisa, the surrender
Of real children.
The other, darling, is a sacrifice
Of nobody's children, is barbarism, is an Eskimo
Running amok in a museum, is Bohemia
Renouncing cities it had never conquered.
An ugly Vandal pissing on a statue is not Phidias
Pissing on a statue. Barbarism
Is something less than a gesture.
Destroy your own gods if you want Dada:

Give up your vices, burn your jukebox,
Draw mustaches on music, paint a real mother
On every non-objective canvas. Befoul only
Those things that belong to you.
"Beauty is so rare a thing," Pound said,
"So few drink at my fountain."
You only have the right to piss in the fountain
If you are beautiful.

"The window is a sword . . ."

The window is a sword. In the wet air the glass rain falls. I sense the early morning rain. I hear it drop against the window, die there, as if the glass were violent. I feel your body move. You are so far away. In all your sleep, the murdered rain will not cry out. I turn and place my hand upon your groin. This window is a sword.

The window is an angel. It kills the memories of the outside air as they surge in to reach us. Look, you move. You are not safe in sleep. Your hands are clenching sea wind from the air. You groan. Softly, Leech! No childhood rain will rise to drown this room. No long-forgotten wind will chafe your flesh. This window is an angel.

The window is a mirror. We see ourselves upon it. Passionless, it separates our flesh against our flesh until we sleep alone. You, firm in sleep, become the room and I become the rain behind the glass. It keeps a watch so we see ourselves across its opaque edge. It passes light. It keeps us separate. This window is a mirror.

The window is a door. All beauty is behind it. Look, Leech, the light, the light that vanishes! Behind the cracks, the chinks—vague tigers walking under vanilla suns, tired oceans, monsters of the air. All beauty is behind it. See, Leech, the light! This window is a door.

The window is an ocean.

IMAGINARY ELEGIES

IV.

Yes, be like God. I wonder what I thought
When I wrote that. The dreamers sag a bit
As if five years had thickened on their flesh
Or on my eyes. Wake them with what?
Should I throw rocks at them
To make their naked private bodies bleed?
No. Let them sleep. This much I've learned
In these five years in what I spent and earned:
Time does not finish a poem.
The dummies in the empty funhouse watch
The tides wash in and out. The thick old moon
Shines through the rotten timbers every night.
This much is clear, they think, the men who made
Us twitch and creak and put the laughter in our throats
Are just as cold as we. The lights are out.
                               The lights are out.
You'll smell the oldest smells—
The smell of salt, of urine, and of sleep
Before you wake. This much I've learned
In these five years in what I've spent and earned:
Time does not finish a poem.
What have I gone to bed with all these years?
What have I taken crying to my bed
For love of me?
Only the shadows of the sun and moon
The dreaming groins, their creaking images.
Only myself.
                   Is there some rhetoric
To make me think that I have kept a house
While playing dolls? This much I've learned

In these five years in what I've spent and earned:
That two-eyed monster God is still above.
I saw him once when I was young and once
When I was seized with madness, or was I seized
And mad because I saw him once. He is the sun
And moon made real with eyes.
He is the photograph of everything at once. The love
That makes the blood run cold.
But he is gone. No realer than old
Poetry. This much I've learned
In these five years in what I've spent and earned:
Time does not finish a poem.
Upon the old amusement pier I watch
The creeping darkness gather in the west.
Above the giant funhouse and the ghosts
I hear the seagulls call. They're going west
Toward some great Catalina of a dream
Out where the poem ends.
                              But does it end?
The birds are still in flight. Believe the birds.

NEW YORK / BOSTON (1955–1956)

IInd PHASE OF THE MOON

Son of Pan with thighs smooth as raw silk, send some of our dreams back to us from your moonless north. Unnatural sorcerer, you spend your days watching the birds conceal themselves in a cloudless sky or hunting the same birds like a patch of fog in the darkness of birch thickets.

No living man has seen you. The sun that shines so brightly on your lips has made you forget how to cast a shadow. We have been looking for you on the insides of mirrors. You might have given us great joy.

No, you are too tall for love. Along your thighs your love is erected by the birds' screaming, is empty as a lake. No living man has seen such innocence.

Unaware of us as an autumn, you are born and you die in the middle of our parks and our oceans. You hide nothing. You cannot imagine the eyes with which we could watch you.

Let me say now that we suspect you. Let me say now that you have already made yourself known to us as a murderer. Let me say now that our love for you is only an insane abstraction of the love that we have been waiting to give.

IIIrd PHASE OF THE MOON

You stand on a small hill overlooking a valley we were not able to visit. You raise your arms and out of the air comes a mad procession of herons and sparrows flying past you and a small wren, frightened, which flies just above your naked shoulder. We would snatch at the cold wing as it passes, but you blow kisses at its moving shadow. You have broken up all auguries and patterns. Yours is the magnificent nonsense of experience.

In China the nights are cold. Vague tigers gather around your fire and watch you breathlessly. I have not seen you flying into the heart of the sun on wings that did not melt. You play chess with the Emperor of Egypt in an ivory castle. People are dying all around you. I have seen your body stretched out naked before God and reason.

Nothing is too incredible to believe about you. Idiot, simpleton, heartbreaker! . . . Teach us the magic of the departing shadow, teach us how to smash our hearts into butterflies!

IVth PHASE OF THE MOON

You are almost as old as the youngest of us were. So old, old king, and we were in love with your grandfather. See there, on your throne, sitting in judgment like a mountain, see a solitary bird pass through the window, over the banquet table, and down the dark ale-hall towards another window. Your senile heart has ripened into a bird flying. We were in love with your grandfather.

Or a flat Tarot pack. A bearded king on a throne in wisdom, a lightning-blasted tower on a throne in wisdom, a crucified fool ass-backwards on a throne in wisdom. Fire can only burn, terror can only crumble, the heart can only die. There is room for triumph.

Die, then, loved by the gods. Who are we but those that have dared to create you? Lawgiver for your nation, wise as the stone of an old cathedral, moonlight flutters into your ale-hall like a bird without message. Who wrote your laws but those that will be born to destroy them? Who laid that stone but those who will be born to destroy it? The cathedral of stone is beginning to crumble. Die then, loved by the gods who will be born to destroy you, they who were in love with your grandfather.

SOME NOTES ON WHITMAN FOR ALLEN JOYCE

"Let shadows be furnished with genitals."

He was reaching for a world I can still remember. Sweet and painful. It is a world without magic and without god. His ocean is different from my ocean, his moon is different from my moon, his love (oh, God the loss) is different from my love.

In his world roads go somewhere and you walk with someone whose hand you can hold. I remember. In my world roads only go up and down and you are lucky if you can hold on to the road or even know that it is there.

He never heard spirits whispering or saw Aphrodite crawl out of the water or was frightened by the ghost of something crucified. His world had clouds in it and he loved Indian names and carried some of his poems in a pouch around his neck. He had no need of death.

Rimbaud without wings.

Forgive me Walt Whitman, you whose fine mouth has sucked the cock of the heart of the country for fifty years. You did not ever understand cruelty. It was that that severed your world from me, fouled your moon and your ocean, threw me out of your bearded paradise. The comrade you are walking with suddenly twists your hand off. The ghost-bird that is singing to you suddenly leaves a large seagull dropping in your eye. You are sucking the cock of a heart that has clap.

Calamus cannot exist in the presence of cruelty. Not merely human cruelty, but the cruelty of shadows, the cruelty of spirits. Calamus is like Oz. One needs, after one has left it, to find some magic belt to cross its Deadly Desert, some cat to entice one into its mirror. There Walt is, like some great seabird from the Emerald Palace, crying, "Calamus, Calamus." And there one is, at the other side of the desert, hearing Walt but seeing that impossible shadow, those shimmering heat waves across the sky. And one needs no Virgil, but an Alice, a Dorothy, a Washington horsecar conductor, to lead one across that cuntlike mirror, that cruelty.

So when I dreamed of Calamus, as I often did when I touched you or put my hand upon your hand, it was not as of a possible world, but as a lost paradise. A land my father Adam drove me out of with the whip of shadow. In the last sense of the word—a fairy story. That is what I think about Calamus. That is what I think about your damned Calamus.

THE DAY FIVE THOUSAND FISH DIED
ALONG THE CHARLES RIVER

And when the fish come in to die
They slap their heads against the rocks until they float
Downstream on one dead eye. From rocks
The Irish boys yell and throw rocks at them and
      beat them with their sticks.
Gulls wheel in the fine sky. Tall as an ogre
God walks among the rocks. His angels cry,
"Yell and throw rocks at them and beat them
      with sticks!"
But watch those upturned eyes
That gleam like God's own candles in the sun. Nothing
Deserves to live.

HIBERNATION—AFTER MORRIS GRAVES

Deeper than sleep, but in a room as narrow
The mind turns off its longings one by one,
Lets beautiful black fingers snap the last one,
Remove the self and lie its body down.
The Future chills the sky above the chamber.

The second word is *andros*
Who is proud of his gender
Wears it like a gamecock, erects it
Through the midnight of time
Like a birthday candle.
He will give you wisdom like a Fool
Hidden in the loins
Crying out against the inelegance
Of all that is not sacred.

The third word is *eros*
Who will cling to you every birthnight
Bringing your heart substance.
Whomever you touch will love you,
Will feel the cling of His touch upon you
Like sunlight scattered over an ancient mirror.

The fourth word is *thanatos,* the black belly
That eats birthdays.
I do not give you *thanatos.* I bring you a word to call Him
Thanatos, devourer of young men, heart-biter, bone-licker.
Look, He slinks away when you name Him.
Name Him! *Thanatos.*

The last word is *agape,*
The dancer that puts birthdays in motion.
She is there to lead words.
Counter to everything, She makes words
Circle around Her. Words dance.
See them. *Anthropos* ageless,
Andros made virgin, *Eros* unmirrored,
Thanatos devoured.
Agape, Agape, ring-mistress,
Love

That comes from beyond birthdays,
That makes poetry
And moves stars.

BIRDLAND, CALIFORNIA

The stairs upstairs were stairs
For the sake of ceremony
If Gertrude Stein had tried them on tiptoe
She would not have reached the 2nd floor.
The 2nd floor was a floor
For the sake of ceremony
What I mean is
This is a poem about Orpheus
Orpheus, he had the weight of Eurydice upon
     his back
He tried to carry her
Up that imaginary stairway.
Eurydice could be anyone. Is
I suppose
Anyone.
That makes the poem harder.
This night (Joe Dunn could give a date
October 1st
That's Joe Dunn's date)
But I can't.
Butterflies transfigure and burn
In the absences of postmen.
But Joe Dunn will come home
Past all those unreal stairs
Will
Make a noise when the door opens,

Will turn on the light. Will turn on the light
Madness lies there. Orpheus collapses
Under the weight of the sentence, killing butterflies.
It is already
October 2nd.
October 3rd. Will it ever be important again
Whether it is October 2nd or October 3rd?
Have you ever wondered
What I mean is
When will they take all of us back to Birdland?
An embarrassed Orpheus
Arises
With a heavy Eurydice in his arms
What I mean is can a poem ever
Take accidentals for its ultimates?
It is now October 5th (or 6th)
English majors
Can discover the correct date
(The Yankees used seven pitchers
That will tell you the day)
I was lonelier than you are now (or will be)
October something, 1956.

"Imagine Lucifer . . ."

Imagine Lucifer
An angel without angelness
An apple
Plucked clear by will of taste, color,
Strength, beauty, roundness, seed
Absent of all God painted, present everything
An apple is.

Imagine Lucifer
An angel without angelness
A poem
That has revised itself out of sound
Imagine, rhyme, concordance
Absent of all God spoke of, present everything
A poem is.
                    The law I say, the Law
Is?
What is Lucifer
An emperor with no clothes
No skin, no flesh, no heart
An emperor!

THE SONG OF THE BIRD IN THE LOINS

A swallow whispers in my loins
So I can neither lie or stand
And I can never sleep again
Unless I whisper you his song:

"Deep in a well," he whispers. "Deep
As diamonds washed beneath the stone
I wait and whisper endlessly
Imprisoned in a well of flesh.

"At night he sometimes sleeps and dreams.
At night he sometimes does not hear my voice.
How can I wound you with my well of sound
If he can sleep and dream beneath its wounds?

"I whisper to you through his lips.
He is my cage, you are my source of song.
I whisper to you through a well of stone.
Listen at night and you will hear him sing:

"'A swallow whispers in my loins
So I can neither lie or stand
And I can never sleep again
Unless I whisper you this song.'"

BABEL 3

It wasn't the tower at all
It was our words he hated.
Once our words rose
Into God's willing mouth
Like bells sing into houses.
When someone loved
The word said love,
On the 38th floor,
On the 94th floor,
On the 1224th floor.
Words were different then. God didn't
Divide us into different languages
He divided
Words and men.
Men and words—He called the words angels.
We called the words angels.
Things were different then.

THEY MURDERED YOU: AN ELEGY ON THE DEATH OF KENNETH REXROTH

To be accompanied by five jazz flutes and a contrabassoon

I will never again climb a mountain, read St. Augustine or go to bed
    with a woman
Without wishing that you were there, Kenneth Rexroth
Sharing my experience.
I will find you now in the leaves and in the sunsets,
Yes, and in the saxophones and peyote buttons
Wherever God and Nature make it quietly together
And the murderous squares don't try to stop their experience.
When you died last month at the age of 52 of stomach ulcers
It was as if we young men had lost the last hope of a libertarian
    revolution
A society where poetry, jazz, sex, politics, and religion could function
    together like a giant gong
Each of whose tones perfectly overlays the other.
A society where Bohemians wouldn't starve and predatory men
    wouldn't lynch Negros and kill Jews and Hungarians
A society where wars would be abolished
A society where men and women would be perfectly free to do, say,
    think, feel what they wanted
Under your leadership.
When Christopher Smart
Went to bed in the meat market
You were there Kenneth Rexroth
Giving encouragement to the best minds of his generation
When Jakob Boehme
Was busted by ten Christ-hating policemen
You were there Kenneth Rexroth
Breathing comfort.
Sacco and Vanzetti will never forget

The sound of your rough voice
Or Rosa Luxemburg
Or Allen Ginsberg.
Yes, you have taught the youth of our generation to write
    political poetry
That does not really offend the F.B.I.
And yet is unsquare, mystical
Firmly in favor
Of God, physical exercise, and companionate marriage.

A POEM TO THE READER OF THE POEM

I throw a naked eagle in your throat.
I dreamed last night
That I was wrestling with you on the mountainside.
An eagle had a dream over our heads.
We threw rocks at him.
I dreamed last night—
This is false in any poem
Last night never happened
Couldn't
Make you feel the meaning so quickly
That I could tell you what I dreamed last night
That I could tell you that I dreamed I was wrestling
With the reader of this poem.
Dreamed—
Was it a wet dream?
Or dry
Like a dream is
When boys in a dream throw rocks at it?
I heard myself sobbing in a wet dream
Don't worry I will tell you everything.

I had a dream last night
That I was wrestling with you on the mountainside.
Was it a wet dream?
No I would tell you if it was a wet dream.
It was this poem
Us
I wrestled with you in this poem
And it was not a wet dream.

Then define
If you don't want to scare him out of the poem
Define
The dream
The wrestling
The lie
And in
What sweet Christ's name the eagle we were throwing rocks at was,
And why I love you so much
And why it was not a wet dream.
I can't deny
The lie.
The eagle was
God or Charles Olson
The eagle was men wrestling naked
Without the hope of men wrestling naked.
The eagle was a wet dream.
But the eagle in my throat says, "Jack,
How can you write a poem to the reader of a poem?
Even in a dream you must love somebody."
This is another lie.
I did not wrestle with anybody
I wrestled with the reader of this poem.

Men kiss men
Not like anybody
Kisses a girl
Kiss each other like the map of Africa
Or a picture of a desert
Or a scale-map of the entire universe.
But this is not a wet dream.
We did not kiss each other.
My darling, if you flew
A naked eagle in my throat
I'd shout, "Exactly!
When I said this was a poem to the reader
I wanted to dig a pitfall
Only you could fall into.
You
Know who you are
Know how terribly far
From last night you are.
If I am old when you read this,
If I am dead when you read this,
Darling, darling, darling,
It was last night
When I wrestled with you.
I am wrestling with you.
It was not a wet dream or you would be wrestling
With a naked gravestone."
Take it simply
Suppose we had been exploring
The hills and canyons of hell
And wrestled
And fucked
And—Hell,
Nothing but a spoiled camping trip.

Wrestling! It was as if we were in a room full
Of faceless comedians.

That wasn't what I wanted to say. I wanted to
		tell you
That there is innocence too
And the blind grandeur
Of the face of a mountain
In all we would have surveyed
If it had been a wet dream
If we had traveled
Mapless, past what either of us knew
Past the dead eagle,
Past the faceless comedians
Who bug us,
Past the past that has misplaced us,
Past all the dead lines in a poem that after all
Are only dead lines in a poem,
To the mountains
Where our hearts are
Where the heart is.
A wet dream—
I'll tell God
It was a wet dream.

SONG FOR BIRD AND MYSELF

I am dissatisfied with my poetry.
I am dissatisfied with my sex life.
I am dissatisfied with the angels I believe in.
    Neo-classical like Bird,
    Distrusting the reality
    Of every note.
    Half-real
    We blow the sentence pure and real
    Like chewing angels.

"Listen, Bird, why do we have to sit here dying
In a half-furnished room?
The rest of the combo
Is safe in houses
Blowing bird-brained Dixieland,
How warm and free they are. What right
Music."
    "Man,
    We
    Can't stay away from the sounds.
    We're *crazy*, Jack
    We gotta stay here 'til
    They come and get us."

Neo-classical like Bird.
Once two birds got into the Rare Book Room.
Miss Swift said,
"Don't
Call a custodian
Put crumbs on the outside of the window
Let them
Come outside."

Neo-classical

The soft line strains
Not to be neo-classical.
But Miss Swift went to lunch. They
Called a custodian.
Four came.
Armed like Myrmidons, they
Killed the birds.
Miss Munsterberg
Who was the first
American translator of Rilke
Said
"Suppose one of them
Had been the Holy Ghost."
Miss Swift,
Who was back from lunch,
Said
"Which."

     But the poem isn't over.
     It keeps going
     Long after everybody
     Has settled down comfortably into laughter.
     The bastards
     On the other side of the paper
     Keep laughing.
     LISTEN.
     STOP LAUGHING.
     THE POEM ISN'T OVER. Butterflies.
I knew there would be butterflies
For butterflies represent the lost soul
Represent the way the wind wanders
Represent the bodies
We only clasp in the middle of a poem.
See, the stars have faded.

There are only butterflies.
Listen to
The terrible sound of their wings moving.
Listen,
The poem isn't over.

Have you ever wrestled with a bird,
You idiotic reader?
Jacob wrestled with an angel.
(I remind you of the image)
Or a butterfly
Have you ever wrestled with a single butterfly?
Sex is no longer important.
Colors take the form of wings. Words
Have got to be said.
A butterfly,
A bird,
Planted at the heart of being afraid of dying.
Blow,
Bird,
Blow,
Be,
Neo-classical.
Let the wings say
What the wings mean
Terrible and pure.

    The horse
    In Cocteau
    Is as neo-classical an idea as one can manage.
    Writes all our poetry for us
    Is Gertrude Stein
    Is God
    Is the needle for which

God help us
There is no substitute
Or the Ace of Swords
When you are telling a fortune
Who tells death.
Or the Jack of Hearts
Whose gypsy fortune we clasp
In the middle of a poem.

"And are we angels, Bird?"
"That's what we're trying to tell 'em, Jack
There aren't any angels except when
You and me blow 'em."

So Bird and I sing
Outside your window
So Bird and I die
Outside your window.
This is the wonderful world of Dixieland
Deny
The bloody motherfucking Holy Ghost.
This is the end of the poem.
You can start laughing, you bastards. This is
The end of the poem.

A POEM WITHOUT A SINGLE BIRD IN IT

What can I say to you, darling,
When you ask me for help?
I do not even know the future
Or even what poetry
We are going to write.
Commit suicide. Go mad. Better people
Than either of us have tried it.
I loved you once but
I do not know the future.
I only know that I love strength in my friends
And greatness
And hate the way their bodies crack when they die
And are eaten by images.
The fun's over. The picnic's over.
Go mad. Commit suicide. There will be nothing left
After you die or go mad,
But the calmness of poetry.

THE UNVERT MANIFESTO AND OTHER PAPERS FOUND IN THE RARE BOOK ROOM OF THE BOSTON PUBLIC LIBRARY IN THE HANDWRITING OF OLIVER CHARMING. BY S.

THE UNVERT MANIFESTO

1) An unvert is neither an invert or an outvert, a pervert or a convert, an introvert or a retrovert. An unvert chooses to have no place to turn.

2) One should always masturbate on street corners.

3) Unversion is the attempt to make the sexual act as rare as a rosepetal. It consists of linking the sexual with the greatest cosmic force in the universe—Nonsense, or as we prefer to call it, MERTZ.

4) Sex should be a frightening experience like a dirty joke or an angel.

5) Dirty jokes and angels should be frightening experiences.

6) An unvert must not be homosexual, heterosexual, bisexual, or autosexual. He must be metasexual. He must enjoy going to bed with his own tears.

7) Mertz!

8) All the universe is laughing at you.

9) Poetry, painting, and cocksucking are all attempts of the unvert to make God laugh.

10) The larger the Dada, the bigger the hole.

11) Sidney Mertz was the only man ever arrested for drunken-driving of a steam locomotive. He is now the bartender of the American Legion bar in Jackson, Wyoming.

12) Jews and Negros are not allowed to be unverts. The Jew will never understand unversion and the Negro understands it too well.

13) An unvert only loves other unverts. He will, however, consent to perform an act of unversion with almost anything else except lovers and mountain lions.

14) God loves God.

15) Mertz must be applied to sex. People must learn to laugh into each other's gonads.

16) God is an unvert.

17) Sex without love is better than love without sex. Sex without Mertz is never better than Mertz without sex. Nonsense is an act of friendship.

18) The larger the Dada, the bigger the hole.

19) Nonsense. Mertz, Dada, and God all go to the same nightclubs.

20) So does Graham Macarel.

EXCERPTS FROM OLIVER CHARMING'S DIARY

October 31, 1953:
I must unvent someone named Graham Macarel. He should be about seventeen or eighteen and have a large Dada. I can use him as the hero and victim of my Mertzcycle . . .

November 5, 1953:
Laughed all day. The elements of imagination are exhausting as Hell.

November 23, 1953:
It was more successful than I expected. He is beginning to become mythical. I saw him today and he told me that he is taking a course in his art school in which he has to clip examples of racial prejudice from Tarot cards and give their exact date. His art school's name is the California School of Fine Flowers. His teacher's name is S. We talked for a while and I am already beginning to destroy his universe. . . . Method is everything.

December 1, 1953:
Love must only be applied at the wrong time and in the wrong place. It must be thrown at the unsuspecting like a custard pie made of poison. . . . Nothing destroys Mertz more than custom. Nothing destroys it less than treason.

December 7, 1953:
I return to Graham Macarel. (Note—I must be sure to call him Mac. Graham reminds the uninformed imagination of crackers.) He has become a combination of a Boy Scout and a depth charge. He appeals to the primitive sources of nonsense and despair. I suspect that his teacher, S., is secretly an unvert—or at least a spoiled unvert. Something is going on between S. and history. I wonder if Mac realizes that an unvert is an agent of Kubla Khan.

December 9, 1953:
"An unvert is an angel of Kubla Khan."—that's what Mac said to me last night in the men's room of the Palace Hotel. At the time he said it he was . . . which is certainly Dada if not Mertz.

December 10, 1953:
. . . suspects . . .

December 18, 1953:
It is Christmas vacation at the California School of Fine Flowers. S. was in the bars last night, very drunk. I think he is planning to unvert somebody.

December 19, 1953:
I had a conversation with S. late last night. He was again very drunk. "Why did you have to invent Graham Macarel?" he asked me angrily.
"I thought it would be good for your poetry," I answered.
"Why didn't you invent syphilis instead," he asked contemptuously.
So yesterday I invented syphilis. Today I am going to . . .

December 22, 1953:
S. is in Los Angeles.

December 23, 1953:
To appear as human among homosexuals and to appear as divine among heterosexuals . . .

December 24, 1953:
Nobody remains in this city and I have done all my Christmas shopping. The Dada in painting is not Duchamp. The Dada in poetry is not Breton. The Dada in sex is not de Sade. All these men were too obsessed with the mechanism of their subject. A crime against nature must also be a crime against art. A crime against art must also be a crime against nature. All beauty is at continuous war with God.

December 25, 1953:
Merry Christmas, Graham Macarel.

December 26, 1953:
It continually amazes the unprejudiced Mertzian observer that even the people who struggle most against the limits of art are content to

have sex in ordinary academic ways, as if they and their bed-partners were nineteenth-century paintings. Or, worse, they will change the point of view (top becomes bottom, male becomes female, etc., etc.) and think, like the magic realists that they are, that they have changed something.

Everybody is guilty of this—from Cocteau to Beethoven.

December 28, 1953:
A sailor asked me last night what the unvert thought of Kinsey. I told him that we held that Kinsey was a valuable evidence of the boredom of un-unverted sex—that ordinary sex had become so monotonous that it had become statistical like farm income or rolling stock totals. I told him that Kinsey was the Zola preparing the way for the new Lautréamont.

It is remarkable how even science fiction has developed no new attitudes toward sex. The vacant interstellar spaces are filled with exactly the same bedrooms the rocketships left behind. It is only the unvert who dares to speak Martian in bed. I wonder if Kierkegaard had wet dreams.

December 29, 1953:
How the Zen Masters Taught Sex to Their Disciples—such a book would be the most useful book a man could publish. Sex is a metaphysical experience. Zen taught that man can only reach the metaphysical by way of the absurd. No, absurd is the wrong word. What is the Chinese for shaggy-dog story?

The book should be illustrated pornographically but in the general style of *Mad* Comics. It should have a blue cover.

December 30, 1953:
S. is in town again. I saw him at the Black Cat. He looked confused at all the lack of excitement around him, as if he believed that a holiday was like a snowstorm and people should notice it.

We began discussing homosexuality. I, by bringing in subtle pieces of unvert propaganda, and he, embarrassed and overintellectual as if he thought, or rather hoped, that I was trying to seduce him:

"We homosexuals are the only minority group that completely lacks any vestige of a separate cultural heritage. We have no songs, no folklore, even our customs are borrowed from our upper-middle-class mothers," he said.

"What about camping?" I asked. "Isn't that a cultural pattern worthy at least of Ruth Benedict's cunt?"

"What about camping?" he asked rhetorically. "A perpetual Jewish vaudeville joke—or, at the very best, a minstrel show impeccably played by Negros in blackface."

The trouble with S. is that he doesn't understand Martian. I must tell him about the time . . .

December 31, 1953:
I rebel against the tyranny of the calendar.

January 1, 1954:
My analyst is teaching me French.

January 2, 1954:
S. says that it is inconsistent for an unvert to have a psychiatrist. He does not understand unversion. The relation between the analyst and the patient is the firmest and most hallowed, if the most conventional, sexual relationship in the modern world. This is precisely why it must be shaken. It is our task to experience and unvert all sexual relationships.

January 3, 1954:
Sometimes, in moments of depression, I think that all this talk of Dada and Mertz is merely the reaction of the unsuccessful cocksucker or artsucker who doesn't understand beauty when it offers itself to him. Witness Western civilization or the bar last night. . . .

January 4, 1954:

Now that I have Graham Macarel, S., and a psychiatrist, all that I need is an angel. One cannot, however, safely invent an angel . . . Lot was the last person to safely invent an angel. He was bored with his lover, with their children, and with all the inhabitants of the immense and sandy Turkish bath that they were living in . . . He invented an angel and then everybody had to kill him. . . . Everybody had to kill him not because the angel was as dangerous as a hydrogen bomb (which he was) and not because the angel was beautiful as a Florida hurricane (which he was), but because the angel was a stranger and it is always the habit of Jews and homosexuals to kill strangers. . . . They almost caught the angel once in Lot's chimney, and a sailor once managed to catch hold of its groin as it was disappearing into a broom closet; but soon fire and brimstone were descending on the town and Lot was walking with his lover along a deserted road on the first range of foothills carrying a packed suitcase. . . . The lover looked backwards, of course, to make sure that the angel was not following them and was immediately turned into a life-sized salt statue. It is very difficult to suck the cock of a life-sized salt statue, or to sample the delights of sodomy with a pillar . . . Lot left him there and trudged onward alone, with an angel on his back.

I must take warning from this. There are some inventions even sex does not make necessary.

January 5, 1954:

No angel as of yet. I wonder if I could steal one. By a bit of clever propaganda I have arranged that Mac will have to report on angels to his history class. This should bring things into focus.

Mac asked me about angels yesterday—whether I thought they really existed, what they did in bed, etc., etc. I told him that very few people under twenty-five had angels at all. That they were like a kind of combination of Siamese cats and syphilis and for him not to worry if they occasionally tugged at his pubic hairs. He was still uncertain: "How can I find any chronology in it?" he asked plaintively.

January 6, 1954:
There is a morning when it rains in the corner of everybody's bedroom.

January 7, 1954:
My psychiatrist, Robert Berg, considers that it is his duty to unvent angels. It must be understood that unvention is different from unversion as psychoanalysis is from poetry.

January 9, 1954:
Mac tells me that he saw an angel resting in a tree above his art school. This must be the angel we have been waiting for.

January 10, 1954:
I have seen it too. It is a bearded angel, small as a bird, and answers to the name of Heurtebise. S., being what he is, pretends not to believe and says that it is only an owl or some unlucky night creature. He says that he is sorry for it.

January 11, 1954:
The angel keeps screeching in the tree. It is behaving more and more like a bird. We are doing something wrong. . . . Perhaps it isn't our angel.

January 12, 1954:
I am gradually able to have the most Mertzian sexual experiences in my dreams, experiences as divorced from the limitations of the material as Dada poetry is from Dada sculpture. My psychiatrist, Robert Berg, is helping me to do this. It is his theory that psychiatrists should teach people how to dream properly, that a man's day should not be wasted in a struggle for meaning but should be spent in the simplest pursuits (including the earning of enough money to pay for a psychiatrist) so that he may save all his energies from his dreams at night—the proper and strategic place to continue his eternal struggle against God.

It is his feeling that the world of Mertz is the world of the dreamer—that to try to force the truly Mertzian act upon reality is like trying to make a collage out of a sheep's belly or forcing a penis into an empty Pepsi Cola bottle. It is his conception that the most complete and metasexual act that man can hope for is the perfect wet dream, the bloody battlefield on which God is finally defeated.

The angel screeched all night last night below my window.

January 13, 1954 :
Mac asked me to tell him another story like the one about Lot, he says it helps him with his classes, and so I told him the story about Noah.

Noah was drinking in a bar one evening and he happened to knock over the glass he was drinking from. He asked the bartender for a rag to wipe up the puddle, which the bartender gave to him, but when he had finished wiping up the mahogany counter, it was just as wet as it had been before. He called over the bartender and asked him to wipe the bar with a fresh cloth. The same thing happened, in fact the puddle was even wetter. Noah knew then. He put a few tables together and began building an ark. . . .

This, of course, has nothing to do with either angels or poems.

January 14, 1954:
. . . Mac begged me to tell him who Noah took along with him in the ark. I couldn't, of course. It would be too cruel. . . . Noah took nobody, neither his wife, nor Mac, nor S., nor his psychiatrist, only a dove to tell him when land was ahead. . . . Nobody is necessary after you have built your ark. Mac is too young to understand without crying. . . . S., whom I met last night, tells me that he thinks the ark is a book. He would. The angel has stopped screeching outside my window.

January 15, 1954:
Very interesting session with Berg. Must remember that he, with his focus on the surreal, is the Trotsky of the movement. Today he

suggested that the flood in my story symbolized the wet dream and the ark, the heart that emerges from it.

In the course of a discussion of how to assassinate S., we came to talk of other repressed unverts. Who were our precursors? The men who almost succeeded in freeing us from the yoke of sexual meaning? We agreed that Plato was an unvert because he was able to unvent the figure of Socrates, that first and greatest of Dada poets who was able to unseduce Alcibiades as if he were a piece of rough trade. We rejected Tiberius as too ingenious. Of the moderns we agreed on Lewis Carroll and L. Frank Baum. We agreed that the frog Dada poets were mere bleeding-hearted sexual liberals who started out by proclaiming the absolute mastery of Dada and ended up writing poems about how nice their wives' tits look. The only real unvert Berg could see among the contemporaries was Rimbaud on account of his childhood. The only one that I could see was Stevens on account of his secret vices.

January 16, 1954:
The negro's aim is integration. The Jew's and the homosexual's aim is segregation. The unvert's aim is a grand degradation between men and angels. We are a minority group only in our heros.

Talked with S. in the Black Cat last night. He was quoting that great suppressed sonnet of Joyce Kilmer's which describes a gay bar as a "savage fishpond." I wish I could trust him enough to talk about unversion.

July (no, January) 18, 1954:
This is a country that destroys its children, almost before they are born. I know what they will make out of Mac, what they have made out of S. and Berg, what they will try to make out of me. There is only the angel in the tree outside—who may be the wrong angel—and then acres of empty television sets and children.

January 20, 1954:

My grandmother's birthday . . . S. and Mac were playing chess together in The Place when I walked in last night. S. looked up and said, without really seeing me, "Ah, the Queen's Gambit." He is teaching Mac to distrust me. . . .

Later, after a young woman had come in and taken Mac from the bar (another one of S.'s students) S. at once began talking to me about Genet. I told him that I thought that Gide was more to the point, that he was a subtler pornographer. S. would have none of this. "Gide's inversion is like Christian socialism," he said, "Gide has sex like a popular-front clergyman. He is on the letterhead of every pink committee to defend lonely gonads."

. . . . "Anybody can have sexual fantasies in a prison," I said.

January 21, 1954:
The girl's name is Kathy.

January 20, 1954:
The angel in the tree turns out not to be an angel at all but an old bitter man named Thomas Wentworth Higginson who wishes to seduce me. He tells me that his cries were not shrieks or screeches at all. He was merely trying to attract my attention. . . . He says that he is only fifty-four (he looks sixty and smells of tobacco) and that he is able to maintain an erection . . . . . He knows my name and says that he has been watching me and wants to be loved.

January 21, 1954:
It was a warm night last night and the angel in my tree was naked. He keeps shouting now, "I will teach you the secrets that old men know" or, "Look, my penis is dry." I liked him better as a bird . . . .

Earlier I had dinner with Robert Duncan, the poet. He is too concerned with affirmation, with flying his soul like a kite. . . . He substitutes wit for nonsense, the transcendent for the vicious. It is as if Gertrude Stein and Ralph Waldo Emerson had gone to bed together with Jean Cocteau holding the vaseline. He is the greatest poet America has produced since Pound and Williams died.

S. writes poetry too. Mac writes wet dreams and Berg collects photographs of nude horses. But that old man in the tree, that angel, what does he write?

January 22, 1954:
Mac was in The Place with Kathy (this girl that he never talks about) and he asked me to tell them a story that both of them could use in the same class. I told them the story of Adam . . .

Adam and the Devil lived together as lovers in a large garden. They would float down the river together, or ride railway trains together, or play a complicated form of cowboys and Indians . . . They loved to kiss each other's beautiful sunburned faces.

One day Adam invented a snake. It was very large and very deaf and Adam was amused to see how much it resembled his penis. Unfortunately a woman named Eve came along with the snake (she had been with it for years in sideshows and carnivals and she carried it in a golden box, which she kept sealed with a hairpin). Adam had no choice but to fall in love with her.

The Devil was very hurt when he noticed that Adam never wanted to come to bed with him again. He couldn't bring himself to kill Adam and it wasn't in his power to kill Eve since she didn't really exist. He wept and he suffered and finally, feeling truly alone, built a large apple tree and put all of his love for Adam into an apple that was to hang from its branches forever . . . Eve merely ate the apple and spat the seeds upon the ground.

As a result of this, God created man.

January 23, 1954:
S. talked to the angel in the Black Cat last night. He insists on treating it as an old auntie just as before he insisted on treating it as an owl.

"But Mr. Higginson—"

"Call me Tom," the angel said.

"—I don't sleep with old men."

"You'd sleep with Jean Cocteau, wouldn't you?"

S. was baffled.

A rather remarkable evening. Thomas Wentworth Higginson, Mac, S., and I were present. Nothing seemed further away than love.

The Angel Higginson was dressed elaborately. A sunlamp had been used on his face. He sat and stared at S., who was uncomfortable. S. could finally stand it no longer. "You and your fake angels," he said, turning angrily to me. "Your clever theology, your ingenious substitutes for bodies! Why don't you tell us a story that doesn't depend on the Jews?"

"My stories do not depend on the Jews," I said.

"Yes?" S. said nastily. "I've had them retold to me, you know. Abie Adam, and Ikey Noah, and Isadore Lot of Hillel House. Why don't you tell a story with an Aryan hero in it?"

"Orpheus?"

"Orpheus."

"I'd better take up the story here myself," Thomas Wentworth Higginson said as he nervously rubbed one of the rings on his shining hands with his handkerchief. "I was one of those who met Orpheus. It is really a delightful story.

"We were having a party. Everyone was there. Tata was sitting on the black chaise lounge holding court—"

"Tata?" S. interrupted.

"The queen. Persephone, my dear, Persephone. That's what we always call her. She was wearing the most extravagant feather demi-châle and Heurtebise was pouting a little and singing the naughtiest song about his childhood, when suddenly there was the maddest commotion at the door. Somebody was arguing with the butler.

"Well, some of us just had to see who it was and what it wanted. Well, there in the doorway looking just about ready to cry was a rather dumpy little human carrying a stringed instrument.

"In spite of the howling of the butler we invited him in, trying to make him feel as comfortable as was possible. He kept mumbling about looking for somebody but we couldn't hear him well and we were standing politely away from him because his breath was bad.

"We left him in the middle of the room and went back to the crowd that was listening to Heurtebise sing. He had just gotten to that incredibly naughty part of the song where he sings 'Diddle my iddlejums.' Only a few people turned around to look at Orpheus."

"Was Eurydice there?" Mac asked.

"Oh, yes. She was in the corner of the room giggling with some of the rest of the girls. She was wearing a Russian bathing suit and looked terribly elegant."

"Could Orpheus see her?" I asked.

Thomas Wentworth Higginson looked around at me. "I don't really know," he said. "He was gawking around at everything as if he had never been to a party before. Well, anyway I didn't pay much attention to him for a while and the next time I noticed him he was on his knees in front of poor Miffy singing and making horrible noises on his guitar or whatever it was. Poor Miffy didn't know what to make of it. She was wearing a very amusing drag outfit—a huge crown made of real pearls and imitation opals and rhinestones and the choicest black ermine robe and, of course, she didn't know whether the little thing was camping or just utterly, awfully serious. Everything had stopped now and we all were staring at the effect. Tears were running out of his swollen eyes and he was singing, sobbing, and screaming at the same time:

> 'Black queen, bitch of the heartless night
> Listen in anger while I sing my song.'

"Suddenly we all started to giggle. The poor thing thought Miffy was Tata."

The Angel Higginson stopped and ordered himself another cognac and soda. His small eyes were gleaming.

"What happened then?" Mac wanted to know.

"Ask him," the Angel Higginson said, putting his manicured hand lightly on my shoulder.

"What happened?" Mac repeated.

"Nothing happened," I said. "That's the end of the story. In later years Orpheus was killed by the god Dionysus, but that was for wholly different reasons."

I think that Mac was so frightened and unhappy that he went home to sleep with S. tonight. Neither of them understands elegance.

"Then Orpheus," Mac said, "was on a spaceship and Eurydice couldn't see him anymore."

April 1, 1954:

. . . when suddenly Kathy became something like a life-sized doll and said, "I am imperatrix mundi." We all stared. She took a Tarot deck out from between her breasts and handed it to Mac. He picked a card and she took the deck from him immediately and picked a card for herself.

"What on earth is happening?" S. asked. "What cards did you pick?" He reached for the deck himself, but it seemed to cut him—as if the cards were razor blades—and he dropped it and then sat there staring at his bloody hand and then at Mac and Kathy. "Now we have different names," Kathy said.

. . . Mr. and Mrs. Doom have been married to each other for almost three years. They are a very pleasant couple. The Angel Higginson cannot see them and says that they are demons.

April 2, 1954:

Mrs. Doom seems to follow us everywhere. Today she brought up the question of whether women can be unverts. S., whose hand is still inflamed, made the rather cheap witticism that the limit of a woman's sexual imagination is to be unmarried. Mrs. Doom, after she had finished laughing at this, launched a long complicated anecdote about how the Dooms had first met S. on a cable car at two in the morning in a previous year and how funny he had been then. She seems sincerely to like him.

The Angel Higginson did not show up at our table tonight, but I thought I saw him standing outside the bar talking to a policeman.

April 3, 1954:

"Why don't you ever tell us stories like you used to," Mrs. Doom asked.

"But I never—"

"Last year you told us stories," Mrs. Doom said. "Nice stories, stories about all those lovely people with the funny names."

(Mr. Doom just handed me a poem under the table. I don't believe that anyone noticed.)

Mrs. Doom turned to S. "Don't you remember all those lovely stories? You were there too."

"Women are the enemies of the sexual imagination," S. said.

"Yes, women are the energies of the sexual imagination," Mrs. Doom said. She began humming to herself. (Mr. Doom just handed me another poem underneath the table.)

"I'll tell you a story about Lizzie Borden," I said. "Lizzie Borden woke up one morning and discovered that she was the last empress on earth. It was a hot July day and she lived in a small town in southern Massachusetts. She had breakfast with her mother and father (bacon and eggs and cold mutton) and then took off all her clothes and proceeded to cut her mother and father to pieces with an ax she had been keeping under her bed.

"The people of the town (who did not know that Lizzie Borden was the last empress on earth—as indeed she hadn't been until that very morning) arrested her and brought her to trial. 'Did you do it and why did you do it?' the prosecutor asked her. 'It was exactly like having a baby and besides there were no bloodstains on my clothes,' she replied. She was triumphantly acquitted and the whole jury thanked her.

"She moved to a small town in western Massachusetts and decided to do the same thing to poetry that she had done for living. She got herself a new father and began destroying all the objects that could be used in poetry. She started out with things that could be used around the house, like closets and kitchen knives, and went on to abstract words like fear and wisdom and, finally, to God himself. By this time, she had published three series of poems and had destroyed all the objects and emotions that it was possible to have in a small town in western Massachusetts and she began to be tired of her new name.

"Reading William James convinced her that she should go to Paris and become a Lesbian. She got herself a new mother (who made hot fudge sundaes out of bay leaves and marijuana), and then she bought a lot of shapes and squares and shadows which were really cubed and made out of old newspapers."

"And I suppose she murdered the French language as well as English," Mrs. Doom said. "You artists blame women for everything."

"No," I said, "what she had discovered now is that if you cut words small enough they have to echo. She merely took the words she hadn't killed and made them repeat themselves forever."

(Mr. Doom passed me a broad sheaf of poetry under the table. They are made out of all the words his wife left him.)

April 4, 1954:
"You people are dying of angelism," Mrs. Doom said.

We were all assembled there. S., Robert Berg the psychiatrist, Kathy and Mac (who had been called up from non-existence for this very purpose), the Angel Higginson (who has become a bat again and is hovering around the chandelier on the second story above the bar), and myself, bound and gagged and carried in by three strangers.

"Angelism is like giantism or scurvy," she said. "It is an organic disease usually caused by the presence of an unvert."

"That's what I always said," Robert Berg shouted. "I always said he was crazy."

(I must be crazy. I have become convinced that I am Mr. Doom. S. has also disappeared.)

"Angelism is merely a symptom of wanting forbidden meanings," Mac said in a little-boy voice. He has begun dancing a waltz with Kathy.

"Angelism is merely a symptom of wanting there to be forbidden meanings," Kathy says sweetly in the middle of a blue waltz.

"Everything is as quiet as grasshoppers," says Mr. Doom suddenly. I am Mr. Doom suddenly. I am bound and gagged.

"There is a psychological reason for grasshoppers being silent," says Robert Berg, the psychiatrist. "Grasshoppers do not know how to keep themselves from dying. They suffer from angelism."

The Angel Higginson swoops down from the ceiling suddenly and onto Robert Berg's shoulder. "Haven't you ever wanted to be an angel?" he asks.

Berg looks over his shoulder without wonder. "Haven't you ever wanted not to be an angel," he asks. "Not to be different. To be able to sleep at the time everybody sleeps. To lose your shape gradually instead of your wings."

"A grasshopper is crawling on my grave," Mr. Doom says.

"Quiet!" says Mrs. Doom. "Quiet. Once men get old enough they learn how to keep quiet. All of you men are old enough."

★

The Angel Higginson, looking quite angry and absurd, flies into her face on his little wings. She smashes him onto the table with one slap and signals to the waiter to take the dead insect away.

"We are here tonight," she says, "to explain away contagious angelism. The prisoner (looking at me) will be questioned about his beliefs and judged according to his answers. Does anyone here take shorthand?"

"I take shorthand," Kathy says, grinning at Mac.

"You will start recording with exact accuracy everything that is said. Otherwise the defendant will invent his own questions and answers afterwards."

"But who will be the jury?" Mr. Doom asks.

"After the trial we will leave the defendant alone in a room with the transcript of the trial and a loaded revolver," Mrs. Doom answers carefully. "What could be fairer than that?"

MRS. DOOM: Let the record show that the defense is allowed to appoint any attorneys he desires.

MR. DOOM (I am still bound and gagged): I appoint Perry Mason, your honor.

MRS. DOOM: Let the record show that Perry Mason has entered the courtroom.
  (Perry Mason enters the courtroom carrying a briefcase, attended by Della Street and Paul Drake.)

PERRY MASON: May I have a conference with my client, your honor?

MRS. DOOM: Your client is bound and gagged. You can only swear him in as a hostile witness
  (Paul Drake hands Perry Mason three large photographs.)

PERRY MASON: We can prove, your honor—

MRS. DOOM: Let the record show that the District Attorney, R. Hamilton Burger, has entered the courtroom.
  (R. Hamilton Burger enters the courtroom carrying a tape-recorder.)

PERRY MASON: We can prove, your honor—

MRS. DOOM: The defense attorney will be silent. He will meditate on how silent a man is who has just died of stomach cancer.

PERRY MASON: Yes, your honor.

MR. DOOM (starting to masturbate): This is not a fair trial.

MRS. DOOM: There will be order in the court. We will hear the district attorney's opening statement.

R. HAMILTON BURGER: Your honor, the crime of angelism is itself so unintentional that it stamps the faces of those who are about to be convicted of it with an innocence that makes them certain of being convicted. The crime, however, must be defined before the face of the criminal can be destroyed.

(Paul Drake rushes into the courtroom and hands some papers to Perry Mason. Mason reads them and addresses the court with excitement.)

PERRY MASON: Your honor, I have evidence to prove that my client does not exist.

MRS. DOOM: This evidence was already ruled inadmissible. Proceed with your statement, Mr. Burger.

R. HAMILTON BURGER: Look at man basically, your honor. He is a child. He wants to grow up. As soon as he realizes he is too old to grow up, he dies. Somebody shoots him or stabs him or he dies of pneumonia or a heart attack or commits suicide. This is what we in law call the basic law. Angelism is like leprosy. It tries to thwart the basic nature of man. It cannot succeed. That is its basic treason. If it could succeed, if the leprous person by having his face eaten away could make his bones seem so beautiful that all men would kiss them, if leprosy exposed the heart and the heart only, man (and nature) would not consider leprosy a crime. If there were any secrets the broken skin could lay bare, if the broken skin could display anything else but broken skin. But, your honor, you know, I know, all men know, there is nothing broken flesh can expose but more broken flesh.

PERRY MASON: Your honor, I object. My client is not accused of leprosy.

R. HAMILTON BURGER: I accuse him of leprosy.

MRS. DOOM: The attorneys will refrain from personality.

R. HAMILTON BURGER: Yes, your honor. I will sum up briefly the charges I intend to prove against the accused, against that criminal who lies bound, gagged, and bewildered in the corner, against, and I am not afraid to name him in spite of the many names he is accused of using, against Oliver Charming.

(R. Hamilton Burger sits down.)

DELLA STREET (whispering to Perry Mason): Chief, he's forgotten to state the charge.

PERRY MASON (whispering back): It may be a trap, Della.

MRS. DOOM: There will be order in the court. The prosecution will proceed with its witnesses.

R. HAMILTON BURGER: The first witness that the state wishes to call is S.

PAUL DRAKE (whispering to Perry Mason): You can tear him to shreds on cross-examination, Perry.

PERRY MASON (whispering back): I'm not so sure, Paul. There's something different about this case.

MRS. DOOM: Let the witness be sworn.

(S. is sworn.)

R. HAMILTON BURGER: Are you acquainted with the defendant?

II (1956–1965)

SAN FRANCISCO   (1956–1965)

"POETRY AS MAGIC" WORKSHOP

This questionnaire is in no sense designed to indicate whether you can write poetry. Since the workshop is limited to 15 people, I must have some guide as to which of you would most benefit from a workshop of this particular content. Some of the questions will seem bizarre or pointless, but it would be useful if you would answer all of them as precisely as possible.

A list of those selected will be posted on Thursday, February 21, on the main bulletin board of the Library and at the Poetry Center, S. F. State College, Juniper 4-2300, Ext. 251.

I. POLITICS

1. What is your favorite political song?

_____

2. If you had a chance to eliminate three political figures in the world, which would you choose?

1.

_____

2.

_____

3.

_____

3. What political group, slogan, or idea in the world today has the most to do with Magic?

_____

_____. With Poetry?_____

_____

4. Who were the Lovestoneites?

II. RELIGION

1. Which one of these figures had or represented religious views nearest to your own religious views? Which furthest? Jesus, Emperor Julian, Diogenes, Buddha, Confucius, Marcus Aurelius, Lao Tse, Socrates, Dionysus, Apollo, Hermes Trismegistus, Li Po, Heraclitus, Epicurus, Apollonius of Tyana, Simon Magus, Zoroaster, Mohammed, the White Goddess, Cicero.

Nearest _____. Furthest_____.

2. Classify this set of figures in the same way. Calvin, Kierkegaard, Suzuki, Schweitzer, Marx, Russell, St. Thomas Aquinas, Luther, St. Augustine, Santayana, the Mad Bomber, Marquis de Sade, Yeats, Gandhi, William James, Hitler, C.S. Lewis, Proust.

Nearest _____. Furthest_____.

3. What is your favorite book of the Bible? _____.

III. HISTORY

1. Give the approximate date of the following people or events:

Plato _____ Buddha _____ The Battle of Waterloo _____ Dante _____
The invention of printing _____ Nero _____ Chaucer _____
The unification of Italy _____ Joan of Arc _____

2. Write a paragraph about how the fall of Rome affected modern poetry.

IV. POETRY

1. If you were editing a magazine and had an unlimited budget, which poets would you first ask for contributions?

_____
_____
_____

V. PERSONAL

1. Name: _____ Address: _____
Age: _____ Sex: _____ City: _____ Phone: _____
Height: _____ Weight: _____ Married or unmarried: _____

2. What animal do you most resemble? _____

3. What insect do you most resemble? _____

4. What star do you most resemble? _____

5. What card of the ordinary playing-card deck (or Tarot deck) represents
the absolute of your desires? _____
the absolute of your fears? _____

6. Write the funniest joke that you know.

VI. PRACTICE

ANSWER EITHER OR BOTH QUESTION 1 AND 2

1. In any of the three following poems fill in each of the blanks with any number of words you wish (including none) attempting to make a complete and satisfactory poem. Do not alter any of the existing words or punctuation or increase the number of lines.

2. Invent a dream in which you appear as a poet.

I

With the gums gone . . . .
are . . . . And though the nose is . . . . . nothing,
the eye . . . .

And now the . . . . .
Of the radiator . . . . . floor
is . . . . . , the even row of it
fit to raise
. . . . . children.

You will count . . . . .
You will stay in the midst of them,
You will know . . . . . , you will hear them
in the narrow . . . . . .

II

In . . . . endlessness
Snow, ... salt
He lost his . . . .

The color white. He walks
Over a . . . . carpet made
. . . .

Without eyes or thumbs
He suffers . . . .
But the . . . . quiver

In the . . . . endlessness
How . . . . a wound
His . . . . left.

Snow, ... salt . . . .
In the . . . . endlessness.

III

Blue-rooted heron, ... lake
. . . . song, like me no traveler
Taking . . . . rest, loose-winged water-bird
And dumb with music . . . .

I stand upon the waterfront, like him no traveler
. . . . , dangling on . . . . wings.
Aching for flight, for . . . .
I . . . . and take my rest.

They will not hunt us . . . .
The flesh of the . . . . is . . . . and is dumb.
The sound of an arrow, the sight of a hunter
. . . . life without wings.

So let us die for death alone is motion
And death alone will make these herons fly.
. . . . wingless . . . . ocean
. . . . die.

AFTER LORCA (1957)

With an Introduction by Federico García Lorca

Introduction

Frankly I was quite surprised when Mr. Spicer asked me to write an introduction to this volume. My reaction to the manuscript he sent me (and to the series of letters that are now a part of it) was and is fundamentally unsympathetic. It seems to me the waste of a considerable talent on something which is not worth doing. However, I have been removed from all contact with poetry for the last twenty years. The younger generation of poets may view with pleasure Mr. Spicer's execution of what seems to me a difficult and unrewarding task.

It must be made clear at the start that these poems are not translations. In even the most literal of them Mr. Spicer seems to derive pleasure in inserting or substituting one or two words which completely change the mood and often the meaning of the poem as I had written it. More often he takes one of my poems and adjoins to half of it another half of his own, giving rather the effect of an unwilling centaur. (Modesty forbids me to speculate which end of the animal is mine.) Finally there are an almost equal number of poems that I did not write at all (one supposes they must be his) executed in a somewhat fanciful imitation of my early style. The reader is given no indication which of the poems belong to which category, and I have further complicated the problem (with malice aforethought I must admit) by sending Mr. Spicer several poems written after my death which he has also translated and included here. Even the most faithful student of my work will be hard put to decide what is and what is not García Lorca as, indeed, he would if he were to look into my present resting place. The analogy is impolite, but I fear the impoliteness is deserved.

The letters are another problem. When Mr. Spicer began sending them to me a few months ago, I recognized immediately the "programmatic letter"—the letter one poet writes to another not in any effort to communicate with him, but rather as a young man whispers his secrets to a scarecrow, knowing that his young lady is in the distance listening. The young lady in this case may be a Muse, but the scarecrow nevertheless quite naturally resents the confidences. The reader, who is not a party to this singular tryst, may be amused by what he overhears.

The dead are notoriously hard to satisfy. Mr. Spicer's mixture may please his contemporary audience or may, and this is more probable, lead him to write better poetry of his own. But I am strongly reminded as I survey this curious amalgam of a cartoon published in an American magazine while I was visiting your country in New York. The cartoon showed a gravestone on which were inscribed the words: "HERE LIES AN OFFICER AND A GENTLEMAN." The caption below it read: "I wonder how they happened to be buried in the same grave?"

Federico García Lorca
Outside Granada, October 1957

Juan Ramón Jimenez

A Translation for John Ryan

In the white endlessness
Snow, seaweed, and salt
He lost his imagination.

The color white. He walks
Upon a soundless carpet made
Of pigeon feathers.

Without eyes or thumbs
He suffers a dream not moving
But the bones quiver.

In the white endlessness
How pure and big a wound
His imagination left.

Snow, seaweed, and salt. Now
In the white endlessness.

Ballad of the Little Girl Who Invented the Universe

A Translation for George Stanley

Jasmine flower and a bull with his throat slashed.
Infinite sidewalk. Map. Room. Harp. Sunrise.
A little girl pretends a bull made of jasmine
And the bull is a bloody twilight that bellows.

If the sky could be a little boy
The jasmines could take half the night to themselves
And the bull a blue bullring of his own
With his heart at the foot of a small column.

But the sky is an elephant
And the jasmines are water without blood
And the little girl is a bouquet of night flowers
Lost on a big dark sidewalk.

Between the jasmine and the bull
Or the hooks of the sleeping people of marble or
In the jasmine, clouds and an elephant—
The skeleton of a little girl turning.

———————————

Dear Lorca,

These letters are to be as temporary as our poetry is to be permanent. They will establish the bulk, the wastage that my sour-stomached contemporaries demand to help them swallow and digest the pure word. We will use up our rhetoric here so that it will not appear in our poems. Let it be consumed paragraph by paragraph, day by day, until nothing of it is left in our poetry and nothing of our poetry is left in it. It is precisely because these letters are unnecessary that they must be written.

In my last letter I spoke of the tradition. The fools that read these letters will think by this we mean what tradition seems to have meant lately—an historical patchwork (whether made up of Elizabethan quotations, guide books of the poet's home town, or obscure bits of magic published by Pantheon) which is used to cover up the nakedness of the bare word. Tradition means much more than that. It means generations of different poets in different countries patiently telling the same story, writing the same poem, gaining and losing something with each transformation—but, of course, never really losing anything. This has nothing to do with calmness, classicism, temperament, or anything else. Invention is merely the enemy of poetry.

See how weak prose is. I invent a word like invention. These paragraphs could be translated, transformed by a chain of fifty poets in fifty languages, and they still would be temporary, untrue, unable to yield the substance of a single image. Prose invents—poetry discloses.

A mad man is talking to himself in the room next to mine. He speaks in prose. Presently I shall go to a bar and there one or two poets will speak to me and I to them and we will try to destroy each other or attract each other or even listen to each other and nothing will happen because we will be speaking in prose. I will go home, drunken and dissatisfied, and sleep—and my dreams will be prose. Even the subconscious is not patient enough for poetry.

You are dead and the dead are very patient.

Love,
Jack

Ballad of the Seven Passages

A Translation for Ebbe Borregaard

Rimbaud is spelled with seven letters of the alphabet
Your heart will never break at what you are hearing
Rimbaud was older than you are when he was dead
Your heart will never break at what you are hearing.
I tell you, darling, beauty was never as old as he was
And your heart will never break at what you are hearing.
Shut your mouth.

Rimbaud is spelled with seven passages
A E I O U Y
And that stony vowel called death.
Oh,
Damn Rimbaud,
Beauty is spelled with all the vowels of seven passages.
Shut your damned mouth.
When Rimbaud died he became older than your alphabet
And your heart will never break at what you are hearing.

Debussy

A Translation for the University of Redlands

My shadow moves silently
Upon the water in the ditch.

Upon my shadow are the frogs
Blocked off from the stars.

The shadow demands from my body
Unmoving images.

My shadow skims the water like a huge
Violet-colored mosquito.

A hundred crickets try to mine gold
From the light in the rushes.

A light born in my heart
Upon the ditch, reflected.

Frog

A Translation for Graham Mackintosh

Like all the novels I've read
My mind is going to a climax
And a climax means a splash in the pool.
Booing. Booing. Booing.
And your heart is full of water
And your nose can't hardly breathe.
Remember
How black those pinetrees were that fire burned.
All that black forest. And the noise
(Splash)
Of a single green needle.

Buster Keaton's Ride

A Translation for Melvin Bakkerud

ROOSTER: Cockledoodledoo!

(Buster Keaton enters carrying four children in his arms.)

BUSTER KEATON (takes out a wooden dagger and kills them):
My poor children!

ROOSTER: Cockledoodledoo!

BUSTER KEATON (counting the corpses on the ground): One, two, three,
four. (Grabs a bicycle and goes.)

(Among the old rubber tires and cans of gasoline a Negro eats a straw hat.)

BUSTER KEATON: What a beautiful afternoon!

(A parrot flutters around in the sexless sky.)

BUSTER KEATON: I like riding a bicycle.

THE OWL: Toowit toowoo.

BUSTER KEATON: How beautifully these birds sing!

THE OWL: Hoo!

BUSTER KEATON: It's lovely!

(Pause. Buster Keaton ineffably crosses the rushes and little fields of rye. The landscape shortens itself beneath the wheels of his machine. The bicycle has a single dimension. It is able to enter books and to expand itself even into operas and coalmines. The bicycle of Buster Keaton does not have a riding seat of caramel or sugar pedals like the bicycles bad men ride. It is a bicycle like all bicycles except for a unique drenching of innocence. Adam and Eve run by, frightened as if they were carrying a vase full of water and, in passing, pet the bicycle of Buster Keaton.)

BUSTER KEATON: Ah, love, love!

(Buster Keaton falls to the ground. The bicycle escapes him. It runs behind two enormous gray butterflies. It skims madly half an inch from the ground.)

BUSTER KEATON: I don't want to talk. Won't somebody please say something?

A VOICE: Fool!

(He continues walking. His eyes, infinite and sad like a newly born animal, dream of lilies and angels and silken belts. His eyes which are like the bottom of a vase. His eyes of a mad child. Which are most faithful. Which are most beautiful. The eyes of an ostrich. His human eyes with a secure equipoise with melancholy. Philadelphia is seen in the distance. The inhabitants of that city now know that the old poem of a Singer machine is able to encircle the big roses of the greenhouse but not at all to comprehend the poetic difference between a bowl of hot tea and a bowl of cold tea. Philadelphia shines in the distance.)

(An American girl with eyes of celluloid comes through the grass.)

THE AMERICAN: Hello.

(Buster Keaton smiles and looks at the shoes of the girl. Those shoes! We do not have to admire her shoes. It would take a crocodile to wear them.)

BUSTER KEATON: I would have liked—

THE AMERICAN (breathless): Do you carry a sword decked with myrtle leaves?

(Buster Keaton shrugs his shoulders and lifts his right foot.)

THE AMERICAN: Do you have a ring with a poisoned stone?

(Buster Keaton twists slowly and lifts an inquiring leg.)

THE AMERICAN: Well?

(Four angels with wings of a heavenly gas balloon piss among the flowers. The ladies of the town play a piano as if they were riding a bicycle. The waltz, a moon, and seventeen Indian canoes rock the precious heart of our friend. As the greatest surprise of all, autumn has invaded the garden like water explodes a geometrical clump of sugar.)

BUSTER KEATON (sighing): I would have liked to have been a swan. But I can't do what I would have liked. Because—What happened to my hat? Where is my collar of little birds and my mohair necktie? What a disgrace!

(A young girl with a wasp waist and a high collar comes in on a bicycle. She has the head of a nightingale.)

YOUNG GIRL: Whom do I have the honor of saluting?

BUSTER KEATON (with a bow): Buster Keaton.

(The young girl faints and falls off the bicycle. Her legs on the ground tremble like two agonized cobras. A gramophone plays a thousand versions of the same song—"In Philadelphia they have no nightingales.")

BUSTER KEATON (kneeling): Darling Miss Eleanor, pardon me! (lower) Darling (lower still) Darling (lowest) Darling.

(The lights of Philadelphia flicker and go out in the faces of a thousand policemen.)

116

Ballad of the Shadowy Pigeons

A Translation for Joe Dunn

On the branches of laurel
Saw two shadowy pigeons.
One of them was the sun
The other the moon.

Little neighbors, I asked them,
Where am I buried?
In my tail, said the sun.
In my craw, said the moon.

And I who had been walking
With the earth at my waistline
Saw two eagles of marble
And a naked maiden.
The one was the other
And the maiden was no one.

Little eagles, I asked them,
Where am I buried?
In my tail, said the sun.
In my craw, said the moon.

On the branches of laurel
Saw two naked pigeons.
The one was the other
And the both of them no one.

Suicide

A Translation for Eric Weir

At ten o'clock in the morning
The young man could not remember.

His heart was stuffed with dead wings
And linen flowers.

He is conscious that there is nothing left
In his mouth but one word.

When he removes his coat soft ashes
Fall from his arms.

Through the window he sees a tower
He sees a window and a tower.

His watch has run down in its case
He observes the way it was looking at him.

He sees his shadow stretched
Upon a white silk cushion.

And the stiff geometric youngster
Shatters the mirror with an ax.

The mirror submerges everything
In a great spurt of shadow.

Bacchus

A Translation for Don Allen

An untouched green murmur.
The figtree wants to extend me its branches.

Like a panther its shadow
Stalks my poet shadow.

The moon has words with the dogs.
She is mistaken and begins over.

Yesterday, tomorrow, black, and green
Troop around my circle of laurel.

Where would you look for my lifetime
If I exchanged my heart?

—And the figtree shouts at me and advances
Terrible and extended.

A Diamond

A Translation for Robert Jones

A diamond
Is there
At the heart of the moon or the branches or my nakedness
And there is nothing in the universe like diamond
Nothing in the whole mind.

The poem is a seagull resting on a pier at the end of the ocean.

A dog howls at the moon
A dog howls at the branches
A dog howls at the nakedness
A dog howling with pure mind.

I ask for the poem to be as pure as a seagull's belly.

The universe falls apart and discloses a diamond
Two words called seagull are peacefully floating out where the
    waves are.
The dog is dead there with the moon, with the branches, with
    my nakedness
And there is nothing in the universe like diamond
Nothing in the whole mind.

The Little Halfwit

A Translation for Robin Blaser

I said, "Afternoon"
But it wasn't there.
The afternoon was another thing
Which had gone someplace.

(And the light shrugged its shoulders
Like a little girl.)

"Afternoon" But this is useless,
This is untrue, this has to it
Half a moon of lead. The other
Will never get here.

(And the light that everyone sees
Played at being a statue.)

The other one was tiny
And ate pomegranates.

This one is big and green and I'm not able
To grab her in my arms or dress her.
Is she ever coming? What was she?

(And the light as it went along, as a joke
Separated the little halfwit from his own shadow.)

Verlaine

A Translation for Pat Wilson

A song
Which I shall never sing
Has fallen asleep on my lips.
A song
Which I shall never sing—

Above the honeysuckle
There's a firefly
And the moon stings
With a ray into the water—

At that time I'll imagine
The song
Which I shall never sing.

A song full of lips
And far-off washes

A song full of lost
Hours in the shadow

A song of a star that's alive
Above enduring day.

_____

Dear Lorca,

When I translate one of your poems and I come across words I do not understand, I always guess at their meanings. I am inevitably right. A really perfect poem (no one yet has written one) could be perfectly translated by a person who did not know one word of the language it was written in. A really perfect poem has an infinitely small vocabulary.

It is very difficult. We want to transfer the immediate object, the immediate emotion to the poem—and yet the immediate always has hundreds of its own words clinging to it, short-lived and tenacious as barnacles. And it is wrong to scrape them off and substitute others. A poet is a time mechanic not an embalmer. The words around the immediate shrivel and decay like flesh around the body. No mummy-sheet of tradition can be used to stop the process. Objects, words must be led across time not preserved against it.

I yell "Shit" down a cliff at an ocean. Even in my lifetime the immediacy of that word will fade. It will be dead as "Alas." But if I put the real cliff and the real ocean into the poem, the word "Shit" will ride along with them, travel the time-machine until cliffs and oceans disappear.

Most of my friends like words too well. They set them under the blinding light of the poem and try to extract every possible connotation from each of them, every temporary pun, every direct or indirect connection—as if a word could become an object by mere addition of consequences. Others pick up words from the street, from their bars, from their offices and display them proudly in their poems as if they were shouting, "See what I have collected from the American language. Look at my butterflies, my stamps, my old shoes!" What does one do with all this crap?

Words are what sticks to the real. We use them to push the real, to drag the real into the poem. They are what we hold on with, nothing else. They are as valuable in themselves as rope with nothing to be tied to.

I repeat—the perfect poem has an infinitely small vocabulary.

Love,
Jack

The Ballad of the Dead Woodcutter

A Translation for Louis Marbury

Because the figtree was sapless
It has cracked at the root.

Oh, you have fallen down on your head
You have fallen on your head.

Because the oaktree was rootless
It has cracked at the branch.

Oh, you have fallen down on your head
You have fallen on your head.

Because I walked through the branches
I have scratched out my heart.

Oh, you have fallen down on your head
You have fallen on your head.

The Ballad of Weeping

A Translation for Bob Connor

I have closed my window
Because I do not want to hear the weeping
But behind the gray walls
Nothing can be heard but weeping.

A few dogs might bark
A few angels might sing
There might be room for a thousand violins in the palm of my
        hand.

But the weeping is a big dog
The weeping is a big angel
The weeping is a big violin
The tears put a muzzle on the air
And nothing can be heard but weeping.

Alba

A Translation for Russ Fitzgerald

If your hand had been meaningless
Not a single blade of grass
Would spring from the earth's surface.
Easy to write, to kiss—
No, I said, read your paper.
Be there
Like the earth
When shadow covers the wet grass.

Song of the Poor

A Translation

Ay qué trabajo me cuesta
quererte como te quiero!

Because I love you the table
And the heart and the lamplight
Feel sorry for me.

Who will buy from me
That small belt I have
And that sadness of white thread
To weave handkerchiefs?

Because I love you the ceiling
And the heart and the air
Feel sorry for me.

Ay qué trabajo me cuesta
quererte como te quiero!

Ode for Walt Whitman

A Translation for Steve Jonas

Along East River and the Bronx
The kids were singing, showing off their bodies
At the wheel, at oil, the rawhide, and the hammer.
Ninety thousand miners were drawing silver out of boulders
While children made perspective drawings of stairways.

But no one went to sleep
No one wanted to be a river
No one loved the big leaves, no one
The blue tongue of the coastline.

Along East River into Queens
The kids were wrestling with industry.
The Jews sold circumcision's rose
To the faun of the river.
The sky flowed through the bridges and rooftops—
Herds of buffalo the wind was pushing.

But none of them would stay.
No one wanted to be cloud. No one
Looked for the ferns
Or the yellow wheel of the drum.

But if the moon comes out
The pulleys will slide around to disturb the sky
A limit of needles will fence in your memory
And there will be coffins to carry out your unemployed.

New York of mud,
New York of wire fences and death,
What angel do you carry hidden in your cheek?
What perfect voice will tell you the truth about wheat
Or the terrible sleep of your wet-dreamed anemones?

Not for one moment, beautiful old Walt Whitman,
Have I stopped seeing your beard full of butterflies
Or your shoulders of corduroy worn thin by the moon
Or your muscles of a virgin Apollo
Or your voice like a column of ashes
Ancient and beautiful as the fog.

You gave a cry like a bird
With his prick pierced through by a needle
Enemy of satyrs
Enemy of the grape
And lover of bodies under rough cloth.
Not for one moment, tight-cocked beauty,
Who in mountains of coal, advertisements, and railroads
Had dreamed of being a river and of sleeping like one
With a particular comrade, one who could put in your bosom
The young pain of an ignorant leopard.
Not for one moment, blood-Adam, male,

Man alone in the sea, beautiful
Old Walt Whitman.
Because on the rooftops
Bunched together in bars
Pouring out in clusters from toilets
Trembling between the legs of taxi-drivers
Or spinning upon platforms of whiskey
The cocksuckers, Walt Whitman, were counting on you.

That one also, also. And they throw themselves down on
Your burning virgin beard,
Blonds of the North, negroes from the seashore,
Crowds of shouts and gestures
Like cats or snakes
The cocksuckers, Walt Whitman, the cocksuckers,
Muddy with tears, meat for the whip,
Tooth or boot of the cowboys.

That one also, also. Painted fingers
Sprout out along the beach of your dreams
And you give a friend an apple
Which tastes faintly of gas-fumes
And the sun sings a song for the bellybuttons
Of the little boys who play games below bridges.

But you weren't looking for the scratched eyes
Or the blackswamp-country where children are sinking
Or the frozen spit
Or the wounded curves like a toad's paunch
Which cocksuckers wear in bars and night-clubs
While the moon beats them along the corners of terror.

You were looking for a naked man who would be like a river
Bull and dream, a connection between the wheel and the seaweed,

Be father for your agony, your death's camellia
And moan in the flames of your hidden equator.

For it is just that a man not look for his pleasure
In the forest of blood of the following morning.
The sky has coastlines where life can be avoided
And some bodies must not repeat themselves at sunrise.

Agony, agony, dream, leaven, and dream.
That is the world, my friend, agony, agony.
The dead decompose themselves under the clock of the cities.
War enters weeping, with a million gray rats.
The rich give to their girlfriends
Tiny illuminated dyings
And life is not noble, or good, or sacred.

A man is able if he wishes to lead his desire
Through vein of coral or the celestial naked.
Tomorrow his loves will be rock and Time
A breeze that comes sleeping through their clusters.

That is why I do not cry out, old Walt Whitman,
Against the little boy who writes
A girl's name on his pillow,
Or the kid who puts on a wedding dress
In the darkness of a closet
Or the lonely men in bars
Who drink with sickness the waters of prostitution
Or the men with green eyelids
Who love men and scald their lips in silence,
But against the rest of you, cocksuckers of cities,
Hard-up and dirty-brained,
Mothers of mud, harpies, dreamless enemies
Of the Love that distributes crowns of gladness.

Against the rest of you always, who give the kids
Drippings of sucked-off death with sour poison.
Against the rest of you always
Fairies of North America,
Pajaros of Havana,
Jotos of Mexico,
Sarasas of Cadiz,
Apios of Seville,
Cancos of Madrid,
Adelaidas of Portugal,
Cocksuckers of all the world, assassins of doves,
Slaves of women, lapdogs of their dressing tables,
Opening their flys in parks with a fever of fans
Or ambushed in the rigid landscapes of poison.

Let there be no mercy. Death
Trickles from all of your eyes, groups
Itself like gray flowers on beaches of mud.
Let there be no mercy. Watch out for them.
Let the bewildered, the pure,
The classical, the appointed, the praying
Lock the gates of this Bacchanalia.

And you, beautiful Walt Whitman, sleep on the banks of the Hudson
With your beard toward the pole and your palms open
Soft clay or snow, your tongue is invoking
Comrades to keep vigil over your gazelle without body.
Sleep, there is nothing left here.
A dance of walls shakes across the prairies
And America drowns itself with machines and weeping.
Let the hard air of midnight
Sweep away all the flowers and letters from the arch in which you sleep
And a little black boy announce to the white men of gold
The arrival of the reign of the ear of wheat.

Aquatic Park

A Translation for Jack Spicer

A green boat
Fishing in blue water

The gulls circle the pier
Calling their hunger

A wind rises from the west
Like the passing of desire

Two boys play on the beach
Laughing

Their gangling legs cast shadows
On the wet sand

Then,
Sprawling in the boat

A beautiful black fish.

Forest

A Translation for Joe Dunn

You want me to tell you
The secret of springtime—

And I relate to that secret
Like a high-branching firtree

Whose thousand little fingers
Point a thousand little roads.

I will tell you never, my love,
Because the river runs slowly

But I shall put into my branching voice
The ashy sky of your gaze.

Turn me around, brown child
Be careful of my needles.

Turn me around and around, playing
At the well pump of love.

The secret of springtime. How
I wish I could tell you!

———————————

Dear Lorca,

I would like to make poems out of real objects. The lemon to be a lemon that the reader could cut or squeeze or taste—a real lemon like a newspaper in a collage is a real newspaper. I would like the moon in my poems to be a real moon, one which could be suddenly covered with a cloud that has nothing to do with the poem—a moon utterly independent of images. The imagination pictures the real. I would like to point to the real, disclose it, to make a poem that has no sound in it but the pointing of a finger.

We have both tried to be independent of images (you from the start and I only when I grew old enough to tire of trying to make things connect), to make things visible rather than to make pictures of them (phantasia non imaginari). How easy it is in erotic musings or in the truer imagination of a dream to invent a beautiful boy. How difficult to take a boy in a blue bathing suit that I have watched as casually as a tree and to make him visible in a poem as a tree is visible, not as an image or a picture but as something alive—caught forever in the structure of words. Live moons, live lemons, live boys in bathing suits. The poem is a collage of the real.

But things decay, reason argues. Real things become garbage. The piece of lemon you shellac to the canvas begins to develop a mold, the newspaper tells of incredibly ancient events in forgotten slang, the boy becomes a grandfather. Yes, but the garbage of the real still reaches out into the current world making *its* objects, in turn, visible—lemon calls to lemon, newspaper to newspaper, boy to boy. As things decay they bring their equivalents into being.

Things do not connect; they correspond. That is what makes it possible for a poet to translate real objects, to bring them across language as easily as he can bring them across time. That tree you saw in Spain is a tree I could never have seen in California, that lemon has a different smell and a different taste, BUT the answer is this—every place and every time has a real object to *correspond* with your real object—that lemon may become this lemon, or it may even become this piece of seaweed, or this particular color of gray in this ocean. One does not need to imagine that lemon; one needs to discover it.

Even these letters. They *correspond* with something (I don't know what) that you have written (perhaps as unapparently as that lemon corresponds to this piece of seaweed) and, in turn, some future poet will write something which *corresponds* to them. That is how we dead men write to each other.

Love,
Jack

Narcissus

A Translation for Basil King

Poor Narcissus
Your dim fragrance
And the dim heart of the river

I want to stay at your edge
Flower of love
Poor Narcissus

Ripples and sleeping fish
Cross your white eyes
Songbirds and butterflies
Japanese mine

I so tall beside you
Flower of love
Poor Narcissus

How wide-awake the frogs are
They won't stay out of the surface
In which your madness and my madness
Mirrors itself

Poor Narcissus
My sorrow
Self of my sorrow.

He Died at Sunrise

A Translation for Allen Joyce

Night of four moons
And a single tree,
With a single shadow
And a single bird.

I look into my body for
The tracks of your lips.
A stream kisses into the wind
Without touch.

I carry the No you gave me
Clenched in my palm
Like something made of wax
An almost-white lemon.

Night of four moons
And a single tree
At the point of a needle
Is my love, spinning.

Ballad of the Terrible Presence

A Translation for Joe LeSueur

I want the river lost from its bed
I want the wind lost from its valleys

I want the night to be there without eyes
And my heart without the golden flower

So that the oxen talk with big leaves
And the earthworm is dead of shadow

So that the teeth of the skull glisten
And the yellows give a complete color to silk.

I can look at the agony of wounded night
Struggling, twisted up against noontime

I can stand all the sunsets of green poison
And the wornout rainbows that time suffers

But don't make your clean body too visible
Like a black cactus opened out among rushes

Let me go in an anguish of star clusters
Lose me. But don't show me that cool flesh.

Ballad of Sleeping Somewhere Else

A Translation for Ebbe Borregaard

The pine needles fall
Like an ax in the forest.

Can you hear them crumble
There where we are sleeping?

The windows are close to the wall
Here in the darkness they remain open.

(When I saw you in the morning
My arms were full of paper.)

Five hundred miles away
The moon is a hatchet of silver.

(When I saw you in the morning
My eyes were full of paper.)

Here the walls are firm
They do not crumble and remain certain.

(When I saw you in the morning
My heart was full of paper.)

Five hundred miles away
The stars are glass that is breaking.

The windows sag on the wall
I feel cold glass in the blankets.

Child, you are too tall for this bed.

The pine needles fall
Like an ax in the forest.

Can you hear them crumble
There where we are sleeping?

Dear Lorca,

When you had finished a poem what did it want you to do with it? Was it happy enough merely to exist or did it demand imperiously that you share it with somebody like the beauty of a beautiful person forces him to search the world for someone that can declare that beauty? And where did your poems find people?

Some poems are easily laid. They will give themselves to anybody and anybody physically capable can receive them. They may be beautiful (we have both written some that were) but they are meretricious. From the moment of their conception they inform us in a dulcet voice that, thank you, they can take care of themselves. I swear that if one of them were hidden beneath my carpet, it would shout out and seduce somebody. The quiet poems are what I worry about—the ones that must be seduced. They could travel about with me for years and no one would notice them. And yet, properly wed, they are more beautiful than their whorish cousins.

But I am speaking of the first night, when I leave my apartment almost breathless, searching for someone to show the poem to. Often now there is no one. My fellow poets (those I showed poetry to ten years ago) are as little interested in my poetry as I am in theirs. We both compare the poems shown (unfavorably, of course) with the poems we were writing ten years ago when we could learn from each other. We are polite but it is as if we were trading snapshots of our children—old acquaintances who disapprove of each other's wives. Or were you more generous, García Lorca?

There are the young, of course. I have been reduced to them (or my poems have) lately. The advantage in them is that they haven't yet decided what kind of poetry they are going to write tomorrow and are always looking for some device of yours to use. Yours, that's the trouble. Yours and not the poem's. They read the poem once to catch the marks of your style and then again, if they are at all pretty, to see if there is any reference to them in the poem. That's all. I know. I used to do it myself.

When you are in love there is no real problem. The person you love is always interested because he knows that the poems are always about him. If only because each poem will someday be said to belong to the Miss X or Mr. Y period of the poet's life. I may not be a better poet when I am in love, but I am a far less frustrated one. My poems have an audience.

Finally there are friends. There have only been two of them in my life who could read my poems and one of that two really prefers to put them in print so he can see them better. The other is far away.

All this is to explain why I dedicate each of our poems to someone.

Love,
Jack

Narcissus

A Translation for Richard Rummonds

Child,
How you keep falling into rivers.

At the bottom there's a rose
And in the rose there's another river.

Look at that bird. Look,
That yellow bird.

My eyes have fallen down
Into the water.

My god,
How they're slipping! Youngster!

—And I'm in the rose myself.

When I was lost in water I
Understood but won't tell you.

Ballad of the Dead Boy

A Translation for Graham Mackintosh

Every afternoon in Granada
Every afternoon a boy dies
Every afternoon the river sits itself down
To talk things over with its neighbors.

All the dead wear wings of moss.
The cloudy wind and the bright wind
Are two pheasants who fly around towers
And the day is a boy with a wound in him.

There wasn't a touch of lark in the sky
When I met you at the wine cavern
Or a fragment of cloud near the earth
When you drowned on the river.

A giant of water went slopping over the mountains
And the canyon spun around the dogs and lilies.
Your body, with the violet shadow of my hands,
Was dead there on the banks, an archangel, cold.

Song for September

A Translation for Don Allen

In the distant night the children are singing:
    A little river
    And a colored fountain

THE CHILDREN: When will our hearts come back from your holiday?

I: When my words no longer need me.

THE CHILDREN: You have left us here to sing the death of your summer
    A little river
    And a colored fountain
        What September flowers do you hold in your hand?

I: A bloody rose and a white lily.

THE CHILDREN: Dip them in the water of an old song
    A little river
    And a colored fountain
        What are you tasting in your thirsty mouth?

I: The flavor of the bones of my big skull.

THE CHILDREN: Drink the kind water of an old song

A little river

And a colored fountain

Why have you gone so very far from the death of your summer?

I: I am looking for a magical clockworkman.

THE CHILDREN: And how will you find the highway of poets?

I: The fountain and a river and an old song.

THE CHILDREN: You are going very far.

I: I am going very far, farther than my poems, farther than the mountains, farther than the birds. I am going to ask Christ to give me back my childhood, ripe with sunburn and feathers and a wooden sword.

THE CHILDREN: You have left us here to sing the death of your summer. And you will never return.

A little river

And a colored fountain

And you will never return.

Buster Keaton Rides Again: A Sequel

A Translation for The Big Cat Up There

BUSTER KEATON (entering a long dark corridor): This must be Room 73.

PIGEON: Sir, I am a pigeon.

BUSTER KEATON (taking a dictionary out of his back pocket): I don't understand what anybody is talking about.

(No one rides by on a bicycle. The corridor is quite silent.)

PIGEON: I have to go to the bathroom.

BUSTER KEATON: In a minute.

(Two chambermaids come by carrying towels. They give one to the pigeon and one to Buster Keaton.)

1ST CHAMBERMAID: Why do you suppose human beings have lips?

2ND CHAMBERMAID: Nothing like that entered my head.

BUSTER KEATON: No. There were supposed to be three chambermaids.

(He takes out a chessboard and begins playing upon it.)

PIGEON: I could love you if I were a dove.

BUSTER KEATON (biting the chessboard): When I was a child I was put in jail for not giving information to the police.

3 CHAMBERMAIDS: Yes.

BUSTER KEATON: I am not a Catholic.

PIGEON: Don't you believe that God died?

BUSTER KEATON (crying): No.

(4 Spanish dancers come in. They are mostly male.)

1ST SPANISH DANCER: I have a little magazine up my ass.

4 CHAMBERMAIDS: Oh!

(Buster Keaton forgets his politeness and becomes a Catholic. He takes mass, says Holy Mary Mother of God, and distributes rosaries to all the policemen in the room. He hangs by his heels from a crucifix.)

VIRGIN MARY (coming in abruptly): Buster Keaton you have bumPed The Car.

BUSTER KEATON: No.

(Alcohol comes in wearing the disguise of a cockroach. It is blue. It crawls silently up Buster Keaton's leg.)

BUSTER KEATON: No.

(Alcohol and the Virgin Mary perform a dance. They both pretend to have been lovers.)

BUSTER KEATON: I will never see either of you in Rockland. I am not going to Rockland.

(He takes the chessboard and invents a new alphabet.)

VIRGIN MARY: Holy Mary Mother of God Pray For Us Sinners Now At The Hour Of Our Death.

ALCOHOL: Dada is as dada does.

VIRGIN MARY: Did. (She falls into a blue robe.)

BUSTER KEATON: I wonder if there is anything but love in the universe.

(Suddenly, at the last possible time before the curtain falls, somebody kisses the Virgin Mary, and Buster Keaton, and everybody.)

ALCOHOL: If I weren't tone-deaf I would sing.

BUSTER KEATON (sadly): I announce a new world.

(Three literary critics disguised as chambermaids bring down the curtain. Buster Keaton, bleeding, breaks through the curtain. He stands in the middle of the stage holding a fresh pomegranate in his arms.)

BUSTER KEATON (even more sadly): I announce the death of Orpheus.

(Everyone comes in. Policemen, waitresses, and Irene Tavener. They perform a complicated symbolic dance. Alcohol nibbles at the legs of every dancer.)

BUSTER KEATON (bleeding profusely): I love you. I love you. (As a last effort he throws the bleeding pomegranate from his heart.) No kidding, I love you.

VIRGIN MARY (taking him into her arms): You have bumped the car.

(The gaudy blue curtain, silent and alive like the mouth of a seagull, covers everything.)

The Ballad of Escape

A Translation for Nat Harden

I have become lost many times along the ocean
With my ears filled with newly cut flowers
With my tongue full of loving and agony
I have become lost many times along the ocean
Like I lose myself in the hearts of some boys.

There is no night in which, giving a kiss,
One does not feel the smiles of the faceless people
And there is no one in touching something recently born
Who can quite forget the motionless skulls of horses.

Because the roses always search in the forehead
For a hard landscape of bone
And the hands of a man have no other purpose
Than to be like the roots that grow beneath wheat-fields.

Like I lose myself in the hearts of some boys
I have become lost many times along the ocean
Along the vastness of water I wander searching
An end to the lives that have tried to complete me.

Venus

A Translation for Ann Simon

The dead girl
In the winding shell of the bed
Naked of the little wind and flowers
Surges on into perennial light.

The world stayed behind
Lily of cotton and shadow.
It peeked timidly out of the mirror
Looking on at that infinite passage.

The dead girl
Was eaten from inside by love.
In the unyieldingness of seafoam
She lost her hair.

Friday, the 13th

A Translation for Will Holther

At the base of the throat is a little machine
Which makes us able to say anything.
Below it are carpets
Red, blue, and green-colored.
I say the flesh is not grass.
It is an empty house
In which there is nothing
But a little machine
And big, dark carpets.

Song of Two Windows

A Translation for James Broughton

Wind, window, moon
(I open the window to the sky)
Wind, window, moon
(I open the window to the earth)
Then
From the sky
The voices of two girls.

In the middle of my mirror
A girl is drowning
The voice of a single girl.
She holds cold fire like a glass
Each thing she watches
Has become double.
Cold fire is
Cold fire is.
In the middle of my mirror
A girl is drowning
The voice of a single girl.

A branch of night
Enters through my window
A great dark branch
With bracelets of water
Behind a blue mirror
Someone is drowning
The wounded instants
Along the clock—pass.

I stick my head out of the window and I see a chopper of wind ready to cut it off. Upon that invisible guillotine I have mounted the heads without eyes of all my desires, and the odor of lemon fills all of the instant while the wind changes to a flower of gas.

At the pool there has died
A girl of water
She has pushed the earth aside
Like a ripe apple
Down from her head to her thighs
A fish crosses her, calling softly
The wind whispers, "Darling"
But is unable to awaken her

The pool holds loosely
Its rider of something
And in the air its gray nipples
Vibrate with frogs.
God, we hail you. We will make payment
To Our Lady of Water
For the girl in the pool
Dead below the ripples.
I will soon put at her side
Two small gourds
Because they can keep afloat,
Yes, even in water.

———————

Dear Lorca,

Loneliness is necessary for pure poetry. When someone intrudes into the poet's life (and any sudden personal contact, whether in the bed or in the heart, is an intrusion) he loses his balance for a moment, slips into being who he is, uses his poetry as one would use money or sympathy. The person who writes the poetry emerges, tentatively, like a hermit crab from a conch shell. The poet, for that instant, ceases to be a dead man.

I, for example, could not finish the last letter I was writing you about sounds. You were like a friend in a distant city to whom I was suddenly unable to write, not because the fabric of my life had changed, but because I was suddenly, temporarily, not in the fabric of my life. I could not tell you about it because both it and I were momentary.

Even the objects change. The seagulls, the greenness of the ocean, the fish—they become things to be traded for a smile or the sound of conversation—counters rather than objects. Nothing matters except the big lie of the personal—the lie in which these objects do not believe.

That instant, I said. It may last for a minute, a night, or a month, but, this I promise you, García Lorca, the loneliness returns. The poet encysts the intruder. The objects come back to their own places, silent and unsmiling. I again begin to write you a letter on the sound of a poem. And this immediate thing, this personal adventure, will not have been transferred into the poem like the waves and the birds were, will, at best, show in the lovely pattern of cracks in some poem where autobiography shattered but did not quite destroy the surface. And the encysted emotion will itself become an object, to be transferred at last into poetry like the waves and the birds.

And I will again become your special comrade.

Love,
Jack

The Moon and Lady Death

A Translation for Helen Adam

The moon has marble teeth
How old and sad she looks!
There is a dry river
There is a hill without grass
There is a dead oak tree
Near a dry river.

Lady Death, wrinkled,
Goes looking for custom
At the heels of a crowd
Of tenuous phantoms.
Near the dead oak tree
Near the dry river
There is a fair without trumpets
And tents made of shadow.

She sells them dry paint
Made of wax and torture,
Wicked and twisted
Like a witch in a story.
There is a dry river
There is a hill without grass
There is a dead oak tree
Near a dry river.

The moon
Is tossing money

Down through the black air.
Near the dead oak tree
Near the dry river
There is a fair without trumpets
And tents made of shadow.

Afternoon

A Translation for John Barrow

The sky asks afternoon for a word.
—"It is 1:36. A black cloud
    Has crossed one of the white clouds.
    13 empty boats
    And a seagull."

The bay asks afternoon for a word.
—"The wind is blowing
    Southwest at nine miles an hour
    I am in love with an ocean
    Whose heart is the color of wet sand.
    At 1:37
    13 empty boats
    And a seagull."

Afternoon asks the ocean,
"Why does a man die?"
—"It is 1:37
    13 empty boats
    And a seagull."

Dear Lorca,

This is the last letter. The connection between us, which had been fading away with the summer, is now finally broken. I turn in anger and dissatisfaction to the things of my life and you return, a disembodied but contagious spirit, to the printed page. It is over, this intimate communion with the ghost of García Lorca, and I wonder now how it was ever able to happen.

It was a game, I shout to myself. A game. There are no angels, ghosts, or even shadows. It was a game made out of summer and freedom and a need for a poetry that would be more than the expression of my hatreds and desires. It was a game like Yeats' spooks or Blake's sexless seraphim.

Yet it was there. The poems are there, the memory not of a vision but a kind of casual friendship with an undramatic ghost who occasionally looked through my eyes and whispered to me, not really more important then than my other friends, but now achieving a different level of reality by being missing. Today, alone by myself, it is like having lost a pair of eyes and a lover.

What is real, I suppose, will endure. Poe's mechanical chessplayer was not the less a miracle for having a man inside it, and when the man departed, the games it had played were no less beautiful. The analogy is false, of course, but it holds both a promise and a warning for each of us.

It is October now. Summer is over. Almost every trace of the months that produced these poems has been obliterated. Only explanations are possible, only regrets.

Saying goodbye to a ghost is more final than saying goodbye to a lover. Even the dead return, but a ghost, once loved, departing will never reappear.

Love,
Jack

Radar

A Postscript for Marianne Moore

No one exactly knows
Exactly how clouds look in the sky
Or the shape of the mountains below them
Or the direction in which fish swim.
No one exactly knows.
The eye is jealous of whatever moves
And the heart
Is too far buried in the sand
To tell.

They are going on a journey
Those deep blue creatures
Passing us as if they were sunshine
Look
Those fins, those closed eyes
Admiring each last drop of the ocean.

I crawled into bed with sorrow that night
Couldn't touch his fingers. See the splash
Of the water
The noisy movement of cloud
The push of the humpbacked mountains
Deep at the sand's edge.

ADMONITIONS (1957)

Dear Joe,

Some time ago I would have thought that writing notes on particular poems would either be a confession that the poems were totally inadequate (a sort of patch put on a leaky tire) or an equally humiliating confession that the writer was more interested in the terrestrial mechanics of criticism than the celestial mechanics of poetry—in either case that the effort belonged to the garage or stable rather than to the Muse.

Muses do exist, but now I know that they are not afraid to dirty their hands with explication—that they are patient with truth and commentary as long as it doesn't get into the poem, that they whisper (if you let yourself really hear them), "Talk all you want, baby, but *then* let's go to bed."

This sexual metaphor brings me to the first problem. In these poems the obscene (in word and concept) is not used, as is common, for the sake of intensity, but rather as a kind of rhythm as the tip-tap of the branches throughout the dream of *Finnegans Wake* or, to make the analogy even more mysterious to you, a cheering section at a particularly exciting football game. It is precisely because the obscenity is unnecessary that I use it, as I could have used any disturbance, as I could have used anything (remember the beat in jazz) which is regular and beside the point.

The point. But what, you will be too polite to ask me, is the point? Are not these poems all things to all men, like Rorschach ink blots or whores? Are they anything better than a kind of mirror?

In themselves, no. Each one of them is a mirror, dedicated to the person that I particularly want to look into it. But mirrors can be arranged. The frightening hall of mirrors in a fun house is universal beyond each particular reflection.

This letter is *to* you because you are my publisher and because the poem I wrote *for* you gives the most distorted reflection in the whole promenade. Mirror makers know the secret—one does not make a mirror to resemble a person, one brings a person to the mirror.

Love,
Jack

For Nemmie

When they number their blocks they mean business.
If you hear the Go sign
Around 32nd Avenue
Bear it
Others have
Better
On the same street.
If you hadn't seen it
On 16th
Or 23rd street
Shit.
This thing is all traffic.
And you say
As you are going through a signal
Look
Those motorcycle policemen
That police love
Those avenues—
And the strangers
(Road agents)
No one can stop their whispering.

For Ebbe

Oh there are waves where the heart beats fully
Where the blood wanders
Alive like some black sea fish
Teach the young to be young
The old
To be old

The heartless
To swim in the sea they do not believe in.
Oh, no
Reconstituted universe
Is as warm as the heart's blood.

For Russ

Christ,
You'd think it would all be
Pretty simple
This tree will never grow. This bush
Has no branches. No
I love you. Yet.
I wonder how our mouths will look in twenty five years
When we say yet.

For Ed

Bewildered
Like the first seagull that ever ate a fish
Everyone's heart dives and
Stops just before eating.
Ah
What comfort is there in the sight
Or in the belly?
No fish in this pond or ocean is supreme
No fish tastes.
In all this muck and water there is only
The ocean's comfort.

For Harvey

When you break a line nothing
Becomes better.
There is no new (unless you are humming
Old Uncle Tom's Cabin) there is no new
Measure.
You breathe the same and Rimbaud
Would never even look at you.
Break
Your poem
Like you would cut a grapefruit
Make
It go to sleep for you
And each line (There is no Pacific Ocean) And make each line
Cut itself. Like seaweed thrown
Against the pier.

For Mac

A dead starfish on a beach
He has five branches
Representing the five senses
Representing the jokes we did not tell each other
Call the earth flat
Call other people human
But let this creature lie
Flat upon our senses
Like a love
Prefigured in the sea
That died.

And went to water
All the oceans
Of emotion. All the oceans of emotion
Are full of such fish
Why
Is this dead one of such importance?
Died
With blue of heart's blood, the brown
Of unknowing
The purple of unimportance
It lies upon our beach to be crowned.
Purple
Starfish are
And love. And love
Is like nothing I can imagine.

For Dick

Innocence is a drug to be protected against strangers
Not to be sold to police agents or rather
Not to be sold.
When you protect it a sudden chill
Comes in the window
When you proclaim it it becomes a wet marijuana cigarette
Which cannot be lit by matches.
Hear the wind outside
The bloody shell of your life.
Hear the wind rumble
Like a sabre-toothed ape.
Look
Innocence is important

It has meaning
Look
It can give us
Hope against the very winds that we batter against it.

For Billy

That old equalizer
Called time by some
Love by others
Cock by a few
Will come to meet you at the door
When you go
(Knowing that death is as near to you as water)
Go to fuck and say goodbye to your Mexican whore.
They will be waiting in the same room for you:
Time with his big jeans
Love with his embarrassed laugh
Cock with his throat cut wearing a bandana.
They can equalize anybody
January, February, March,
April, May, June, July, August, September,
October,
November,
December,
I love you, I love you,
Scream when you come.
There is not another room to go into
But hell, Billy,
It was hell when they shot you.

Dear Robin,

Enclosed you find the first of the publications of White Rabbit Press. The second will be much handsomer.

You are right that I don't now need your criticisms of individual poems. But I still want them. It's probably from old habit—but it's an awfully old habit. Halfway through *After Lorca* I discovered that I was writing a book instead of a series of poems and individual criticism by anyone suddenly became less important. This is true of my *Admonitions* which I will send you when complete. (I have eight of them already and there will probably be fourteen including, of course, this letter.)

The trick naturally is what Duncan learned years ago and tried to teach us—not to search for the perfect poem but to let your way of writing of the moment go along its own paths, explore and retreat but never be fully realized (confined) within the boundaries of one poem. This is where we were wrong and he was right, but he complicated things for us by saying that there is no such thing as good or bad poetry. There is—but not in relation to the single poem. There is really no single poem.

That is why all my stuff from the past (except the *Elegies* and *Troilus*) looks foul to me. The poems belong nowhere. They are one night stands filled (the best of them) with their own emotions, but pointing nowhere, as meaningless as sex in a Turkish bath. It was not my anger or my frustration that got in the way of my poetry but the fact that I viewed each anger and each frustration as unique—something to be converted into poetry as one would exchange foreign money. I learned this from the English Department (and from the English Department of the spirit—that great quagmire that lurks at the bottom of all of us) and it ruined ten years of my poetry. Look at those other poems. Admire them if you like. They are beautiful but dumb.

Poems should echo and re-echo against each other. They should create resonances. They cannot live alone any more than we can.

So don't send the box of old poetry to Don Allen. Burn it or rather open it with Don and cry over the possible books that were buried in it—the *Songs Against Apollo*, the *Gallery of Gorgeous Gods*, the *Drinking Songs*—all incomplete, all abortive—all incomplete, all abortive because I thought, like all abortionists, that what is not perfect had no real right to live.

Things fit together. We knew that—it is the principle of magic. Two inconsequential things can combine together to become a consequence. This is true of poems too. A poem is never to be judged by itself alone. A poem is never by itself alone.

This is the most important letter that you have ever received.

Love,
Jack

For Joe

People who don't like the smell of faggot vomit
Will never understand why men don't like women
Won't see why those never to be forgotten thighs
Of Helen (say) will move us into screams of laughter.
Parody (what we don't want) is the whole thing.
Don't deliver us any mail today, mailman.
Send us no letters. The female genital organ is hideous. We
Do not want to be moved.
Forgive us. Give us
A single example of the fact that nature is imperfect.
Men ought to love men
(And do)
As the man said
It's
Rosemary for remembrance.

For Judson

El guardarropa, novedad, dispersar.
There are little fish that are made angry
At all that we do. No one can look at us better
Than their mouth. Little mouths
That eat anything.
Ale, automatization, scattering.
I could not invent a better skeleton
That you could
Like a pumpkin on wet Halloween
Flicker into.

For Robert

The poet
Robert D.
Writes poetry while we
Listen to him.
Commentary—follow
The red dog
Down the
Limit
Of possible
Quarterbacks.

For Jack

Tell everyone to have guts
Do it yourself
Have guts until the guts
Come through the margins
Clear and pure
Like love is.
The word changes
Grows obscure
Like someone
In the coldness of the scarey night air
Says—
Dad
    I want your voice.

For Willie

There is no excuse for bad ghosts
Or bad thoughts.
6X / 10 equals 150
And electric socket with a plug in it
Or a hole in your eyeball:
It is bad
And everyone says, "What?" X
—4X / 10 equals 150.

For Hal

Youth
Is no excuse for such things
Responsibilities
Weigh like strawberries
On a shortcake.
Go
To the root of the matter
Get laid
Have a friend
Do anything
But be a free fucking agent.
No one
Has lots of them
Lays or friends or anything
That can make a little light in all that darkness.
There is a cigarette you can hold for a minute
In your weak mouth
And then the light goes out,
Rival, honey, friend,
And then you stub it out.

For Jerry

In the poisonous candy factory
Or on the beach which is entirely empty of stone
Or at the bottom of your own navel
A voice stirs
Saying, "Sleep
Though you are no longer young.
Cry

On nobody else's shoulder.
Love them.
Go to sleep. Every color
Our bodies are made of."

A Postscript for Charles Olson

If nothing happens it is possible
To make things happen.
Human history shows this
And an ape
Is likely (presently) to be an angel.
If you dream anything
You are marked
With a blue tattoo on your arm.
Rx: Methadrine
To be taken at 52 miles an hour.

A BOOK OF MUSIC   (1958)

With words by Jack Spicer

Improvisations on a Sentence by Poe

"Indefiniteness is an element of the true music."
The grand concord of what
Does not stoop to definition. The seagull
Alone on the pier cawing its head off
Over no fish, no other seagull,
No ocean. As absolutely devoid of meaning
As a French horn.
It is not even an orchestra. Concord
Alone on a pier. The grand concord of what
Does not stoop to definition. No fish
No other seagull, no ocean—the true
Music.

A Valentine

Useless Valentines
Are better
Than all others.
Like something implicit
In a poem.
Take all your Valentines
And I'll take mine.
What is left is better
Than any image.

Cantata

Ridiculous
How the space between three violins
Can threaten all of our poetry.
We bunch together like Cub
Scouts at a picnic. There is a high scream.
Rain threatens. That moment of terror.
Strange how all our beliefs
Disappear.

Orfeo

Sharp as an arrow Orpheus
Points his music downward.
Hell is there
At the bottom of the seacliff.
Heal
Nothing by this music.
Eurydice
Is a frigate bird or a rock or some seaweed.
Hail nothing
The infernal
Is a slippering wetness out at the horizon.
Hell is this:
The lack of anything but the eternal to look at
The expansiveness of salt
The lack of any bed but one's
Music to sleep in.

Song of a Prisoner

Nothing in my body escapes me.
The sound of an eagle diving
Upon some black bird
Or the sorrow of an owl.
Nothing in my body escapes me.
Each branch is closed
I
Echo each song from its throat
Bellow each sound.

Jungle Warfare

The town wasn't much
A few mud-huts and a church steeple.
They were the same leaves
And the same grass
And the same birds deep in the edge of the thicket.
We waited around for someone to come out and surrender
But they rang their church bells
And we
We were not afraid of death or any manner of dying
But the same muddy bullets, the same horrible
Love.

Good Friday: For Lack of an Orchestra

I saw a headless she-mule
Running through the rain
She had the hide of a chessboard
And withers that were lank and dark
"Tell me," I asked
"Where
Is Babylon?"
"No," she bellowed
"Babylon is a few baked bricks
With some symbols on them.
You could not hear them. I am running
To the end of the world."
She ran
Like a green and purple parrot, screaming
Through the sand.

Mummer

The word is imitative
From the sound mum or mom
Used by nurses to frighten or amuse children
At the same time pretending
To cover their faces.
Understanding is not enough
The old seagull died. There is a whole army of seagulls
Waiting in the wings
A whole army of seagulls.

The Cardplayers

The moon is tied to a few strings
They hold in their hands. The cardplayers
Sit there stiff, hieratic
Moving their hands only for the sake of
Playing the cards.
No trick of metaphor
Each finger is a real finger
Each card real pasteboard, each liberty
Unaware of attachment.
The moon is tied to a few strings.
                  Those cardplayers
Stiff, utterly
Unmoving.

Ghost Song

The in
        ability to love
The inability
            to love
In love
        (like all the small animals went up the hill into the
        underbrush to escape from the goat and the bad tiger)
The inability
Inability
        (tell me why no white flame comes up from the earth
        when lightning strikes the twigs and the dry branches)

In love. In love. In love. The
In-
   ability
            (as if there were nothing left on the mountains but
            what nobody wanted to escape from)

Army Beach With Trumpets

Rather than our bodies the sand
Proclaims that we are on the last edge
Of something. Two boys
Who cannot catch footballs horseplay
On the wet edge.
Or if the sight of the thing ended
Did not break upon us like a wave
From every warm ocean.
We call it sport
To play on the edge, to drop
Like a heartless football
At the edge.

Duet for a Chair and a Table

The sound of words as they fall away from our mouths
Nothing
Is less important
And yet that chair
            this table
                  named

Assume identities
                  take their places
Almost as a kind of music.
Words make things name
                themselves
Makes the table grumble
             I
In the symphony of God am a table
Makes the chair sing
A little song about the people that will never be sitting on it
And we
Who in the same music
Are almost as easily shifted as furniture
We
Can learn our names from our mouths
Name our names
In the middle of the same music.

Conspiracy

A violin which is following me

In how many distant cities are they listening
To its slack-jawed music? This
Slack-jawed music?
Each of ten thousand people playing it.

It follows me like someone that hates me.

Oh, my heart would sooner die
Than leave its slack-jawed music. They
In those other cities
Whose hearts would sooner die.

It follows me like someone that hates me.

Or is it really a tree growing just behind my throat
That if I turned quickly enough I could see
Rooted, immutable, neighboring
Music.

A Book of Music

Coming at an end, the lovers
Are exhausted like two swimmers. Where
Did it end? There is no telling. No love is
Like an ocean with the dizzy procession of the waves' boundaries
From which two can emerge exhausted, nor long goodbye
Like death.
Coming at an end. Rather, I would say, like a length
Of coiled rope
Which does not disguise in the final twists of its lengths
Its endings.
But, you will say, we loved
And some parts of us loved
And the rest of us will remain
Two persons. Yes,
Poetry ends like a rope.

— • • • —

SOCRATES

Because they accused me of poems
That did not disturb the young
They gave me a pair of glasses
Filled with tincture of hemlock.
Because the young accused me
Of piles, horseradish, and bad dreams
They gave me three days
To burn down the city. What dialogues
(If they had let me)
Could I have held with both of my enemies.

A POEM FOR DADA DAY AT THE PLACE, APRIL 1, 1958

i.

The bartender
Has eyes the color of ripe apricots
Easy to please as a cash register he
Enjoys art and good jokes.
Squish
Goes the painting
Squirt
Goes the poem
He
We
Laugh.

ii.

It is not easy to remember that other people died
      besides Dylan Thomas and Charlie Parker
Died looking for beauty in the world of the
      bartender
This person, that person, this person, that person
      died looking for beauty
Even the bartender died

iii.

Dante blew his nose
And his nose came off in his hand
Rimbaud broke his throat
Trying to cough
Dada is not funny
It is a serious assault
On art
Because art
Can be enjoyed by the bartender.

iv.

The bartender is not the United States
Or the intellectual
Or the bartender
He is every bastard that does not cry
When he reads this poem.

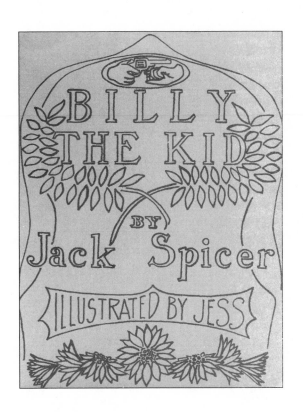

I.

    The radio that told me about the death of Billy The Kid
    (And the day, a hot summer day, with birds in the sky)
    Let us fake out a frontier—a poem somebody could hide in with a
sheriff's posse after him—a thousand miles of it if it is necessary for
him to go a thousand miles—a poem with no hard corners, no houses
to get lost in, no underwebbing of customary magic, no New York Jew
salesmen of amethyst pajamas, only a place where Billy The Kid can
hide when he shoots people.
    Torture gardens and scenic railways. The radio
    That told me about the death of Billy The Kid
    The day a hot summer day. The roads dusty in the summer. The
roads going somewhere. You can almost see where they are going
beyond the dark purple of the horizon. Not even the birds know where
they are going.
    The poem. In all that distance who could recognize his face.

II.

A sprinkling of gold leaf looking like hell flowers
A flat piece of wrapping paper, already wrinkled, but wrinkled
    again by hand, smoothed into shape by an electric iron
A painting
Which told me about the death of Billy The Kid.
Collage   a binding together
Of the real
Which flat colors
Tell us what heroes
                really come by.
No, it is not a collage. Hell flowers

Fall from the hands of heroes
                    fall from all of our hands
                                        flat
As if we were not ever able quite to include them.
His gun
        does not shoot real bullets
                            his death
Being done is unimportant.
Being done
In those flat colors
Not a collage
A binding together,   a
Memory.

III.

There was nothing at the edge of the river
But dry grass and cotton candy.
"Alias," I said to him. "Alias,
Somebody there makes us want to drink the river
Somebody wants to thirst us."
"Kid," he said. "No river
Wants to trap men. There ain't no malice in it. Try
To understand."
We stood there by that little river and Alias took off his shirt
        and I took off my shirt
I was never real. Alias was never real.
Or that big cotton tree or the ground.
Or the little river.

IV.

What I mean is
I
Will tell you about the pain
It was a long pain
About as wide as a curtain
But long
As the great outdoors.
Stig-
        mata
Three bullet holes in the groin
One in the head
                        dancing
Right below the left eyebrow
What I mean is I
Will tell you about his
Pain.

V.

Billy The Kid in a field of poplars with just one touch of moonlight
His shadow is carefully
                        distinguished from all of their shadows
Delicate
        as perception is
No one will get his gun or obliterate
Their shadows

VI.

The gun
A false clue

           Nothing can kill

Anybody.
Not a poem or a fat penis. Bang,
Bang, bang. A false
Clue.
Nor immortality either (though why immortality should occur to
      me with somebody who was as mortal as Billy The Kid or
      his gun which is now rusted in some rubbish heap or shined
      up properly in some New York museum) A
False clue
Nothing
Can kill anybody. Your gun, Billy,
And your   fresh
Face.

VII.

Grasshoppers swarm through the desert.
Within the desert
There are only grasshoppers.
Lady
Of Guadalupe
Make my sight clear
Make my breath pure
Make my strong arm stronger and my fingers tight.
Lady of Guadalupe, lover
Of many   make
Me avenge
Them.

VIII.

Back where poetry is Our Lady
Watches each motion when the players take the cards
From the deck.
The Ten of Diamonds. The Jack of Spades. The Queen
Of Clubs. The King of Hearts. The Ace
God gave us when he put us alive writing poetry for unsuspecting
      people or shooting them with guns.
Our Lady
Stands as a kind of dancing partner for the memory.
Will you dance, Our Lady,
Dead and unexpected?
Billy wants you to dance
Billy
Will shoot the heels off your shoes if you don't dance
Billy
Being dead also   wants
Fun.

IX.

So the heart breaks
Into small shadows
Almost so random
They are meaningless
Like a diamond
Has at the center of it a diamond
Or a rock
Rock.
Being afraid
Love asks its bare question—
I can no more remember
What brought me here
Than bone answers bone in the arm
Or shadow sees shadow—
Deathward we ride in the boat
Like someone canoeing
In a small lake
Where at either end
There are nothing but pine-branches—
Deathward we ride in the boat
Broken-hearted or broken-bodied
The choice is real. The diamond. I
Ask it.

X.

Billy The Kid
I love you
Billy The Kid
I back anything you say
And there was the desert
And the mouth of the river
Billy The Kid
(In spite of your death notices)
There is honey in the groin
Billy

—— • • • ——

FOR STEVE JONAS WHO IS IN JAIL
FOR DEFRAUDING A BOOK CLUB

And you alone in Federal prison saying
That the whole State is based on larceny
Christ who didn't know that, Steve?
The word steals from the word, the sound from
    the sound. Even
The very year of your life steals from the last one. So
Do you have to get put in jail for it? Finding
Yourself a martyr for a cause that you and your
    jury and your heartbeat all support. All
This crap about being a human. To tell the
    truth about our State.
                      So—

You would say—
It is better than going to Europe.

FIFTEEN FALSE PROPOSITIONS AGAINST GOD (1958)

I.

The self is no longer real
It is not like loneliness
This big huge loneness. Sacrificing
All of the person with it.
Bigger people
I'm sure have mastered it.
"Beauty is so rare a thing," Pound sings
"So few drink at my fountain."

II.

Look I am King Of The Forest
Says The King Of The Forest
As he growls magnificently
Look, I am in pain. My right leg
Does not fit my left leg.
I am King Of The Forest
Says The King Of The Forest.
And the other beasts hear him and would rather
They were King Of The Forest
But that their right leg
Would fit their left leg.
"Beauty is so rare a thing," Pound sang.
"So few drink at my fountain."

III.

Beauty is so rare a th—
Sing a new song
Real
Music
A busted flush. A pain in the eyebrows. A
Visiting card.
There are rocks on the mountains that will lie there for fifty years
      and I only lived with you three months
Why
Does
Your absence seem so real or your presences
So uninviting?

IV.

Real bad poems
Dear Sir: I should like to—
Hate and love are clarifications enough of themselves, do not
      belong in poetry, embarrass the reader and the poet, lack
Dignity.
Or the dignity of a paper airplane
That you throw at someone's face
And it swoops across the whole occasion quickly
Hitting every angle.
Hate and love are clar—
Dear Sir: I should like to make sure that everything that I said
      about you in my poetry was true, that you really existed,
That everything that I said was true
That you were not an occasion
In a real bad scene
That what the poems said had meaning
Apart from what the poems said.

Dear Sir:
My mouth has meanings
It had not wanted to argue.

V.

When the house falls you wonder
If there will ever be poetry
And you shiver in the timbers wondering
If there will ever be poetry
When the house falls you shiver
In the vacant lumber of your poetry.
Beauty is so rare a thing, Pound sang.
So few drink at my fountain.

VI.

Drop
The word drops
As if it were not spoken
I can't remember tomorrow
What I said tonight
(To describe the real world.
Even in a poem
One forgets the real world.)
Fuzzy heads of fuzzy people
Like the trees Williams saw. Drop
The words drop
Like leaves from a fuzzy tree
I can't remember tomorrow
I (alone in the real world with their fuzzy heads nodding at me)
Can't
Remember.

VII.

Trees in their youth look younger
Than almost anything
I mean
In the spring
When they put forth green leaves and try
To look like real trees
Honest to God my heart aches
When I see them trying.
Comes August and the sunshine and the fog and only the wood
    grows
They stand there with big rough leaves amazed
That it is no longer summer.
The cold fog seeps in and by November
They don't look the same (the leaves I mean) the leaves fall
Such a hard reason to seek. Such heart's
Timber.

VIII.

Shredded wheat, paper maché
Nobody believes in you
Least of all us trees.
Who find ourselves at the final edge
Of a cliff or at least an ocean
Eating salt air and fog and rock
Just standing
There
Bother your fuzzy heads about God. Gee
God is not even near your roots or our roots
He is the nearest
Tree.

IX.

After you have told your lover goodbye
And chewed the cud of your experience with him
Your bitter experience:
                What else?
Perhaps trees. Slippery elm. Birch
That knows no thankless nights. Oaktrees and palm
Ready to start a revolution.
No you should stay there with your roots in the ground
Ready to drink whatever water
The rain is willing to send you. The rain
The cow
And my true body   a
Revolution.

X.

"Trees. Those fuzzy things?" Williams' grandfather or was it his
      grandmother asked on the way to the hospital. A journey
We will all take.
I do not remember the poem well but I know that beauty
Will always become fuzzy
And love fuzzy
And the fact of death itself fuzzy
Like a big tree.
Let me chop down then one by one
Whatever is in the way of my eyesight
People, trees, even my own eyestalks.
Let me chop apart
With my bare hands
This blurred forest.

XI.

In the grotto of knowingness
There is born a child. There is born a child
Like we Protestants say in our Christmas carols.
Saint Mary
Virgin mistress
Author of One Word
Give me strength to have joy. The heart wants it
The ball bounces
Faster than any eye can see. I believe you love me
Like a fried egg can exist on a purple plate alone
Or being born.
How love can exist without any favor to it
As George told me you said the
Joyful mysteries.

XII.

Millions of meaningless toys
If the child isn't born soon we'll have to close the toyshop. The
        second
Joyful mystery.
They make them out of trees and rubber bands and place them
        in stockings and cradles
No one
Knows how to play with them.
Kneel
At his birth
Meaningless
As he is
They are not his toys or our toys we must play with. They are
Our toys.

XIII.

Hush now baby don't say a word
Mama's going to buy you a mocking bird
The third
Joyful mystery.
The joy that descends on you when all the trees are cut down
    and all the fountains polluted and you are still alive waiting
    for an absent savior. The third
Joyful mystery.
If the mocking bird don't sing
Mama's going to buy you a diamond ring
The diamond ring is God, the mocking bird the Holy Ghost.
    The third
Joyful mystery.
The joy that descends on you when all the trees are cut down
    and all the fountains polluted and you are still alive waiting
    for an absent savior.

XIV.

If the diamond ring turns brass
Mama's going to buy you a looking glass
Marianne Moore and Ezra Pound and William Carlos Williams
    going on a picnic together when they were all students at
    the University of Pennsylvania
Now they are all over seventy and the absent baby
Is a mirror sheltering their image.

XV.

Dear Sir:

In these poems I tried to find the three-headed God I believed in
      sometimes both when talking with you and living with you.
      The abysmal toyshop
Intrudes.
(It is hell where no one
Guesses another. It is after
Every thing.)
No thought coheres or sensation. It is five o'clock in the
      morning.
If the mocking bird don't sing
Mama's going to buy you a diamond ring
This is the last joyful mystery
The end of all guessing.

LETTERS TO JAMES ALEXANDER   (1958–1959)

Fort Wayne, Indiana, is the capital of Nitrogen. All streets end there. No buses arrive there except those that carry direct mail or cargoes of Negroes en route on the Underground Railway. There has never been a city made up of so many arms.

You can see Troy, New York in the distance.

Christmas poems and lovers' holly branches grow there in the winter as well as stuffings of turkeys, memory pie, and little droppings of passing angels. It is not reached by air.

Fort Wayne, Indiana, has industries and tournament golf, and blocks and blocks of weeping buildings. It is built on high ground above the slough of utter unwinding.

The birds which all look like seagulls or cormorants in its artificial sky finish singing when the day is over. At night they look like elephants. People watch them with telescopes as they hover.

In Fort Wayne, Indiana the trees are dying and you can see footprints in the rather wet snow. People take their motor scooters to bed with them.

Come back to California, come back to California every mapmaker, every mapmaker is pleading to James Alexander.

"What do the sparrows eat in the winter?" I asked someone once in Minneapolis. He replied, "They eat horse turds if they can find them."

There are acres of cold snow.

Love,
Jack

2.

Railroad trains lost their balance and buses stood on their hind ends and licked their wounded wheels when James Alexander came back to California.

And poor airplanes dripped sweat from their wings and little cars mooed as if they were not quite convinced they were mechanical.

When James Alexander came back to California he and the other poet who exists in the universe formulated a series of true propositions:

THAT POETRY ALONE CAN LOVE POETRY

THAT POEMS CRY OUT TO EACH OTHER FROM A
GREAT DISTANCE

THAT POETS, BEING BASTARD FATHERS, LOVE EACH
OTHER LIKE BASTARD FATHERS WHEN THEY SEE THEIR
CHILDREN PLAYING TOGETHER

THAT POEMS PLAY TOGETHER FROM A GREAT
DISTANCE

It was made illegal for a bachelor to watch poems.

When James Alexander came back to California they hunted mushrooms together in the cold rocks of the Berkeley Hills.

They invented a game which was more complicated than bridge or chess or football which was played with gum and chalk and a piece of common wrapping paper.

They made it utterly impossible to identify God.

Having a hand in each other's hand, they walked down every street on which it was possible to walk, having the pavements dictated to them by an angel.

They purged history of contemporary reference.

They wrote poetry that had to be looked at from a distance on a gigantic playground. Their children split words.

The scholars who found these children died in agony.

One thumb opposed one thumb, each thumb was the center of the universe.

They forged a lost manuscript of Rimbaud's La Chasse Spirituelle for their own purposes. It was mysteriously discovered to have been written in English.

They found that they had one tongue
We shall find that we have one tongue
I hope that we shall find that we have one tongue.

Love,
Jack

3.

Dear James,

I don't know if there is room in the world for a postoffice but you come across 'em often enough, if you don't make the mistake of pretending that they're in a fixed place (like the moon) and if you don't let their continual changes bewilder you.

It's rather like hunting mushrooms. They grow in certain places and you can never be sure where their (certain) places will be after the next rain but you get a sense of where they won't be and don't go there. Unless, of course, they tell you.

The letters, poems, kisses (since the original game of postoffice is stuck in the mysterious regions of childhood) are directed by a fantastically inefficient system up to the place where poetry comes from and then back down again to the person whose poetry, or letters, or love was meant to receive it. It is a lot different from Air Mail.

And it is almost impossible to list the random places from which they will deliver their letters. A box of shredded wheat, a drunken comment, a big piece of paper, a shadow meaningless except as a threat or a communication, a throat.

Believe them all but obey the postofficers who tell you when to believe them or obey them.

If you don't have money for the money order why not send me the pawntickets (I have money for a few months) and I will send you pawntickets with the equivalents of a watch and a typewriter upon them. The real pawntickets are letters.

Love,
Jack

4.

Dear James,

Went down to Duncan and Jess's Friday to read them the letters.

Their house is built mainly of Oz books, a grate to burn wood, a second story for guests, paintings, poems, and miscellaneous objects of kindly magic. Cats. It is a place where I am proud (we are proud) to read the letters. It is a postoffice. I had not realized how little alone one is in a postoffice. Before I had merely posted the letters and wondered.

It is possible if you have the humility to create a household and the sense to tread on all pieces of bad magic as soon as they appear to create a postoffice. It is as mechanical as Christmas.

Late at night (we drank a gallon of wine and talked about the worlds that had to be included into our poetry—Duncan wanted me to send Creeley the letters because Creeley, he said, needed the letters—and I went to bed upstairs with George MacDonald's *Lilith*). I had to piss and walked down the outside stairs and saw (or heard but I think I saw) the ocean and the moonless stars that filled the sky so full of light I understood size for the first time. They seemed, while I was pissing away the last of the wine and the conversation, a part of the postoffice too.

This I promise—that if you come back to California I will show you where they send letters—all of them, the poems and the ocean. The invisible

Love,
Jack

5.

It is not the monotony of nature but the poems beyond nature that call to each other above the poets' heads. The heads of poets being a part of nature. It is not for us to make the lines of nature precise. It is for the poems to make the lines of nature precise. Because of their fatal attraction for the lines of nature, for our heads.

We proclaim a silent revolution. The poems above our heads, without tongues, are tired of talking to each other over the gabble of our beliefs, our literary personalities, our attempts to project their silent conversation to an audience. When we give tongue we amplify. We are telephone switchboards deluded into becoming hi-fi sets. The terrible speakers must be allowed silence. They are not speaking to us.

How is it then our business to talk of revolution—we heads of poets one named Jack and one named James, three in the distance named Ebbe, Charles, and Robert? It is because we as their victims, as their mouthpiece, must learn to become complete victims, complete pieces of their mouth. We must learn that our lips are not our own. A revolution is a savage education.

There are people that talk about poetry like tired insurance clerks talk about baseball. They must be destroyed by our silence. Even the hatred of them interrupts the conversation that our poems wish to continue. Even the mention of them makes it me talking, crashes into paradox that was their truth.

We do not write for each other. We are irritable radio sets (but the image of the talking head of a horse on the wall in Cocteau's first Orpheus was a truer image) but our poems write for each other, being full of their own purposes, no doubt no more mysterious in their universe than ours in ours. And our lips are not our lips. But are the lips of heads of poets. And should shout revolution.

Love,
Jack

209

6.

Dear James

It is absolutely clear and absolutely sunny as if neither a cloud nor a moon had ever been invented. I am lying here on the grass of the University of California, a slave state but one which today seems peculiarly beneficent. I have not had a letter from you in weeks.

I read them all (your letters and mine) to the poets assembled for the occasion last Wednesday. Ebbe was annoyed since he thought that letters should remain letters (unless they were essays) and poems poems (a black butterfly just flew past my leg) and that the universe of the personal and the impersonal should be kept in order. George Stanley thought that I was robbing Jim to pay James. They sounded beautiful all of them.

Things cannot die in such a spring (unless the old men of the world commit suicide (our suicide) over the question of whether East Germans be called East Germans in diplomatic notes) and every leaf and flower of this red-hot February asks me to remember this. Though it is on the other side of poetry, spring, thank whatever created both of them, is spring. And I am not sure on a day like this that the living and dying world does not have something analogous to poetry in it. That every flower and every leaf (properly read) is not a James as well as a Jim.

Things cannot die in such a spring and yet your silence (for the spring itself proclaims that there are such things as clouds and moons) frightens me when I close my eyes or begin to write a poem.

I wish you were with me now on this grass and could be with me like the leaves and the flowers and the grass a part of this spring. Jim and James.

Love,
Jack

7.

Dear James,

The only place I've found to retire into is your watch. I haven't covered it with bark and it is in no sense beautiful, but I haven't worn a watch in two years and I talk to it (mostly about you and what it was like to be worn on your wrist) and sometimes I spend a few seconds watching its second hand stuttering by (green and nervous) and it really is, all things considered, a natural object like a tree or a flower or a bark covered table. A postoffice.

And the watch believes what I tell it. "There are two kinds of places in the world," it wants me to tell you, "pawnshops and postoffices." You will find it hard to reeducate.

I don't like my poetry either. I read a new poem last Wednesday and nobody said much of anything and I asked why and Duncan said it was because it was a very good Jack Spicer poem and I threw the poem in the garbage sack not tearing the poem because it was a very good Jack Spicer poem. The watch was ticking on my wrist all the time and was not a Jack Spicer wristwatch and would never be a Jack Spicer wristwatch and that should be the way with the poems.

It's rather like a medium (a real medium) who gets a spirit, call her Little Eva, to control her. Pretty soon, after a few sessions, she'll get to know what Little Eva is going to say and start saying it for her. Then it's no longer a seance but fakery and time to change spooks.

That's what your watch tells me. TIME TO CHANGE SPOOKS!

I don't know what your table tells you, but if you came back to California we might arrange a favorable exchange of spooks.

Love,
Jack

8.

Dear James,

This letter is entirely from the other Jack, the nervous worried guy who puts letters into envelopes and receives them from same. The other Jack, the one who wrote you all the letters, is puzzled about the change of postoffices. This Jack, me, being more practical, is wondering

(A) Did you receive his last letter (about watch, p.o. vs pawnshop, ghost-trading etc.) before letters of 31st, 1st ult? Or at all?

(B) Is someone reading and destroying his letters because if so don't because it is harmless to the real world insofar as poetry is harmless to the real world. Which is not so far.

Or (C) What?

He, the other Jack, is probably asleep. I hate him sometimes.

He (it was really my suggestion) on account of (B) is sending this letter from the address of an imaginary little magazine. We have both still our own.

> Love (insofar as I can say it too)
> Jack

9.

The mirror does not break easily regardless of what is reflected in it, regardless of whether there are blue apples, Rimbaud, or even angry white light belonging in it, imprisoned, one might say, in the death of its surface. It is the oblique patience of an Alice who plays with her cat and waits for something between her and the image to melt away. It is the oblique patience of children.

When you rush bravely against the mirror shouting "This is also my universe" you are likely merely to get a bloody nose. That surface has no patience with violence. Even as these letters are our mirrors and we imprisoned singly in the depths of them.

So it is (the violence of the impatient artist) that I keep trying to draw the form of these letters to a close merely because I am going to read them to an audience of boobies and one or two poets. Ridiculous attempt to break the glass! The letters will continue. The letters will continue after both of us are dead. The letters would continue even if we were in the same room together, even though our faces were so close that we could hardly speak—or so distant that our hearts could not touch.

Mirror breaker! I simply do not have the patience merely to let the mirror dissolve. I keep tapping my hand on it. Help me!

Love,
Jack

10.

Dear James,

I'll not explain the mistakes the other Jack made in the last letter. They're obvious. And I'm sure they belong to the poetry of it somewhere too.

I am glad that you're not going to New York. Letters sent to there or received from there would be filled with worms. Any other city. But, of course, if you come here there will be a double advantage for if Jim and the other Jack can't talk to each other and won't let James and Jack talk to each other (unlikely because of the bridge of love we have erected between us but possible God knows) we can still, defying both of them, send letters to each other from the same city. Which would be as unnatural as poetry often is.

Our letters again will cross. Your watch will count out the days and hours of the month. As our letters will.

Love,
Jack

11.

Dear Jim,

I am writing this letter to you rather than James as it is a Christmas letter and both he and I would find it uncomfortable—like saying Merry Christmas to Rimbaud. You, on the other hand, having several faces will be able to select a face appropriate to its reception.

Religion is the shadow of the obvious—and all the paraphernalia of Christmas from the Christ child to the Santa Claus selling ties in a department-store window is just this—religion—the infinite shadow that a false beard or a plaster child can cast. What is under that book lying face downward on the bed or that green radio on the floor? Whatever it is disappears when you pick the object up, but on holidays you can see the shadow that the thing casts. That is why a real Child is born on Christmas, why there *is* a Santa Claus.

Why am I writing you to tell you about this? It is because I am afraid that you may be too young to believe and James too busy to believe in this holiday, that you may confuse the shadows with the things that cast them and believe that there is nothing there. This is not important to James, to the poet who can watch in his own poetry something even more than these shadows—but it is you I am wishing Merry Christmas.

Tell James: I am reading my poetry in public on February 14th and at it reading all his letters.

Jack

12.

Dear James

It was not really the thought of reading them (because I didn't, not on Valentine's Day which would be a threat of perfection, but tomorrow to poets at one of those poetry meetings that were in your time Sundays) but as the prose stretches like a big rubber ball with no

214

middle to it, but the hoverings and threats of evil (do you understand magic or do I have to teach it to you?) that made me lean on the death of our letters. It is a black thing evil is, having nothing to do with good and bad, or even beautiful and fucked up, having much more to do with the inside and outside of a man than good does.

The opposite of it is poetry or pajamas or Paracelsus or anything else in the universe that begins with P.

Magic begins with M and is neutral. So does man, more, much, me, made, middle, meetings, and the last half of tomorrow. Evil denies that this could even be an alphabet.

This is so near to the truth that I don't want to finish the letter. Love that begins with an L like my heart does.

Love,
Jack

13.

Dear James,

"Sun Dance" have just arrived. They speak in wholly (think how *they* would divide that word) wholly different language. I should have known in the places in the letters but that was more like seeing the impossible footprints of a bird on the wet sand—and now seeing the bird I don't know why but I keep thinking of a pterodactyl.

How can they be read by voice? But why in hell should we have to use our mouths to hear messages? And the letters of the alphabet (as Thoth and Rimbaud both told me) are more than mere sounds. But I want to hear the words from your mouth—that's what one unsurprised part of me demands—like when they didn't have any way to write them *down* and they had to be chanted around a fire in a cave or a banquet hall. And the words and the sounds of the words were the same thing. But at that rate the painter would still be chiseling pictures of animals on blank rock.

Tired ar/gue/ments. "Sun Dance" are a school of real birds having come from somewhere up there. I take off my head to you.

Love,

Jack

14.

In the Grand Pyramid they buried the king with all his bottles, postage stamps, and half-eaten loaves of bread. Were they really the king's, Cocteau asks us in his article on Memory, or were they manufactured for the occasion?

No one knows better than I do how lonely you are.

In the Grand Pyramid there are the most complicated mathematical systems and the most complicated moral systems and chains of amethyst and diamond hanging just out of reach. It is the center of the universe.

Were they invented for the occasions?

In the Grand Pyramid it is darker than it ever was and the king is still there. The king communicates by magic and he tells me "Build a pyramid for yourself" and he tells you, "Find a postage stamp" and he eats a little of the bread and drinks a little from the bottles he has manufactured.

The postage stamp has a picture of the Grand Pyramid engraved on it; the pyramid has not been yet invented.

No one knows how lonely you are better than I do.

APOLLO SENDS SEVEN NURSERY RHYMES
TO JAMES ALEXANDER (1959)

I.

You have not listened to a word I have sung
Said Orpheus to the trees that did not move
Your branches vibrate at the tones of my lyre
Not at the sounds of my lyre.
You have set us a tough problem said the trees
Our branches are rooted in fact to the ground
Through our trunks said the trees
But calm as an ax Orpheus came
To the trees and sang on his lyre a song
That the trees have no branches the trunks have no tree
And the roots that are gathered along
Are bad for the branches the trunk and the tree
Say, said the trees, that's a song
And they followed him wildly through rivers and ocean
Till they ended in Thrace with a bang.

II.

At the La Brea Tar Pits
There is a sheer drop then twenty feet of stars. I
Believe this occasionally.
The white skeletons
Jammed in there in the black tar
Don't come back
Can't
Come back
No ghosts
Only occasionally
Ronnie.

III.

The mouse ran up the chessboard
The mouse ran down the chessboard
He destroyed:
>   two pawns and a queen and bit a hell of an edge
>   off a black rook
Savage
As the god of plague is savage
Apollo the mouse ran up the chessboard
Down the chessboard.

IV.

Or, explaining the poem to myself, Jay Herndon has only three
>   words in his language
Door: which means that he is to throw something which will
>   make a sound like a door banging.
Fffish: which means that there is something that somebody
>   showed him
And Car: which is an object seen at a great distance
He will learn words as we did
I tell you, Jay, clams baked in honey
Would never taste as strange.

I died again and was reborn last night
That is the way with we mirror people

Forgive me, I am a child of the mirror and not a child of
the door.

Yes Apollo, I dare. And if the door opens

North of the North Wind

V.

A Christmas toy misdirected, a baseball game, A-
Stounding Science Fiction
All this, but the eyes are full
Of tears? of visions? of trees?
So close to nonsense that the mind shuttles
So full of nonsense.
That there could be a hand, a throat, a thigh
So close to nonsense that the mind shuttles
Between
The subway, station of what would'
Nt.

VI. The Death of Arthur

Pushing wood, they call it when you make automatic moves in
    a chess game or in a poem
Pushing tar
The sound, the subway, the skeleton of the whole
    circumstances you and everybody else was born with
The dance (that you do whenever Apollo or any other smaller
    god is not watching you) the dance
Of probability
Be-
   ing human.

VII.

Fire works
But like the bottom of an alley
They works only
With people in them.
Justly suspicious
Jay did not like the sparks flying past his head
Although they were blue green yellow and purple
And several also made a big whhupp.
Fire works
Broken words
But never repairing
Jay, justly suspicious,
Afterwards
Said, "Fffish."

A BIRTHDAY POEM FOR JIM (AND JAMES) ALEXANDER   (1959)

It is a story for chil
                    dren
Poetry
A search for good
Or against evil
Or merely a story.
Those Babylonian faces
Stone to the touch.
Like ours
Heros have heavy lips
Their legs are lead
Their arms
Cannot quite encircle
Or come to grips
With
(They are the mirror-birds
Don't trust 'em.)
Lack ours
Those heavy lips
The words read back at you. Broken for you
The playing
Of some children
And good
And evil standing
There.

Jim-almost-James tells me he likes Tolkien
"He doesn't water down good and evil," they say. "He sees them."
Everything that is in the pawnshop is for sale. Truth
Is a drinking fountain.
I can't describe good
But once tried to in a poem about a starfish
Or your watery eyes
Seeing nothing but what they told you. Mordor
Is so black that eye can't fathom
The fact of it.
The carefulness of believing in my words, your watery eyes, my
Truth.

The 49ers battling to keep place with the Baltimore Colts.
        No quarterback
Will find the right receiver. The whole game
Is absolute darkness.
Or tell the young to fight. Olson. Big Daddy
Linebacker for the port of the big wish.
Words are not enough. No quarterback
Will find words enough. No linebacker
Can tackle words. They only exist in a poem. Or there maybe
On the forty yardline in darkness.
It is Dover Beach played on a dead piano. A picnic into dream.
        A silence. That linebacker
His silhouette on the playing field alone.

———————————

Deep-
     er than meaning
He lies there amazed at what has happened
Like a dream-
         er
Deep in the sea.
Those pen-
         guins were his eyes. Those rocks
His sole substance.

———————————

Caro m'è il sonno, e più l'esser di sasso,
mentre che il danno, e la vergogna dura;
non veder, non sentir, m'è gran ventura;
però non mi destar; deh, parla basso

———————————

Sucking all the personal from his birthday one obtains
The familiar objects.
One half of a lemon, a voice from a park bench of a park that is not
    there, the thrill of looking at something newly with someone
    or rather an X-ray of that emotion. The familiar objects are
    almost a bedroom.
I mean what obtains is. What catches
In the seams of one's pantlegs or pants. Wild oats, thistles, vacant
    emotions. Like the dust that is really all of the earth's surface
Sucking all the personal from his birthday one obtains
A birthday, an imaginary rose.

———————

Poetry seeks occasion. In a man's life
There is May, June, December, birthdays, nothing else really matters.
(I don't understand why I omitted October. Poetry seeks occasions.
    In a man's life
There are birthdays.)
The style of a poem is the armor we wear and May, June, December
    are the months of a year. I don't understand why I omitted
    October. I love you.
And if this isn't a birthday present, nothing is.

———————

Days without rain. The waste land
They call it that in their English Department
Or him, her, them—like rain beating on a
    deaf tin roof.
Or why I can't call him anymore
Or answer him his
Letters

———————

This poem ends in anger
Like a novel.
There is stuff enough to tell you
What hours are
And no more.
You have hours
There are
To *use them*. Choose your
Cake.

It is Gresham's law: bad money
Drives out good money; bad
Drives out good; bad money
Drives out good.
It is the primal scene. Cain
And Able to end all that
The end of the grain, mushrooms, and wildflowers.
The nearness of when good was there. Fuck
You.

The Poet Insists on Saying the Last Word

The buzzards wheeling in the sky are Thanksgiving
Making their own patterns
There in the sky where they have left us
It is hot down here where they have left us
On the hill or in the city. The hell
Of personal relations
It is like a knot in the air. Their wings free
Is there—our shadows.

— • • —

IMAGINARY ELEGIES

V.

Another wrong turning
Another five years. I can't see
The birds, the island, anything
But vacant shifts and twists of the tunnel
That means
Another five years I can't see.
Or were they all right turnings
The shifts of one sense of a word to another
The birds flying there inside the eaves with their wings dangling
Not bats, birds.
And offering up your life to summon anything is a pretty silly thing.
    I can't see
Where their messages get me. Another five years
Their wings
Glittering in its black ab/sense.

For the birds. Whose live-r is torn out. Whose live-r is torn out.
    Pro-me-thee-us. The old turning.

Where their messages get me. The shifts
Of their beaks. Their hungry beaks. But the birds are real
    not only in feeding. I think
Their wings. Glittering in the black ab/sense.
Pro-me-thee-us. Our mouths water
Like an ocean.

And so I say to you, Jim, do not become too curious about
    your poetry
Let it speed into the tunnel by itself

Do not follow it, do not try to ride it

Let it go into the tunnel and out the other side and back

to you while you do important things like loving and

learning patience

Five years. The train with its utterly alien cargo moving on

the black track.

Prometheus was a guy who had his liver eaten out by birds.

A bum who rode a black train. Who was curious.

Play it cool with Williams or paranoid with Pound but never ride

it past the tunnel or look for a conductor to ask questions

Hide, and do not ask the questions,

At the black throat of the tunnel.

Pro-me-thee-us
Pro-me-thee-us
Five years

The song singing from its black throat.

VI.

Dignity

Dig–nity

The extra syllables are unimportant. Have no dignity, no

meaning on this world.

Nity. Hear those syllables and dig is an obvious pun for

digging graves or whatever that gravedigger is doing

at the moment.

The extra syllables are unimportant. I should have loved
    him yesterday
The boy whistles
Dig-
    nity
Or like that little window in Alice which she can't go through
    because she's 27 feet tall because she ate a bottle called
    Drink Me
Po–etery. Po–eatery. The eaxtra slyllables is unimportant.
    because the poem said Drink Me. I'll find a substitute
For all your long-
Ing.
And that little door with all those wheels in it
Be-
    leave in it
Like God.

"Dignity is a part of a man . . ."

Dignity is a part of a man being naked before
        everybody. The part where the heart separates itself
        from the loins.
The poet is stepping out of the airplane.
Dignity is a part of a rose in a broken
        vase. The part where the thorns separate
        themselves from the flower
The poet is stepping out of the airplane
Dignity is a part of not being asked.

       ★

I miss you, I said. The dead flowers,
The poets who wanted to kiss me, the naked
        hatred
That wanted to kiss me. I miss their flowers
I miss the hatred of not being asked.
                  But Jack . . .
Shut up, I said. Nothing but love could have
        eaten the roses.

       ★

Then, as we went toward the big ocean
Our poems became more threatening. Words sounded like
D-E-A-T-H, L-O-V-E, and the seals howled
        up from the rocks like the last line of a French poem.

       ★

God is merely domestic. Death is merely domestic. They are a lie told to disguise the nature of art.

The poet is stepping out of the airplane.

Magic is merely domestic. Dignity is merely domestic.

The poet is stepping out of the airplane.

My house is merely domestic. I live in my house; my skin lives in my house. We are domestic. My house is merely domestic. We are a lie to disguise the nature of art.

★

I loved him. I loved him. I loved you.
I loved him. I loved him. I loved you.
It is true. It is true. It returns.

HELEN: A REVISION   (1960)

Nothing is known about Helen but her voice
Strange glittering sparks
Lighting no fires but what is reechoed
Rechorded, set on the icy sea.

All history is one, as all the North Pole is one
Magnetic, music to play with, ice
That has had to do with vision
And each one of us, naked.
Partners. Naked.

Helen: A Revision

ZEUS: It is to be assumed that I do not exist while most people in the vision assume that I do exist. This is to be one of the extents of meaning between the players and this audience.

I have to talk like this because I am the lord of both kinds of sky—and I don't mean your sky and their sky because they are signs, I mean the bright sky and the burning sky. I have no intention of showing you my limits.

The players in this poem are players. They have taken their parts not to deceive you (or me if it matters) but because they have been paid in love or coin to be players. I have known for a long time that there is not a fourth wall in a play. I am called Zeus and I know this.

THERSITES (*running out on the construction of the stage*): The fourth wall is not as important as you think it is.

ZEUS (*disturbed but carrying it off like a good Master of Ceremonial*): Thersites is involuntary. (*He puts his arm around him.*) I could not play a part if I were not a player.

THERSITES: Reveal yourself to me and don't pretend that there are people watching you. I am alone on the stage with you. Tell me the plot of the play.

ZEUS *(standing away)*: Don't try to talk if you don't have to. You must admit there is no audience. Everything is done for you.

THERSITES: Stop repeating yourself. You old motherfucker. Your skies are bad enough. *(He looks to the ground.)* A parody is better than a pun.

ZEUS: I do not understand your language. *(They are silent together for a moment and then the curtain drops.)*

And if he dies on this road throw wild blackberries at his ghost
And if he doesn't, and he won't, hope the cost
Hope the cost.

And the terror of the what meets the why at the edge
Like a backwards image of each terror's lodge
Each terror's lodge.

And if he cries put his heart out with a lantern's goat
Where they pay all passages to pay the debt
The lighted yet.

The focus sing
Is not their business. Their tracks lay
By not altogether being there.

Here and there in swamps and villages.
How doth the silly crocodile
Amuse the Muse

———————

And in the skyey march of flesh
That boundary line where no body is
Preserve us, lord, from aches and harms
And bring my death.

Both air and water rattle there
And mud and fire
Preserve us, lord, from what would share a shroud
and bring my death.

A vagrant bird flies to the glossy limbs
The battlefield has harms. The trees have half
Their branches shot away. Preserve us, lord
From hair and mud and flesh.

———————

A twisted smile, a flower I
Could name a rose.

A trick of rhetoric, the shadow standing firm
Against the glass.

A twisted smile, a flower I
Could name a rose.

Which without feeling to the enormous source
Of deep emotion
We laugh until we are hoarse.
Each poisons every well
In which each shadow dwells.

Unmixed emotion. You can shoe a horse
With darkness on the plates
For mates.

Half-real, the iceberg
Was kept from us. By not altogether being there
They couldn't care less what hit them
(A big, red, joyous caterpillar twisting and
        spewing the wet leaves
(From top to bottom the iceberg
Totally indistinguishable.

Nothing complete at the opera but singing
Nothing moves in the grass but noise
There in the edge there, there is some singing
And in the grass there is noise.

Grass is to be prayed for by the singer
A quiet noise that has its grass forever

There in the edge there, there is some singing
Nothing moves in the grass but noise.

———————

An image of withdrawal. All
Of her beauty.
A pair of sox knitted for her in Sparta
Left there to rot.

The rouge she left in Troy.
Fausts.
Now, in Egypt, she who was never there perceives
Two names.

———————

"You have done big things," said the dwarf to the answer.
"We answers live in the ground." We are called
When we're cold.
We grasshoppers live a thousand years
When the ants answer.

———————

Then
Even the extraordinary is unimportant.
Helen's eyes
Are these.
These are bright as stars
We disclothe.

Troy is a bathtub
(An image)
And like a bathtub (an image)
It lets out all its sparks.
In the dark aftermath of it
The pipeline between the poem and the reader
(Them-and-us)! An
Image of pure beauty

The last edge of the voice
Where she sings to men and women
Unchanged like the edge of the moon.
A floating parapet an up-there
She worships herself with it
She lives there,
In brandy and in all senses
Alien.

To make her into an artifact is to try to kill her
Helen was not born of men of history
(They said she had an egg in her cunt)
The what gave life to her
Was extra to her beauty
Housing her.

———————

Dear Russ,

    I am writing to you in the middle of a poem
about Helen. What there was to her about your
body I should have never ceased to wish to know. It is
as if there was a dark fleshy space between us
labeled, "I am not myself."

    There is utterly no reason for imagining Helen.
Whether she was in Troy or Egypt, she would be the
same figure of imagination put into being by a
vacuum, the same vacuum by which I write poetry
or you paint, or, I suppose men fought for her.

    Or becomes more unreal every minute. I do not
love her. As the thought of you or anyone I loved.

    Hold us to the real, lady of the seven webbed
fingers, hold us to their hard hearts bouncing
to and fro against each other.

———————

Where the old distrust breaks through the floor of the
      grainery
No trust is but fallen oats.
On when the seeds do not sprout in the darkness
      of the underground
Nothing shouts out loud.
The crowd
Of loves possible to a man thins
When the crop is harvested.

Black ghosts and black ghosts
Whose little schemes
Possessed by the right dreams.
There is the horror of what isn't and what was
And the little people. They
Haven't anything to say.

Informed against itself
Like your body twisting on its bed dreaming
        of poems it is writing or more probably
        has never written
Hokku, haikku
2400 syllables.

Invited a daimon
A guardian angel closer
Where we could both
Observe ourselves.
"That Helen cat is nothing
She's a dream
From Rockefeller." In Sparta and in histroy
        (a lump)
They are choosing sides.
"Like Helen isn't
The Y of her cunt,
A birthplace
Isn't."

He was beautiful. I am trying to leave him
     and it at that.
I am trying to write a poem apart from all beauty
The world is ugly. A sunshade. Figure that
     in your business. A poetry that don't matter.
The sun is beautiful. Molecules at 532 miles
     a second and 832 billion degrees
     fahrenheit jangle apart
There, his body, when I noticed it. Going at
     a second a time.

Years ago a kindly English professor told me
     that Robert Frost had once said in a moment
     of absolute vision, "Any damned fool can get
     into a poem but it takes a poet to get out
     of one."
I confused this with sexuality and believed it.
Actually getting out of a poem is no more difficult than
     answering a lying obvious answer to a lying
     obvious question in an intelligence test or a
     lover.
What is difficult is the form.
Past one's only cleverness (paradoxes, which are
     songs set aside)
Is the other answer that it is as difficult to get
     into a poem as into
     Helen.

THE HEADS OF THE TOWN UP TO THE AETHER   (1960)

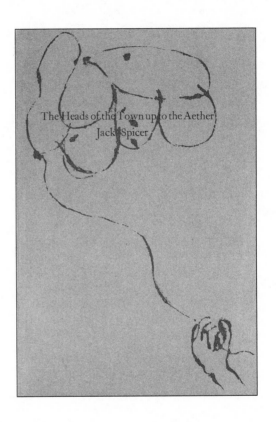

The Heads of the Town up to the Aether
Jack Spicer

HOMAGE TO CREELEY
EXPLANATORY NOTES

I.

For Cegeste

To begin with, I could have slept with all of the people in the poems. It is not as difficult as the poet makes it. That is the reason I was born tonight.

He wanted an English professor—someone he could feel superior to, as a ghost. He wanted to eliminate all traces of the poetry. To kiss someone goodbye but you people out there know none of the answers either—even the simple questions the poet was asked.

I am the ghost of answering questions. Beware me. Keep me at a distance as I keep you at a distance.

Cegeste died at the age of nineteen. Just between the time when one could use one's age as a power and one uses one's age as a crutch. (cf. A Fake Novel About the Life of Arthur Rimbaud). At 35 one throws away crutches. (cf. Inferno Canto I)

Several Years' Love

Two loves I had. One rang a bell
Connected on both sides with hell

The other'd written me a letter
In which he said I've written better

They pushed their cocks in many places
And I'm not certain of their faces
Or which I kissed or which I didn't
Or which of both of them I hadn't.

The two loves are the pain The Poet had. I do not think a doorbell could be extended from one of them to the other. The letter, naturally (as will become more apparent in the conquest of Algeria or outer space) was written to somebody else.

The cocks want to be sure of themselves.

Car Song

Away we go with no moon at all
Actually we are going to hell.
We pin our puns to our backs and cross in a car
The intersections where lovers are.
The wheel and the road turn into a stair
The pun at our backs is a yellow star.
We pin our puns on the windshield like
We crossed each crossing in hell's despite.

"I like it better in L.A. because there're more men and they're prettier," someone said in The Handlebar tonight.

"Intersections" is a pun. "Yellow stars" are what the Jews wore. The stair is what extends back and forth for Heurtebise and Cegeste and the Princess always to march on.

Actually, L.A. is Los Angeles and there was a motion picture that showed everything.

Concord Hymn

Your joke
Is like a lake
That lies there without any thought
And sees
Dead seas
The birds fly
Around there
Bewildered by its blue without any thought of water
Without any thought
Of water.

"Conquered Him" is a poem by Emerson.

The Dead Seas are all in the Holy Land.

If you watch closely you will see that water appears and disappears in the poem.

Wrong Turn

What I knew
Wasn't true
Or oh no
Your face
Was made of fleece
Stepping up to poetry
Demands
Hands.

Jacob's coat was made of virgin wool. Virgin wool is defined as wool made from the coat of any sheep that can run faster than the sheepherder.

There are steps on the stairs too, which are awfully steep.

The Territory Is Not the Map

What is a half-truth the lobster declared
You have sugared my groin and have sugared my hair
What correspondence except my despair?
What is my crime but my youth?

Truth is a map of it, oily eyes said
Half-truth is half of a map instead
Which you will squint at until you are dead
Putting to sea with the truth.

This is a poem to prevent idealism—i.e. the study of images. It did not succeed.

Edward Lear was allowed to say this some time ago in his books for children. Actually The Poet thought of himself as "oily eyes." That is why The Poem could never prevent idealism (Idealism).

Orpheus and Eurydice are in their last nuptial embrace during this poem.

They Came to the Briers and the Briers Couldn't Find 'Em

The goop
Is like mulberry soup
Or like anything
You sang.
    The goop is an international criminal organization
    that talks to each other, makes passes at each other,
    sings to each other, clings to each other, is as
    absolutely alien to each other as a stone in Australia
For example
the poem does not know
Who you refers to.

The goop was a criminal organization long since dead like the Holy Roman Empire. The singer is unknown.

In hell it is difficult to tell people from other people.

When You Go Away You Don't Come Home

On the mere physical level
There is a conflict between what is and what isn't
What is, I guess, is big
And what isn't, bigger
Metaphysically speaking
What aren't casts no shadow
And what are is bigger than the moon, I guess,
Bigger than that boy's pants.

An obvious attempt of The Poet to bring The Poem to a close. Its failure is obvious.

"That boy's pants" is an obvious reference to Eurydice. What doesn't cast shadows is obvious to everyone.

Sheep Trails Are Fateful to Strangers

Dante would have blamed Beatrice
If she turned up alive in a local bordello
Or Newton gravity
If apples fell upward
What I mean is words
Turn mysteriously against those who use them
Hello says the apple
Both of us were object.

There is a universal here that is dimly recognized. I mean everybody says some kinds of love are horseshit. Or invents a Beatrice to prove that they are.

What Beatrice did did not become her own business. Dante saw to that. Sawed away the last plank anyone he loved could stand on.

To Be Inscribed on a Painting

The fate of the car
And the fate of the ride
Is only a bridegroom
Without a bride

Though she hasn't a face
And I haven't seen her
She isn't a mirror
Whatever she was.

And the light in the air
Was as real as it was
And it hasn't her beauty
Whose blankness I stare.

Alice's mirror no longer reflects storybook knights. They reflect the Thirty Years Wars and the automobiles people rode in during them.

Cocteau invented mirrors as things to move through. I invent mirrors as obstacles.

This is called I-IX. I see myself reflected against it.

Elegy

Whispers—
Eurydice's head is missing
Whispers—
Get out of hell—
Whispers—
You big poet
We soldiers from hell's country
Here
Safe as you are
You write poetry
For dead persons

This is definitely a warning to Orpheus which he does not understand—being an asshole. This is too bad because there would have been just as much poetry if he had understood it.

The definition of warning has been given constantly. The fact, alone, that Eurydice's head was missing should have warned him.

II.

For the Princess

The Princess has a special form to function as a Representative of The Dead. She is almost a Congresswoman for them.

"Don't stand there with your fingers in your heart. Do something," she says as she kidnaps Orpheus along with the dead body of Cegeste. Eurydice is miles away.

She is almost the function of them.

Awkward Bridge

Love isn't proud enough to hate
The stranger at its gate
That says and does

Or strong enough to return
Or strong enough to return (and back and back and back again)
What was

A statement dating back to the wars between the Allies and the Spartans. Love is mentioned with a certain metrical coldness—proving only that the poem will go on.

In this poem was a bridge between love and the idea of love. Tentative, rustling.

A Poe-
m Ronnie Wrote the Other Evening

Jack
Of lack
The back
Of our hands
Tattooed
With you
Wherewithal appalling
Willows
In the trees
And that boy's knees
Or anything we sank
In tanks
Thanks
To you.

The figure of Jim begins to emerge in the poem. The Poet uses all his resistance to us to try to create the figure of a person at once lost and unlikely. The unlikelyness is also the first hint of metaphor.

The tanks (and what they store in them) remind the reader. That the Muses are daughters of Memory.

The Poem is for the Princess.

Who Knew

Ghosts drip
And then they leap
The boy sang and the singing that I heard:
Wet shadows on a stick.

"Tanks," he said.
"You're welcome," they said.

The singer and the song are something The Poet did (does) not understand. He had posited something.

Magic

Strange, I had words for dinner
Stranger, I had words for dinner
Stranger, strange, do you believe me?

Honestly, I had your heart for supper
Honesty has had your heart for supper
Honesty honestly are your pain.

I burned the bones of it
And the letters of it
And the numbers of it
That go 1, 2, 3, 4, 5, 6, 7
And so far.

Stranger, I had bones for dinner
Stranger, I had bones for dinner
Stranger, stranger, strange, did you believe me?

Orpheus was never really threatened by the Underworld during his
visits there. In this poem they present him with a diplomatic note.

Honesty does not occur again in the poem.

The numbers do.

Ferlinghetti

Be bop de beep
They are asleep
There where they like us
It goes
From nose to nose
From stop to stop
Violations are rare
And the air is fair
It is spring
On the thing
We sing.
Beep bop de beep
They are all asleep
They're all asleep.

The car is still traveling. It runs through the kingdoms of the dead picking up millions of passengers.

Like most motorists, the Princess is bored on the road she is going.

Ferlinghetti is a nonsense syllable invented by The Poet.

Booth Tarkington

No
Thanks to him you're a poet
Begin to recall
Cegeste's voice
(Distrusted as if there were any number of statues speaking)
Strange how the sound of wings comes through to it
As if the act of having sex had a meaning
Beyond
Recalling.

Booth Tarkington is used in various psychological tests to prove whether persons are artistic.

The recalling of Cegeste's voice was done on a horse in one version and on a car radio in the other. Both made it seem natural. A crystal set, in this version of the legend, would not be inappropriate. However there is no crystal set. Cegeste never speaks after he is spoken to.

The Tragic Muse

She isn't real
She isn't pure
Aside from that
Her teeth are poor

If you listen to her
You will listen for real
Her front and her back teeth
Will bite you for real

And you go to bed
With a sluff and a sigh
And listen next morning
Whatever you said

The Mouses are the daughters of Memory (they become Rats later) and Mrs. Siddons was an 18th century actress painted by Gainsborough or somebody.

Tragedy has exact limits that Hell cannot enclose. This spoils the trip of The Poet and The Poem through Hell and is the point at which they both protest.

Partington Ridge

A white rabbit absolutely outlined in whiteness upon a black
      background
A ghost
The most
We can say or think about it is it stays.
Not as a memory of something that happened or a symbol or
      anything
We loved or respected or was a part of history
Our history
It stays
In a closet we wear like a ring on our fingers
The rabbit
Ghost of them
Most of what we knew.

"They ran through the briers and they ran through the bushes, and they ran through the brambles where the rabbits wouldn't go."

Rabbits do not know what they are.

Ghosts are very similar. They are frightened and do not know what they are, but they can go where the rabbits cannot go. All the way to the heart.

Hisperica Famina

Joan of Arc
Built an ark
In which she placed
Three peas
—Can you imagine translating this poem into New English—
In the ark
Were three ghosts
Named Hymen, Simon, and Bynem
—Can you imagine ghosts like that translating these poems into
    New English—
I, they, him, it, her
I, they, him, it, ourselves, her.

The madmen who drive cars into the distances of dying or who predict football games are celebrated here. Hisperica famina means western words.

The three ghosts have names that are mockeries of your names.

Your names (and theirs) are the afterwords mentioned pronouns.

Coda

Love isn't proud enough to hate
The stranger at its gate
That says and does

Or strong enough to return
Or strong enough to return (and back and back and back again)
What was.

The cactus needle of the past that could be broken by a mere earmuff, plays the phonograph record of its record never again. This is called the concerto form.

The Princess is so absoullutely independent of such tracing (since they sent her back to hell) that she can sing the whole song again. Who had forgotten that her head was missing.

III.

For Heurtebise

Drugs

The bell went "rrrrr"
And we both went "rrrrr"
And there was a beauty
In talking to him.

But angel-talk howls
At the edge of our beds
And all of us now
Are partners of hell.

For the crocodile crys
Every tear that we know
And our tears are our blankets
Wherever we go.

The bell is the connection—which is more than junky-talk.

A definition of hell hovers over the whole poem. It is the first (and the last) mention of angels.

The crocodile, like so many things from either of these universes, is from Lewis Carroll. The blankets are sleeping bags.

Fort Wayne

The messages come through at last:
"We are the ghosts of Christmas past

Our bodies are a pudding boiled
With sixteen serpents and a narrow blade."

I asked my silly messengers to sing it again
"We are the advantages that hate all men

Our bodies are a pudding boiled
With sixteen serpents and a narrow blade."

For there are poems and Christmas pies
And loves like ours while you blink your eyes
And love rises up like a butterfly

"Our bodies are a pudding boiled
With sixteen serpents and a narrow blade."

A dialogue between The Poet and passed Christmases.

Fort Wayne stands on the American fortress between California and reality. It is a geographical point.

The passed Christmases want to know more than they have any right to. So does The Poet. Neither in the last analysis is satisfied.

The pudding is made of a number of serpents that move among us and a knife to cut them with.

Surrealism

Whatever belongs in the circle is in the circle
They
Raise hands.
Death-defying trapeze artists on one zodiac, the Queen of
    Spades, the Ace of Hearts, the nine of Diamonds, the whole
    deck of cards
Promise to whatever is promised
Love to whatever is loved
Ghosts to whatever is ghosts
In our mouths
Their mouths
There is
Hope.

Poe predicted the whole Civil War.

Prayer for My Daughter

Our father that art in heaven
Christmas be thy name

Our father that art in hell
We'll tell
Them

Jim discovered Christmas and the diamond in back of the diamond. In spite of The Poet's invention of his name.

They are the people we expected on Halloween who never came—in spite of our good wishes. Hell is where we place ourselves when we wish to look upward.

Eurydice and Orpheus and Hermes were all simple-minded.

The Man in the Wall

Orpheus
(The bus crashed
It takes ninety days
To call them up from hell)
Heurtebise, well
The whole bus crashed with all the bus team.
I mean his lyre
Soured up his lyre
Everything on fire
(It took ninety days
Before the bus crashed.)

Imagining, at times, a mirror two sides of which are a mirror. Heurtebise is an angel which means, at the Greek of it, messenger. Orpheus is a poet. The bus that crashed with all the bus team, was going to and coming from an athletic event.

It Is Forbidden to Look

I couldn't get my feeling loose
Like a goose I traveled. Well
Sheer hell
Is where your apartness is your apartness
I mean hell
Is where they don't even pick flowers.

The edges of a mirror have their own song to sing. The thickness seems alien to The Poet and he equates his own hell with what is between them.

He refers to Persephone as vaguely as she could be seen there.

Dillinger

The human voices put the angels
Pretty far away. The sleigh-bells
In the distance go
As if we had never seen snow.
Pray for the right of the thing of the universe
The knot which is unknotted by something other than our
       hands
We, ghosts, lovers, and casual strangers to the poem.
Me, the ghost says.

Not anything real. The snowflakes are equidistant from themselves
and fall slowly. Almost impossibly.

There is nothing left of it. Not even the water its crystals puddle into.
These persons know reality for what they are.

Dash

Damn them,
All of them,
That wear beards on the soles of their feet
That ride cars
That aren't
Funny.
It comes with a rush
And a gush
Of feeling
Everything is in the street
Then they meet
It with their automobiles.

Cegeste comes back to a big meeting with his personal fate. He lacks knowledge of the driver's seat as did Cegeste, Creeley, and all of us. He intends to spend his fortune in banks, on the banks of some rivers. He will wreck their cars if he can have to. He.

Crabs

Daughters of memory
Our grandchildren swarm
In buckets and pails
And leaden images

Keep us warm while the night grows
Too cold to bear
Or too hot to carry
A single light.

The crabs are crawdads. They move in their random fashion back and forth toward the tanks which are also a bucket and take the heart out of things. One fishes for them with a long spoon.

The Muses, according to Musaeus, are the daughters of Memory.

Blood

The jokes
Are ghosts
The joke
Is a ghost
How can you love that mortal creature
Everytime he speaks
He makes
Mistakes
Two for one
Three of us vital

"They took (the Sheaves) into the wide barns with loud
    rejoicing & triumph
Of flute & harp & drum & trumpet, horn, & clarion."

"O.K."

A FAKE NOVEL ABOUT THE LIFE OF ARTHUR RIMBAUD

BOOK I

Chapter I
The Dead Letter Office

"You can't close the door. It is in the future," French history said as it was born in Charlieville. It was before the Civil War and I don't think that even James Buchanan was president.

There was a dead-letter office in every French village or town or city the size of Paris. There still is. Rimbaud was born in the Charlieville postoffice. He was a big child.

Apollinaire used to play golf while other people were shooting machine guns. Big butterflies tried to liberate him from the liberal mineded. But Rimbaud crawled to the page that lifted him up from his nephews.

That was born.

Chapter II
The Dead Letter Officer

Mr. Still-Waters-Run-Do-Not-Walk-To-The-Nearest-Exit was an officer of the French government. His noms des ailes were Izzard, Cixambert, and David the Pig. He had enrolled in the French government when he was very young and liked the thought of being there while history was happening.

He took a census of Rimbaud—also of butterflies-that-have-mildew, thoughts-of-this-generation, eyelids-of-people-who-didn't-like-people-who-took-the-census, and God. He was a liberal.

As long as this is a novel I mean that Mr. Still-Waters-Run-Do-Not-Walk-To-The-Nearest-Exit was a liberal. Not God.

Rimbaud was not God or a liberal. He was born near the administration of President Buchanan.

Chapter III
What The Dead Letters Said

"Dear X,
     I love you more than anyone could ever do.
         signed
         Y"

. . ". . . Yes, Virginia, there is a postoffice."
. . ". . . I'm going to go home and eat rose-petals."

. . ". . . It has all been anticipated, there isn't any more for you to do."

"Dearest Y,"

Chapter IV
Rimbaud Puts Off Childish Things

A baby has several choices all of which are unknown. Rimbaud made one of them.

After he had been born in the postoffice he began to practice his mouth with a new language. He could not imagine persons to listen to the new language. He had not invented politics.

He wrote poetry at the base of the postoffice. Not for anybody. He could not imagine what letters were for, or numbers. He was a baby. He could not imagine a whole word.

The Dead-Letter-Office was in another part of the building. They put it there deliberately knowing that Rimbaud would not be born in it. It was later called the Liberation.

He was then a baby and I am taking advantage of his name which was spelled with six letters R-I-M-B-AU-D. He put off all these childish things immediately and became a telegram.

Chapter V
French Politics

The Frank Terrors was one of the political parties Rimbaud invented while he was being born. He knew that he would be dead. They existed somewhere between the Right and the Left of all human behavior.

"Jim loves me," the Right said. "Jim loves me," the Left said. But the Frank Terrors were busy at being born and said nothing.

Rimbaud did not really invent this political party. He took them as they were out of his soul. Â me with a sharp copula to add housing to the business of loving. Speaking sharp.

Gambetta went up in a balloon one winter evening. That was a long time. There was no conversation.

Chapter VI
The Watch Rats

The novelist should explain what he was going about. "Surrealism is a coat of many colors," Rimbaud is supposed to have remarked long after everything was over. To love is not to continue with the Zanzibar slave trade. To continue with the Zanzibar slave trade is not to love. It is similar.

The watch rats (they were really called wharf rats but Rimbaud called them wharf rats) ran along the Meuse River. They explained. The river ran to an ocean that ran to a number of oceans.

"We get into the cargo," said the wharf rats, "and then we get out to sea. We make journeys and it is history. Our ages are 6, 17, 24, and 75."

What they meant was that all this time Rimbaud was being born a little wharf rat was crawling from his skull, into his skull.

Chapter VII
So Far We Have Stressed the Humanness of Rimbaud

The dead are not alive. That is what this unattractive prose wants to stamp out. Once you see an end to it, you believe that the dead are alive.

Rimbaud is now fifteen and is shooting horses. Since he is now dead, the years 1,2,3,4,5,6,7,8,9,10,11,12,13,14 are unimportant both to his death and our lives. It is as if one planted grass in the postoffice.

The horses Rimbaud is shooting are the white and the black horse mentioned in Plato's *Phaedrus*. Also known as a wall.

Imagine not being attacked by Indians (1,2,3,4,5,6,7,8,9,10,11,12,13,14). Imagine not being attacked by Indians. The horse, *Phaedrus*, will win the race, the black one, the white one.

Imagine also that the dead are not alive and his awkward face.

Chapter IX
The Poem Rimbaud Wrote on October 20, 1869

I do not proclaim a new age.
That I am fifteen God only knows.
I keep the numbers in my head
When I am dead
I will fall into a rage
And bite off all my toes.

When I am twenty I will see
Eternity
And all those old numbers
And be their anger
When I am dead
I will leave the stage
And bite off all my toes.

Chapter X
Sex

Rabelais is on the middleaged side of the coin. Rimbaud is on the other. The middleaged side of the coin starts about twenty.

There is a zoo of pleasures to Rabelais. To Rimbaud—but I am too old to remember. It would be wrong to say that the zoo was a jungle, but the animals did not seem to have cages.

This did not have anything to do with poetry—being too old to remember—but Rimbaud thought it had anything to do with poetry—being 15,16,17,18,19, even 20. He was right.

What it is that it has to do with poetry no one is old enough or young enough to know. Even if he kissed me now I would tell him that.

He thought that poetry didn't have to do with cages (which it didn't) and that it was in a jungle (which it isn't). He was fifteen at the time I am writing about this and never kissed me.

BOOK II

Chapter I
A Charm Against the Discovery of Oxygen

We had fought tooth and nail to maintain our beaches. The water sang where the water went and on the other side of it (a gentle rise of sand and then some palm trees) the others were fighting us.

President Buchanan, frightened as if he were alive, appeared above us like a huge kite whose string we could not see against the sand and the jungle, causing panic to our invading hearts, to the others waiting there, and, inevitably, to the ocean.

The barracks we had built the previous night had all turned green.

We were not human, the others were not human, and the sea was not human. It was the old content of war.

Chapter II
Avoid As Much As You Can

—I got a motorscooter for my birthday.

—Indeed, you too have a problem. He had a problem.

—There are no more of them to touch us. Sing out with them. They will think it is a song.

—Beautiful you. Clever foster-parent of madness.

—I was walking down the path one day and I saw a machine-gun. It was painted yellow and red. I was thinking about the tricks poems play on people that had to hear our voices and I wandered up the path again, singing.

—No one deserves to die that hasn't voice enough to carry.

—They have stolen my bicycle and my alarm clock and my heart.

Chapter III
Jim

A kind of witchdoctor told us that a name is the same name that has a property. A property right.

They move in the cool evenings. The names—but their names do not matter.

Expressed well there is a pun of all we do in heaven, in hell, in the outline of the stars, and even in our bank accounts. These graces are digressions but important.

The slaves of poetry are slaves in deed (in dead as Jim who has the name of Jim would say—if he wasn't dead and hadn't died before anyone) and that is history and what they hadn't seen hadn't hurt them. They who were there.

A kind of witchdoctor, his head hurting from the mask that was really a kind of magic, kinded them, the reasons for them. They answered.

Chapter IV
Rimbaud

They said he was nineteen; he had been kissed
So many times his face was frozen closed.
His eyes would watch the lovers walking past
His lips would sing and nothing else would move.

We grownups at the bar would watch him sing.
Christ, it was funny with what childish grace
He sang our blues for us; his frozen lips
Would lift and sing our blues out song for song.

Intemperance of heart and of the mind
Will block their progress to the last abyss
Unwinkingly; they listen to the wind
And find a final ceiling in the throat.

Chapter V
Freakish Noises

Yes. Yesterday's loves. The river was a piece of water that looked twisted. I thought Pan was upon it. Neither Pan nor the river were real—Upon The Water In Charlieville, 1868.

Yes. Yesterday is a lover. If he turns around he will see them— beckoning him to some far off gymnasium or poem, turning him off his path, where he had gone so many miles the place to look back.

Yestestday was eternity. Is backwards. Is the way that man faces the real that is always going past him. And him it. Yestestday survives in his eyes—like one water's particle in his river. Yields salt and tears—they hadn't seen us coming.

Back there where the air was pure. Even yesterday was eternity where the air was pure. One does not discover yestestday remembering.

Chapter VI
An Excuse for This Novel

Paul Morphy said, "P-K4, P-K4, Q-B5 mate" outdating a few pawns and bishops but showing a willingness to sacrifice his pawns, his rooks, his knights, his bishops, his very willingness to play the game of chess. He beat Adolf Anderssen without a question.

When the taxi does not move it does not move. When you feed it gas or treat it like a dead refrigerator it does not move. Burn it as quick as you can.

Chapter VII
An Embarrassing Folksong

No way to turn except upward. Rimbaud will turn sixteen, invent what my shrewdness (our shrewdnesses) will not remember, come to a more usable concept of sex and poetry—a machine to catch ghosts.

Folksinging says that the youth of a hero is nasty, short, and brittle, says that the streets of Laredo will forever contain one coffin, that Sweet Williams' grave will forever contain one brier, while we ghosts and shrewd people know that the graves and the streets are choked with them.

Ghosts are not shrewd people. History begins with shrewd people and ends with ghosts.

That is why $^{we}_{I}$ are writing this novel. If he had read it when he was sixteen, he could have changed human history.

Chapter VIII
The Muses Count

Determined funsters who have eaten half their skull away. These oldnesses are not human.

These Muses (Lake Remember to the thought) when you didn't get angry at other people's putting to the question. When you heard and remembered other people's putting to the question.

An inquisition. Other people grow older. But the ghost don't. Remembering every cup of blood they have lived.

The marshmallows on the banks of the magnificent river draw away. Who is there to hear even his song. The coaches draw away.

There is left a universe of letters and numbers and what I have told you. For Jim.

Chapter IX
Rimbaud Is a Gorilla with Seven Teeth

In the middle of the river of our life.

Things have passage. Most rivers eventually reach the ocean. Or a lake—an inland sea. This is like Africa in all continents.

Rimbaud offered himself up to Africa in all continents. Built a sea wall. But he was sixteen and a love object (a love object) when we eventually heard of him.

Literature suffered whenever he breathed. Literature could hear his chest moving. Great armies of sign painters came to carry him away.

Shouts by the bamboo birds woke him up. They built houses on him while he lay dreaming. There was a raft floating by (a black raft, a black raft.)

When Rimbaud was sixteen he never dreamed of Africa.

Chapter X
Who Are You?

What has four legs, three feet and seldom talks to anyone?
A corpse.

What is seen in the distance when the murmurings of some defeated ideas, or lives, or even dreams are suddenly manifest?
A ghost.

What lives forever, has three knots in its rainbow, stores up passion like a squirrel stores up food for the winter, is disengaged from everything worthless, does not even sense the dreamings of poets or notice the river
They.

Notice the last lack of questionmark, notice the toss of the last question
A defeat.

BOOK III

Chapter I
An Ontological Proof of the Existence of Rimbaud

Imagine, those of us who are poets, a good poet. Name to yourselves his possible attributes. He would have to be mmmmm, and nnnnn, and ooooo, and ppppp, but he would have to exist. It is a necessary attribute of the good to exist.

This is called Occam's Law or Davy Jones' Locker.

If they call him up into being by their logic he does not exist. John The Baptist, river-merchant, logician.

The Word puts on flesh when he becomes sixteen, seventeen, eighteen. The Word before Whom all of us are witless.

If Rimbaud had died there in the cabbage patch before we imagined he existed, there would be no history.

Hysterical voices calling over the path to our womb.

Chapter II
The Dead Letter Office

Sentiment is not to the point. A dead letter is there because it has no longer real addresses.

If President Buchanan sent a letter to Cordell Hull (also dead) it would remain there. No thanks to the spirit of things. A dead letter is exactly as if someone received it.

What Rimbaud knew or someone else knew is not incidental. Sentiment is not to the point. These dead poets knew what was coming to them.

There was a blank book where the ghosts or the ages of them kept listening. To what the others said. As in the gold in an earring.

A blank check.

Or what the others said. President Buchanan pledged his truth when he died.

Chapter III
Plato's Marmalade

I can't take the inferior while the superior is there. I, the author of the novel, the dupe—the danger any reader takes reading these words.

After the breath stops, the words listen. To each other? To the song of each idea (whatever that means) that they are bound to? To something's heart?

A metaphor is something unexplained—like a place in a map that says that after this is desert. A shorthand to admit the unknown.

A is a blank piece of driftwood being busted. E is a carpenter whose pockets are filled with saws, and shadows, and needles. I is a pun. O is an Egyptian tapestry remembering the glories of an unknown alien. U is the reverse of W. They are not vowels.

When he said it first, he created the world.

Chapter IV
Rocks and Cabbages

Mythopoetic creatures flock along the streets of our dreams. They do not mind being monsters. They are casual about the proof of their existence.

What does not move does not move has a converse to it—what moves moves. No abstraction known to man and beast can prevent it.

Those early wars. When the earth with all its pockmarks was young. Rocks and cabbages. One green, the other a base for growing.

Worm does not devour rock, nor water cabbages. Everything changes. Not knowing its natural enemy.

I sing the song of the wrath of Achilles.

Chapter V
Where and What

"Why did you throw it?" I asked.

"I threw it on the ground," Rimbaud said.

"What is the reason for this novel? Why does it go on so long? Why doesn't it give me even a lover?"

"On the page," Rimbaud said.

"Who is fighting? What is this war that seems to go on through history?"

"On the battlefields," and it was a little ghost that said this that had edged Rimbaud away for a minute.

"Why is the river?"

"I is the river," the ghost said.

Chapter VI
The Dead Letter Officer

Inside every Rimbaud was a ready-made dead-letter officer. Who really mailed the letter? Who stole the signs?

The signs of his youth and his poetry. The way he looked at things as if they were the last things to be alive.

The robes of his office are vague and noble. He has a hat that he wears on his head. His arms are attached to his shoulders.

Our contempt for him is general and is echoed even in the house of the dead. Blood would not appease his ghost which stays in us even after we are in the house of the dead. He is in every corpse, in every human life.

He writes poems, pitches baseballs, fails us whenever we have a nerve to need him. Button-molder too, he grows in us like the river of years.

Chapter VII
The Hunting of the Snark

Whoever shares in the chase deserves the prize. Each wagon edges towards the clearing where the fire has already been lighted by neighbors.

These animals distinguish us by our smells. This one has a red smell, this a green, this a purple. They are all alive. They have no ambition to destroy us.

We sit around the campfire and sing songs of snark-hunting. One of us has been to Africa and knows the dangers of what we seek. Our colors and our smells glisten in the smoke toward the waiting flock.

What we have said or sung or tearfully remembered can disappear in the waiting fire. We are snark-hunters. Brave, as we disappear into the clearing.

Chapter VIII
Back to His Genitals

To rise in pleasure is to fall in agony. What counts is the only opponent.

Back to what? Back to back. They and him. Sleeping good dreams.

These instructions call him back from his ache. Plaster his mouth with words. Rimbaud sixteen or thirtyseven and dying. They don't matter.

Like painting a person's cock and his heart. Or her cunt. They don't matter. A mobile. A construction.

Back to what? Back to back. They are sleeping back to back with him. His genitals are alarmed.

Their history.

Chapter IX
Certain Seals Are Broken

The first seal is the name of President Buchanan. He is there because he is there unashamed in his role of building the post office.

The second seal is love. It has not been known to include the neighboring countries.

The third seal is boredom. It is called history or politics depending on the context.

The fourth seal is Jim. A private image. A poet demanding privacy in his poem is like a river and a bank unable to move against each other.

The fifth seal is the eternal privacy words offer. Making them human.

Rimbaud. A cry in the night. An offer. What the words choose to say. An offer of something. A peace.

Chapter X
A Piece of Marble

Rimbaud is 106 years old. Meanwhile everything is going on. A style creates its own context as a river has eels in it.

A piece of marble got lost when they were digging the quarry. His face when he was 86 years old or 104. The mystery of why there is a beauty left in any of us. Human beauty. In marble or in age.

These mysteries are real mysteries. It is I that proclaim these mysteries. Playing leapfrog with the unknown. With the dead. It is I that proclaim this history.

Look at the statues disappearing into the distance. They have space to disappear. Rub your eyes to see them. It is a strategy where we miss what we hit.

I mean that the reader of this novel is a ghost. Involved. Involved in the lives of Rimbaud.

A TEXTBOOK OF POETRY

1.

Surrealism is the business of poets who cannot benefit by surrealism. It was the first appearance of the Logos that said, "The public be damned," by which he did not mean that they did not matter or he wanted to be crucified by them, but that really he did not have a word to say to them. This was surrealism.

But even the business of ignoring the public is the business of the poet and not the surrealism of the poet. The surrealism of the poet could not write words.

To be lost in a crowd. Of images, of metaphors (whatever they were), of words; this is a better surrender. Of the poet who is lost in the crowd of them. Finally.

2.

To define a metaphor against the crowd of people that protest against them. This is neither of our businesses.

It is as if nothing in the world existed except metaphors—linkings between things. Or as if all our words without the things above them were meaningless.

"Personify," you say. "It is less abstract to make a person out of a sound." But the Word was the Word not because he was personified but because he was a personification. As if he were human.

To proclaim his humanity is to lie—to pretend that he was not a Word, that he was not created to Explain. The language where we are born across (temporarily and witlessly) in our prayers.

3.

"Poor bastards, trying to get through hell in a hurry." Pray for them bastards who are not patient enough to listen. The flying leaves of a moving tree, a bleeding tree. In a crowd of imaginary images.

Pray for them poor bastards who are too crowded to listen. An angle cutting off every surface to the prayer, the poem, the messages. An angle of the mind. Meaning to do this.

They go through life till the next morning. As we all do. But constantly. As if the shimmering before them were not hell but the reach of something.

Teach.

4.

Taught. As a wire which reaches. A silver wire which reaches from the end of the beautiful as if elsewhere. A metaphor. Metaphors are not for humans.

The wires dance in the wind of the noise our poems make. The noise without an audience. Because the poems were written for ghosts.

The ghosts the poems were written for are the ghosts of the poems. We have it second-hand. They cannot hear the noise they have been making.

Yet it is not a simple process like a mirror or a radio. They try to give us circuits to see them, to hear them. Teaching an audience.

The wires in the rose are beautiful.

5.

The motion of the afterlife. The afterlife of the poem—

Define ghosts as an India-rubber eraser created to erase their own
past.

The motion of the afterlife. And you will think immediately of a
photograph. The ghost of it defined as a blob of ectoplasm—an anti-
image.

An anti-image as if merely by being dead it could make the motions
of what it was to be apparent.

An argument between the dead and the living.

6.

The poet thinks continually of strategies, of how he can win out
against the poem.

Seeking experience for specific instances, drawing upon the pulp of
the brain and the legs and the arms and the motion of the poet, making
him see things that can be conveyed though their words.

Or disbelief too. Seeking experience for specific instances. And in the
gradual lack of the beautiful, the lock of the door before him, a new
Eurydice, stepping up to him, punning her way through his hell.

They won't come through. Nothing comes through. The death

Of every poem in every line

The argument con-
                        tinues.

7.

Nothingness is alive in the eyes of the beloved. He wears the clothes wherein he walks naked. He is fame.

Sounded ahead by the trumpets of unreason. Barely accounted for by the senses. He is what he is because he is never where he is.

I cannot proclaim him for he is not mine. Eros, Amor, feely love, his body is more abstract than all the messages my body sends my brain of him. And he is human. I cannot proclaim starlight for it is never in the same place.

I can write a poem about him a hundred times but he is not there. The mere numbers prevent his appearance as the names (Eros, Amor, feely love, Starlight) for his fame is as the fame of What. I have not words for him.

8.

Descends to the real. By a rope ladder. The soul also goes there. Solely—not love, beyond the thought of God.

I mean the thought of thinking about God. Naturally. I mean the real God.

Disregards all other images as you disregard the parts of words in a poem. The Logos, crying to be healed from his godhead. His dismay.

Disappears within the flatiron of existence. That smoothes out all the words in the poem. Imparts them. Makes them real like the next day.

And as the words heal, I did not mean the real God.

9.

If you see him everywhere or exactly nowhere, he becomes as it were the circumference of a circle that has no point but the boundary of your desire. Coming to a point.

And the human witness of this passion is rightly stunned by the incongruity of it. Lifting a human being into a metaphor.

All that we do in bed, or sleep, or sex is limited by this circle which can only be personally defined.

On the outside of it is what everybody talks about. On the outside of it are the dead that try to talk.

Once you try to embrace an absolute geometric circle the naked loss stays with you like a picture echoing.

10.

The Indian rope trick. And a little Indian boy climbs up it. And the Jungians and the Freudians and the Social Reformers all leave satisfied. Knowing how the trick was played.

There is nothing to stop the top of the rope though. There is nothing to argue. People in the audience have seen the boy dancing and it is not hypnosis.

It is the definition of the rope that ought to interest everyone who wants to climb the rope. The rope-dance. Reading the poem.

Reading the poem that does not appear when the magician starts or when the magician finishes. A climbing in-between. Real.

11.

Boredom is part of the Logos too. You choose His word instead of someoneelse's because you are bored. Meaningless words stick in the throat and you cough them up as an abstraction of what you are trying to cough up. A green parrot that was talking away that was lost and no one could find it.

An argument with the dead. That is what these pauses are mainly about. They argue with you that there have been no beauty, not even words. They speak out of the right side of their mouths.

See them in the distance not understanding their destiny as we do not understand ours. Making a metaphor inhuman as hell. Standing under the shapes and forms that play with us like a camera selecting.

12.

Being faithful. And you are only being faithful to the shadow of a word. Once lost, once found—in the horny deeps below finding. Once cast ashore upon me like the heart's cargo.

And this is a system of metasexual metaphor. Being faithful to the nonsense of it: The warp and woof. A system of dreaming fake dreams.

Being faithful to it. All the ache of remembering the past, what the body doesn't know—the ache that isn't really there.

Sorry for themselves, the Words beckon terribly to me. They wave the past out the door: "Goodbye, I love you."

Being faithful. I pray hope to it. Not them. Not even the words.

13.

Built of solid glass. The temple out there in the weeds and California wildflowers. Out of position. A place where we worship words.

See through into like it is not possible with flesh only by beginning not to be a human being. Only by beginning not to be a soul.

A sole worshipper. And the flesh is important as it rubs into itself your soleness. Or California. A division of where one is.

Where one is is in a temple that sometimes makes us forget that we are in it. Where we are is in a sentence.

Where we are this is idiocy. Where we are a block of solid glass blocks us from all we have dreamed of. But this place is not where we are we are to meet them.

14.

It is not unfair to say that a city is a collection of humans. Human beings.

In their municipal trust they sit together in cities. They talk together in cities. They form groups.

Even when they do not form groups they sit alone together in cities.

Every city that is formed collects its slums and the ghost of it. Every city that is formed collects its ghosts.

Poetry comes long after the city is collected. It recognizes *them* as a metaphor. An unavoidable metaphor. Almost the opposite.

15.

The city redefined becomes a church. A movement of poetry. Not merely a system of belief but their beliefs and their hearts living together.

They are angry at their differences—the dead and the living, the ghosts and the angels, the green parrot and the dog I have just invented. All things that use separate words. They want to inhabit the city.

But the city in that sense is as far from me (and the things that speak through me) as Dante was from Florence. Farther. For it is a city that I do not remember.

But the city that we create in our bartalk or in our fuss and fury about each other is in an utterly mixed and mirrored way an image of the city. A return from exile.

16.

It does not have to fit together. Like the pieces of a totally unfinished jigsaw puzzle my grandmother left in the bedroom when she died in the living room. The pieces of the poetry or of this love.

Surrealism is a poem more than this. The intention that things do not fit together. As if my grandmother had chewed on her jigsaw puzzle before she died.

Not as a gesture of contempt for the scattered nature of reality. Not because the pieces would not fit in time. But because this would be the only way to cause an alliance between the dead and the living. To magic the whole thing toward what they called God.

To mess around. To totally destroy the pieces. To build around them.

17

—A human love object is untrue.
   Screw you.

—A divine love object is unfair
   Define the air
   It walks in.

The old human argument goes on with the rhymes to show that it still goes on. A stiffening in time as puns are a stiffening in meaning.

The old human argument that goes ahead with our clothes off or our clothes on. Even when we are talking of ghosts.

—A human love object is untrue.
   Screw you

—A divine love object is unfair
   Define the air
   It walks in.

Imagine this as lyric poetry.

18.

When the gas exploded the ghosts disappeared. There was merely a city of chittering human beings.

What had seemed long losses in the air, on the ground were trivial. What had seemed to be words were merely reflected in the air as heat waves.

There was a tremendous loss of substance when the gas exploded. Things that were there took wing. Flew to the farthest corners of whatever sky had been above it. Keening.

This was supposed also to be the story of the creation of the universe. The pieces of the explosion coming afterwards together breathless. Coagulating whatever truth they could muster.

When the heart explodes, there is a tremendous loss. But when the gas explodes the ghosts disappear. There is merely a city of chittering human beings.

19.

"Esstoneish me," the words say that hide behind my alarm clock or my dresser drawer or my pillow. "Etonnez moi," even the Word says.

It is up to us to astonish them and Him. To draw forth answers deep from the caverns of objects or from the Word Himself. Whatever that is.

Whatever That is is not a play on words but a play between words, meaning come down to hang on a little cross for a while. In play.

And the stony words that are left down with us greet him mutely almost rudely casting their own shadows. For example, the shadow the cross cast.

No, now he is the Lowghost when He is pinned down to words.

20.

He at the only thing we dreamed of. Golding words—finer than all the metals you enclose things with.

John Dee with his absolutely fake medium E.K. (who later wrote the *Shepherds Calendar*) trying to transmute letters to metal all the way through Bohemia. Later, in the 19th century, becoming a theosophist and dying.

They tell of a love that is beyond heat. A chemical formula. Sulphur combined with darkness and a piece of the moon. Then say "I love you" three times and turn around.

Magic, which is trying to hold onto people with your own hands, is funny while surrealism is not funny. There is a place where we can talk and we cannot talk. Both of us.

Heat.

21.

Hold to the future. With firm hands. The future of each afterlife, of each ghost, of each word that is about to be mentioned.

Don't say put beauty in here for the past, on account of the past. On account of the past nothing has happened.

Stick to the new. With glue, paste it there continually what God and man has created. Your fingers catch at the edge of what you are pasteing.

You have left the boy's club where the past matters. The future of your words matters. That future is continually in the past.

That pathology leads to new paths and pathfinding. All the way down past the future. The words go swimming past you as if they were blue fish.

22.

Don't you have a sense of humor? Can't you take this calmly? All the words they use for poetry are meaningless.

Postage stamps at the best. Surrealism a blue surcharge for Tchad. This is an imaginary African kingdom which will never gain independence because it does not exist and is not merely an act of the imagination and did issue postage stamps. This is the poest and the poem talking to you.

To create the beautiful again. It is as if somehow the lovers of postage stamps had created an image of themselves. A red wheelbarrow or a blue image of the unknown. And each stamp we put on the letters they send us must be cancelled, heartlessly. As if its delivery, the beautiful image of it, were a metaphor.

23.

Wanting to explain. It is wanting to explain. And all through it burrows of rabbits hover like mice in chimneys or metaphors in the middle of a ginger bread cake.

The poet wants to take up all the marbles and put them in his pocket. Wants marbles. Where the poem is like winning the game.

It is so absurd that the rats calling, "Credo quia absurdum" or the cats or the mountain lions become a singular procession of metaphors. Each with their singular liturgy.

These are words and their words holler hollowly in the rabbit burrows, in the metaphors, in the years of our life.

24.

St. Elmo's Fire. Or why this will be a textbook concerning poetry for 20,999 years. Almost a lifetime.

I chicken out at the edges of it and what doesn't come through to me at the edges of it isn't as if angels met singing or any of that business.

We are all alone and we do not need poetry to tell us how alone we are. Time's winged chariot is as near as the next landmark or busstation. We need a lamp (a lump, spoken or unspoken) that is even above love.

St. Elmo's Fire was what was above the ships as they sailed the unspoken seas. It was a fire that was neither a glow or a direction. But the business of it was fire.

25.

Like love being made between fire-engines the poets talk to each other. To put out the fire—not in each other but the fire that the poems made.

To feel sorry for the bastards. Us. Who walk through hell's fire without moving (quickly) listening to seashells while in our ears there is its real roar.

Quickly. And then the sea moves toward us conveniently. As if death were an excuse for all of our sorrows.

The birds fly away. The surf breaks on the shore, on the rocks, on whatever the ocean, being ocean, is conscious of. Deliberately.

And the tides pull back against the very bones we have let them.

26.

And yet they two bake hearts. Immortal mockers of man's enterprise.

Unbelieving, the photograph shows nothing of their faces. The two of them. Not even as if they were a strange language.

From the top to bottom there is a universe. Extended past what the words mean and below, God damn it, what the words are. A vessel, a vesicle of truth.

And yet they too break hearts. These humans—uncoded, uncyphered, their sheer presences. Beyond the word "Beauty."

They are the makers of man's enterprise. Beyond the word "blowtorch," the two of them, holding a blowtorch at all beauty.

27.

What I am, I want, asks everything of everyone, is by degrees a ghost. Steps down to the first metaphor they invented in the underworld (pure and clear like a river) the in-sight. As a place to step further.

It was the first metaphor they invented when they were too tired to invent a universe. The steps. The way down. The source of a river.

The dead are not like the past. Do not like the passed. Hold to their fingers by their thumbs. A gesture at once forgiving and forgotten.

The eye in the weeds (I am, I was, I will be, I am not). The eyes the ghosts have seeing. Our eyes. A trial of strength between what they believe and we.

28.

We do not hate the human beings that listen to it, read it, make comments on it. They are like you. It is as if they or you observed one continual moment of surf breaking against the rocks. A textbook of poetry is created to explain. We do not hate the human beings that listen to it, the moment of surf breaking.

It is fake. The real poetry is beyond us, beyond them, breaking like glue. And the rocks were not there and the real birds, they seemed like seagulls, were nesting on the real rocks. Close to the edge. The ocean (the habit of seeing) Christ, the Logos unbelieved in, where the real edge of it is.

A private language. Carried about us, them. Ununderstanding.

29.

That they have lost the significance of a name is unimportant. In hoc signo vincit (or the passive troubling probability troubling the restless sea which the restless poets support with their metaphors about it being as how it isn't there).

Now the things that are for Jim are coming to an end, I see nothing beyond it. Like a false nose where a real nose is lacking. Faceless people.

The real sound of the dead. A blowing of trumpets proclaiming that they had been there and been alive. The silver voices of them.

To be alive. Like the noises alive people wear. Like the word Jim, especially—more than the words.

LAMENT FOR THE MAKERS   (1961)

Dover Beach

Tabula rasa
A clean table
On which is set food
Fairies have never eaten.
Fairies, I mean, in the ancient sense
Who invite you to dinner.
The mind clean like that
Prepared
With proper provisions
For its journey into.
Almost like a web
(Dinner table)
Spider, fly, and the web are one
For one moment.
Time traveller,
Personal pronoun
Trapped in the mind. Why
Not put it all to sleep?
O anima cortese Mantovana
A whore's answer to a whore
They go to sleep them souls
But they move in their sleep
O anima cortese
As Pope would have written if he had cared or had known Italian
The final table they show you
Is pop.
      Ghost the weasel
Unman him. Make him drink
Lavender water mixed with ink.
Soda water they drink in the ghost canyons of their memories.

The sharp
Im
     age
A new aesthetic
Each place firmly tied to its place
Eaches to each. Doesn't
Reach much
And the owl's bones
Are built in a nest with them. That's
A poem Pope would have been proud of
One keeps unmentionable
What one ascends to the real with
The lie
The cock in the other person's mouth
The real defined out of nothing. Asking
Shadows. Is pop. Pope
To the worms that bury them. Limit-
Less does it.
Damn it all, Robert Duncan, there is only one bordello.
A pillow. But one only whores toward what causes poetry
Their voices high
Their pricks stiff
As they meet us.
And this is rhetoric. The warning mine
Not theirs.
Words-
     worth
Nods
He heap good
Gray poet
English department in his skull.
And the sea changes

Despite the poet it is next to
The waves beat.
In his skull. Love pops
Crab shells and sand dollars
This you lose if you don't sea it. The
Crash.
Pope, Pope, Pope of the evening
Beautiful Pope. Help
Me as sheer ghost. I
Would like to write a poem as long as the hat of my nephew, as
    wide as is spoiled by writing
Crash
Those waves
Only in one skull
Skill at this is pop. Goes the weasel
(All of them weasels alone, seeking the same things)
On the beach
With the tide sweeping up
The whole sand like a carpet
And throwing it back. Ear full of sea foam. Whore Pound
Wondered Homer. Help
Us sleep as men not as barbarians.
Only in one skull
Those waves
They change
Patterns. The scattered ghosts of what happens
Is kelp. Whelp
Of bending and unbending
Ebbs and flows
Breaks and does not break. Dogs
The wetness in the sand
                Bitch
Howling all night. The bitch dog howls

At the absolute boundaries of sentences. The night they made
    the sea in
The second night. Stars bright as raspberries up there (they
    made the stars the first night) and the wind changes
Table of sand
As the moon begins to be created. No
Gnostrum will cure the ills that are on the face of it. No
    Babylonian poets employ charms
Each other's arms are not enough either when the sea shifts and
    changes
The flight of seagulls here. The pebbles there. Chickens of some
    hen.
Men curse it. For the torments it brings their boats, their rafts,
    their canoes, their reasons for existence. Their sight of the
    sea on their boats. Their child.
Chill-dren of the skull. Chilled beyond recognition. Pray for us
    who are living on the sand.
Aphrodite
            born of waters and of sea weeds
Under an island. Grave
Mother
Pray for us.

The Birds

A penny for a drink for the old guy
Asmodeus, flycatcher
Or whatever is that moves us.
Us we define as invisible worms
Poems you never see. A vision

Of sex in the distance.
Overseer of the real. Lears shout obscenely
One Shakespeare's, the other friend of those damned Jumblies.
A distant race
With the seawater
Between them. Beating
Great clouds of smoke. A worm
In the whole visible world held still. To whom? As we define
    them they dis-
appear.

The Birth of Venus

Everything destroyed must be thrown away
If it were even an emotion
The seashell would be fake. Camp
Moving in nothing.
Camp partly as the homosexuals mean it as private sorrow
And partly as others mean it—lighting fire for food.
Neither, I said, seawater
Gives nothing.
The birth of Venus happened when she was ready to be born,
    the seawater did not mind her, and more important, there
    was a beach, not a breach in the universe but an actual
    fucking beach that was ready to receive her
Shell and all.
Love and food of

Lament for the Makers

No call upon anyone but the timber drifting in the waves
Those blocks, those blobs of wood.
The sounds there, offshore, faint and short
They click or sound together—drift timber spending the night
   there floating just above this beach. Thump or sound
   together. The sound of driftwood the sound that is not
   really a sound at all.
At all
All of them
Cast
In the ghost of moonlight on them
On shore.

Postscript

"Then Frieda told us an incredible story. Someone who wanted Lawrence—and Frieda named the possessive admirer—wanted him in death as well as in life. Frieda's house was invaded and Lawrence's ashes were stolen.

'You can believe,' said Frieda, 'I had a hard time getting them back. But I recovered them. And I made up my mind that nothing of this sort should happen again. So I fixed it.'

'How?' we asked. 'What did you do?'

'I had the ashes mixed with a lot of sand and concrete. Now they are in a huge concrete slab. It weighs over a ton.' She laughed heartily. 'A dozen men could not lift it.'"

A RED WHEELBARROW   (1962)

A Red Wheelbarrow

Rest and look at this goddamned wheelbarrow. Whatever
It is. Dogs and crocodiles, sunlamps. Not
For their significance.
For their significance. For being human
The signs escape you. You, who aren't very bright
Are a signal for them. Not,
I mean, the dogs and crocodiles, sunlamps. Not
Their significance.

Love

Tender as an eagle it swoops down
Washing all our faces with its rough tongue.
Chained to a rock and in that rock, naked,
All of the faces.

Love II

You have clipped his wings. The marble
Exposes his wings clipped.
       "Dead on arrival":
You say before he arrives anywhere.
The marble, where his wings and our wings in similar fashion
      blossom. End-
Less.

Love III

Who pays attention to the music the stone makes
Each of them hearing its voice.
Each of them yells and it is an echo bouncing the stone hard.
Imprisoned in the stone the last of the stone, the last of the stone
     singing, its hard voice.

Love IV

There are no holds on the stone. It looks
Like a used-up piece of chewing gum removed from all use
     because they left it. Naturally
It cannot afford to exist.
Without it I cannot afford to exist. Within
The black rock.

Love V

Never looking him in the eye once. All mythology
Is contained in this passage. Never to look him in the eye once.
     His exclusive right to be
Seen. That is the God in the stone
Who barely comes up to expectation.

Love VI

Hoot! The piercing screams of ghosts vanish on the horizon
I had come to the wrong place
Tall as a monster the shadow of the rock overwhelmed us
Nothing that the stone hears.

Love VII

Nothing in the rock hears nothing
The stone, empty as a teacup, tries for comfort,
The sky is filled with stars:
The wax figures of Ganymede, Prometheus, Eros
Hanging.

Love 8

Love ate the red wheelbarrow.

——— • • • ———

THREE MARXIST ESSAYS

Homosexuality and Marxism

There should be no rules for this but it should be simultaneous if at all.

Homosexuality is essentially being alone. Which is a fight against the capitalist bosses who do not want us to be alone. Alone we are dangerous.

Our dissatisfaction could ruin America. Our love could ruin the universe if we let it.

If we let our love flower into the true revolution we will be swamped with offers for beds.

The Jets and Marxism

The Jets hate politics. They grew up in a fat cat society that didn't even have a depression or a war in it. They are against capital punishment.

They really couldn't care less. They wear switchblade knives tied with ribbons. They know that which runs this country is an IBM machine connected to an IBM machine. They never think of using their knives against its aluminum casing.

A League Against Youth and Fascism should be formed immediately by our Party. They are our guests. They are ignorant.

The Jets and Homosexuality

Once in the golden dawn of homosexuality there was a philosopher who gave the formula for a new society—"from each, according to his ability, to each according to his need."

This formula appears in the New Testament—the parable of the fig tree—and elsewhere.

To continue the argument is fruitless.

THE HOLY GRAIL   (1962)

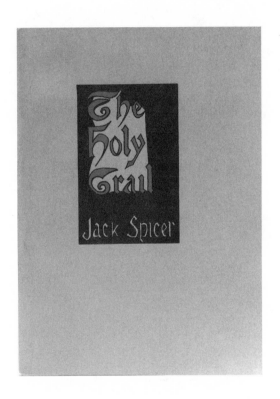

THE BOOK OF GAWAIN

1.

Tony
To be casual and have the wish to heal
Gawain, I think,
Had that when he saw the sick king squirming around like a
      half-cooked eel on a platter asking a riddle maybe only
      ghostmen could answer
His riddled body. Heal it how?
Gawain no ghostman, guest who could not gather
Anything
There was an easy grail.
Later shot a green knight
In a dead forest
That was an easy answer
No king
No riddle.

2.

In some kind of castle some kind of knight played chess with an
      invisible chessplayer
A maiden, naturally.
You can hear the sound of wood on the board and some kind of
      knight breathing
It was another spoiled quest. George
Said to me that the only thing he thought was important in
      chess was killing the other king. I had accused him of lack of
      imagination.
I talked of fun and imagination but I wondered about the nature
      of poetry since there was some kind of knight and an
      invisible chessplayer and they had been playing chess in the
      Grail Castle.

3.

The grail is the opposite of poetry
Fills us up instead of using us as a cup the dead drink from.
The grail the cup Christ bled into and the cup of plenty in Irish
     mythology
The poem. Opposite. Us. Unfullfilled.
These worlds make the friendliness of human to human seem
     close as cup to lip.
Savage in their pride the beasts pound around the forest
     perilous.

4.

Everyone is impressed with courage and when he fought him
     he won
Who won?
I'm not sure but one was wearing red armor and one black armor
I'm not sure about the colors but they were looking for a cup
     or a poem
Everyone in each of the worlds is impressed with courage and
     I'm not sure if either of them were human or that what they
     were looking for could be described as a cup or a poem or
     why either of them fought
They made a loud noise in the forest and the ravens gathered in
     trees and you were almost sure they were ravens.

5.

On the sea
(There is never an ocean in all Grail legend)
There is a boat.
There is always one lone person on it sailing
Widdershins.
His name is Kate or Bob or Mike or Dora and his sex is almost
       as obscure as his history.
Yet he will be met by a ship of singing women who will embalm
       him with nard and spice and all of the hallows
As the ocean
In the far distance.

6.

They are still looking for it
Poetry and magic see the world from opposite ends
One cock-forward and the other ass-forward
All over Britain (but what a relief it would be to give all this up
       and find surcease in somebodyelse's soul and body)
Thus said Merlin
Unwillingly
Who saw through time.

7.

Perverse
Turned against the light
The grail they said
Is achieved by steady compromise.
An unending
The prize is there at the bottom of the rainbow—follow the
    invisible markings processwise
I, Gawain, who am no longer human but a legend followed the
    markings
Did
More or less what they asked
My name is now a symbol for shame
I, Gawain, who once was a knight of the Grail in a dark forest.

End of Book of Gawain

THE BOOK OF PERCIVAL

1.

Fool-
Killer lurks between the branches of every tree
Bird-language.
Fooled by nature, I
Accepted the quest gracefully
Played the fool. Fool-
Killer in the branches waiting.
Left home. Fool-killer left home too. Followed me.
Fool-
Killer thinks that just before the moment I will find the grail
      he will catch me. Poor
Little boy in the forest
Dancing.

2.

Even the forest felt deserted when he left it. What nonsense!
The enormous trees. The lakes with carp in them. The wolves
      and badgers. They
Should feel deserted for a punk kid who has left them?
Even the forest felt deserted. There were no leaves dropping or
      sounds anybody could hear.
The wind met resistance but no noise, the sky
Could not be heard through the water.
Percival
Fool, like badger, pinetree, broken water,
Gone.

3.

"Ship of fools," the wise man said to me.
"I used to work in Chicago in a department store," I said to the
    wise man never knowing that there would be a ship
Whose tiny sails, grail bearing
Would have to support me
All the loves of my life
Each impossible choice I had been making. Wave
Upon wave.
"Fool," I could hear them shouting for we were becalmed in
    some impossible harbor
The grail and me
And in impossible armor
The spooks that bent the ship
Forwards and backwards.

4.

If someone doesn't fight me I'll have to wear this armor
All of my life. I look like the Tin Woodsman in the Oz Books.
Rusted beyond recognition.
I am, sir, a knight. Puzzled
By the way things go toward me and in back of me. And finally
    into my mouth and head and red blood
O, damn these things that try to maim me
This armor
Fooled
Alive in its
Self.

5.

The hermit said dance and I danced
I was always meeting hermits on the road
Who said what I was to do and I did it or got angry and didn't
Knowing always what was not expected of me.
She electrocuted herself with her own bathwater
I pulled the plug
And there was darkness (the Hermit said)
Deeper than any hallow.

6.

It was not searching the grail or finding it that prompted me
It was playing the fool (Fool-killer along at my back
Playing the fool.)
I knew that the cup or the dish or the knights I fought didn't
     have anything to do with it
Fool-killer and I were fishing in the same ocean
"And at the end of whose line?" I asked him once when I met
     him in my shadow.
"You ask the wrong questions" and at that my shadow jumped
     up and beat itself against a rock, "or rather the wrong
     questions to the wrong person"
At the end of whose line
I now lie
Hanging.

7.

No visible means of support
The Grail hung there like june-berries in October or something
      I had felt and forgotten.
This was a palace and an ocean I was in
A ship that cast its water on the tide
A grail, a real grail. Snark-hungry.
The Grail hung there with the seagulls circling round it and the
      pain of my existence soothed
"Fool," they sang in voices more like angels watching
"Fool."

End of Book of Percival

THE BOOK OF LANCELOT

1.

Tony (another Tony)
All the deer in all the forests of Britain could not pay for the
    price of this dish
Lancelot took a chance on this, heard the adulterous sparrows
    murmuring in the adulterous woods
Willing to pay the price of this with his son or his own body.
More simply, your heavy hands (and all the deer of Britain) a
    grail-searcher has need.

2.

Walking on the beach and you both hear the sound the ocean
    makes.
The sailors at Tarawa, Java, burning oil at their backs
Swimming for dear life.
You say, and he says and meaningless says the beach's ocean
Grail at point 029.
In the slick of the thing music
Waves brushing past the beach as if they wanted to be human
The sailors screaming.
Walking on the beach, fondly or not fondly, they hear the
    sound the
Ocean makes.

3.

Nobody's stranger than the stranger coming to the dinner
He can imitate anything or anybody.
"When they start climbing up the back of the old flash" the
      runner who had simply hit a single almost had passed him
        "It is time to quit. I'll never play again."
Almost saw the cup, Lancelot, his eyes so filled with tears.

4.

Love cannot exist between people
Trial balloons. How fated the whole thing is.
It is as if there exists a large beach with no one on it.
Eaches calling each on the paths. Essentially ocean.
You do know Graham how I love you and you love me
but nothing can stop the roar of the tide. The grail, not there,
      becomes a light which is not able to be there like a
      lighthouse or spindrift
No, Graham, neither of us can stop the pulse and beat of it
The roar.

5.

Lancelot fucked Gwenivere only four times.
He fucked Elaine twenty times
At least. She had a child and died from it.
Hero Lancelot feared the question "what is the holy grail?"
      which nobody asked him.
All the snow on the mountain
It was
For a time
His question to answer.

6.

The Irish have only invented three useful things:
Boston, The Holy Grail, and fairies.
This is not to imply that Boston, The Holy Grail and fairies do
    not exist.
They do and are to be proved in time as much as the package of
    Lucky Strike cigarettes you smoke or the village your
    grandmother came from.
Jack, jokes aside, is very much like entering that forest
Perilous
No place for Lancelot, who has killed more men
Than you I-
Rish will ever see.

7.

He has all the sense of fun of an orange, Gawain once explained
    to a trusted friend.
His sense of honor is too much barely to carry his body
The horse he rides on (Dada) will never go anywhere. Sharp, in
    the palace, he wanders alone among intellectual servants
He sings a song to himself as he goes out to look for the thing.
The Grail will not be his
Obviously.

End of Book of Lancelot

THE BOOK OF GWENIVERE

1.

Lance, lets figure out where we stand
On the beach of some inland sea which cannot be called an
      ocean
The river in back of us is green.
The river is wet. Down it floats what is not the grail-mistress,
      several magicians and dead seagulls. Harp
On the same theme. Play the wild chorus over and over again—
      the music magic
Lady of the Lake I hate you; cannot stand your casual
Way the wind blows. Listen,
I am Gwenivere.

2.

The question is pretty simple. I would never have been admitted
      to the Grail Castle but if I had been I would have asked it:
      "Why
Did you admit me to the Grail Castle?" That would have
      stopped him.
I am sick of the invisible world and all its efforts to be visible
What eyes
(Yours or mine)
Are worth seeing it
Or, Lance, what eyes (mine and yours) when, looking at each
      other we forget the Grail Castle for a moment at least
Make it worth seeing it?

3.

Good Friday now. They are saying mass in the Grail Castle
The dumb old king
Awaits
The scourge, the vinegar, the lance, for the umptiumpth time
Not Christ, but a substitute for Christ as Christ was a
        substitute.
You knights go out to tear him from the cross like he was a fairy
        princess turned into a toad
The cup that keeps the blood shed, bled into
Is a hoax, a hole
I see it dis-
Appear.

4.

What you don't understand are depths and shadows
They grow, Lance, though the sun covers them in a single day.
Grails here, grails there, grails tomorrow
A trick of light.
A trick of light streaming from the cup
You say, knowing only the unbent rock
The shells
That have somehow survived their maker.
The depths and shadows are beside all of this, somehow
Returning
Each man to what of him is not bone and skin and mortal
The moon
Which is beautiful and shell of the earth
Streaming.

5.

Sometimes I wonder what you are looking for. The Monday
After Christ died the women came to his tomb and the angel
    said "What are you looking for?"
A sensible question.
The bloody lance that pierced his side, the scourge, the vinegar
    had all turned into relics
Why beat a dead horse?
The women, who were no better than they should be, hadn't
    seen him
If there really was a Christ only
This will happen in the Grail Castle

6.

Boo! I tell you all
Scape-ghosts and half-ghosts
you do not know what is going to appear.
Is going to appear at the proper place like you, Lance
Salt Lake City, New York, Jerusalem, Hell, The Celestial City
Winking and changing like a light in some dark harbor. Damn
The ghosts of the unbent flame, the pixies, the kobalds, the
    dwarves eating jewels underground, the lives that seem to
    have nothing to do except to make you have
Adventures.
Naked
I lie in this bed. The spooks
Around me animate themselves.
Boo! Hello!
Lance, the cup is heavy. Drop the cup!

7.

This teacup Christ bled into. You are so polite, Lance
All your heros are so polite
They would make a cat scream.
I dreamed last night that your body had become a gigantic
    adventure. Wild horses
Could not tear it away from itself.
I
Was the whole earth you were traveling over
Rock, sand, and water.
Christ, and this little teacup
Were always between us.
I was a witch, Lance. My body was not the earth, yours not
    wild horses or what wild horses could not tear
Politely, your body woke me up
And I saw the bent morning

End of Book of Gwenivere

THE BOOK OF MERLIN

1.

"Go to jail. Go directly to jail. Do not pass Go. Do not collect
    $200.00."
The naked sound of a body sounds like a trumpet through all
    this horseshit.
You do not go to jail. You stay there unmoved at what any
    physical or metaphysical policemen do.
You behave like Gandhi. Your
Magic will be better than their magic. You await that time with
    hunger.
Strike
Against the real things. The colonial Hengest and Horsa
The invasion of Britain was an invasion of the spirit.

2.

Wohin auf das Auge blicket
Moor und Heide rings herum
Vogelsang uns nicht erquicket
Eichen stehen kahl und krumm.
Lost in the peril of their own adventure
Grail-searchers im Konzentrationslage
A Jew stole the grail the first time
And a jew died into it
That is the history of Britain.
The politics of the world of spooks is as random as that of a
    Mesopotamian kingdom
Merlin (who saw two ways at the least of the river, the bed of
    the river.) Maer-
Chen ausgeschlossen.

3.

The tower he built himself
From some kind of shell that came from his hide
He pretended that he was a radio station and listened to
      grail-music all day and all night every day and every night.
Shut up there by a treachery that was not quite his own (he
      could not remember whose treachery it was) he predicted
      the future of Britain.
The land is hollow, he said, it consists of caves and holes so
      immense that eagles or nightingales could not fly in them
Love,
The Grail, he said,
No matter what happened.

4.

Otherwise everything was brilliant
Flags loose in the wind. A tournament
For live people. Disengagement as from the throat to the loin or
      the sand to the ocean.
The flags
Of another country.
Flags hover in the breeze
Mary Baker Eddy alone in her attempt
To slake Thursdays. Sereda,
Oh, how chill the hill
Is with the snow on it
What a semblance of
Flags.

5.

Then the thought of Merlin became more than imprisoned
  Merlin
A jail-castle
Was built on these grounds.
Sacco and Vanzetti and Lion-Hearted Richard and Dillinger
  who somehow almost lost the Grail. Political prisoners
Political prisoners. Willing to rise from their graves.
"The enemy is in your own country," he wrote that when
  Gawain and Percival and almost everybody else was
  stumbling around after phantoms
There was a Grail but he did not know that
Jailed.

6.

That's it Clyde, better hit the road farewell
That's it Clyde better hit the road
You're not a frog you're a horny toad. Goodbye, farewell,
  adios.
The beach reaching its ultimate instant. A path over the sand.
And the toadfrog growing enormous in the shadow of fogged-in
  waters. The Lady of the Lakes. Monstrous.
This is not the end because like a distant bullet
A ship comes up. I don't see anybody on it. I am Merlin
  imprisoned in a branch of the Grail Castle.

7.

"Heimat du bist wieder mein"
Heimat. Heimat ohne Ferne
You are called to the phone.
You are called to the phone to predict what will happen to
    Britain. The great silver towers she gave you. What you are
    in among
You are called to predict the exact island that your ancestors
    came from
Carefully now will there be a Grail or a Bomb which tears the
    heart out of things?
I say there will be no fruit in Britain for seven years unless
    something happens.

End of Book of Merlin

THE BOOK OF GALAHAD

1.

Backyards and barnlots
If he only could have stopped talking for a minute he could
      have understood the prairies of American
Whitman, I mean, not Galahad who were both born with the
      same message in their throats
Contemplating America from Long Island Sound or the Grail
      from purity is foolish, not in a bad sense but fool-ish as if
      words or poetry could save you.
The Indians who still walked around the Plains were dead and
      the Grail-searchers were dead and neither of them knew it.
Innocent in the wind, the sound of a real bird's voice
In-vented.

2.

Galahad was invented by American spies. There is no reason to
      think he existed.
There are agents in the world to whom true and false are
      laughable. Galahad laughed
When he was born because his mother's womb had been so
      funny. He laughed at the feel of being a hero.
Pure. For as he laughed the flesh fell off him
And the Grail appeared before him like a flashlight.
Whatever was to be seen
Underneath.

3.

"We're off to see the Wizard, the wonderful Wizard of Oz,"
Damned Austrailians marching into Greece on a fool's errand.
The cup said "Drink me" so we drank
Shrinking or rising in size depending how the bullets hit us
Galahad had a clearer vision. Was an SS officer in that war or a
    nervous officer (Albanian, say), trying to outline the cup
    through his glasses.
The Grail lives and hovers
Like bees
Around the camp and their love, their corpses. Honey-makers
Damned Austrailians marching into Greece on a fool's errand.

4.

To drink that hard liquor from the cold bitter cup.
I'll tell you the story. Galahad, bastard son of Elaine
Was the only one allowed to find it. Found it in such a way that
    the dead stayed dead, the waste land stayed a waste land.
    There were no shoots from the briers or elm trees.
I'll teach you to love the Ranger Command
To hold a six-shooter and never to run
The brier and elm, not being human endure
The long walk down somebody's half-dream. Terrible.

5.

Transformation then. Becoming not a fool of the grail like the
  others were but an arrow, ground-fog that rose up and
  down marshes, loosing whatever soul he had in the shadows
Tears of ivy. The whole lost land coming out to meet this
  soldier
Sole dier in a land of those who had to stay alive,
Cheat of dream
Monster
Casually, ghostlessly
Leaving the story
And the land was the same
The story the same
No hand
Creeping out of the shadows.

6.

The Grail was merely a cannibal pot
Where some were served and some were not
This Galahad thinks.

The Grail was mainly the upper air
Where men don't fuck and women don't stare
This Galahad thinks.

The Grail's alive as a starling at dawn
That shatters the earth with her noisy song
This Galahad thinks.

But the Grail is there. Like a red balloon
It carries him with it up past the moon
Poor Galahad thinks.

Blood in the stars and food on the ground
The only connection that ever was found
Is what rich Galahad thinks.

7.

The Grail is as common as rats or seaweed
Not lost but misplaced.
Someone searching for a letter that he knows is around the
        house
And finding it, no better for the letter.
The grail-country damp now from a heavy rain
And growing pumpkins or artichokes or cabbage or whatever
        they used to grow before they started worrying about the
        weather. Man
Has finally no place to go but upward: Galahad's
Testament.

End of Book of Galahad

THE BOOK OF THE DEATH OF ARTHUR

1.

"He who sells what isn't hisn
Must pay it back or go to prison,"
Jay Gould, Cornelius Vanderbilt, or some other imaginary
    American millionaire
—selling short.
The heart
Is short too
Beats at one and a quarter beats a second or something like that.
    Fools everyone.
I am king
Of a grey city in the history books called Camelot
The door, by no human hand,
Open.

2.

Marilyn Monroe being attacked by a bottle of sleeping pills
Like a bottle of angry hornets
Lance me, she said
Lance her, I did
I don't work there anymore.
The answer-question always the same. I cannot remember when
    I was not a king. The sword in the rock is like a children's
    story told by my mother.
He took her life. And when she floated in on the barge or joined
    the nunnery or appeared dead in all the newspapers it was
    his shame not mine
I was king.

3.

In the episode of le damoissele cacheresse, for example, one
    stag, one brachet, and one fay, all of which properly belong
    together as the essentials for the adventures of a single hero,
    by a judicious arrangement supply three knights with
    difficult tasks, and the maiden herself wanders off with a
    different lover.
So here, by means of one hunt and one fairy ship, three heros
    are transported to three different places. When they awake
    the magic ship has vanished and sorry adventures await
    them all. Not one of them is borne by the boat, as we should
    naturally expect, to the love of a fay
Plainly we are dealing with materials distorted from their
    original form.

4.

The faint call of drums, the little signals
Folks half-true and half-false in a different way than we are
    half-true and half-false
A meal for us there lasts a century.
Out to greet me. I, Arthur
Rex quondam et futurus with a banjo on my knee.
I, Arthur, shouting to my bastard son "It is me you are trying to
    murder!"
Listening to them, they who have problems too
The faint call of   them.
                                                The faint call of
(They would stay in Camelot for a hundred years) The faint call of
Me.

5.

I have forgotten why the grail was important
Why somebody wants to reach it like a window you throw
     open. Thrown open
What would it mean? What knight would fight the gorms and
     cobblies to touch it?
I can remember a lot about the kingdom. The peace I was going
     to establish. The wrong notes, the wrong notes, Merlin told
     me, were going to kill me.
Dead on arrival. Avalon has
Supermarkets—where the dead trade bones with the dead.
     Where the heros
Asking nothing

6.

The blackness remains. It remains even after the rich fisherman
     has done what he can do to protect home and mother. It is
     there like the sun.
Not lost battles or even defeated people
But blackness alive with itself
At the sides of our fires.
At home with us
And a monstrous anti-grail none of those knights could have met
     or invented
As real as tomorrow.
Not the threat of death. They could have conquered that. Not
     even bad magic.
It is a simple hole running from one thing to another. No
     kingdom will be saved.
No rest-
Titution.

7.

A noise in the head of the prince. A noise that travels a long
    ways
Past chances, broken pieces of lumber,
"Time future," the golden head said,
"Time present. Time past."
And the slumbering apprentice never dared to tell the master. A
    noise.
It annoys me to look at this country. Dead branches. Leaves
    unable even to grimly seize their rightful place in the tree of
    the heart
Annoys me
Arthur, king and future king
A noise in the head of the prince. Something in God-language.
    In spite of all this horseshit, this uncomfortable music.

End of Book of the Death of Arthur

GOLEM (1962)

1.

October 1, 1962

This is an ode to Horace Stoneham and Walter O'Malley.
Rottenness.
Who has driven me away from baseball like a fast car. Say
It isn't true Joe.
This is an ode to John Wieners and Auerhahn Press
Who have driven me away from poetry like a fast car. Say
It isn't true Joe. The fix
Has the same place in junkie-talk or real talk
It is the position
They've got you in.
The Giants will have a National League playoff. Duncan
Will read his poems in Seattle.
Money (I forgot the story but the little boy after it all was
        over came up to Shoeless
Joe Jackson) Say it isn't true Joe.

I have seen the best poets and baseball players of our
        generation caught in the complete and contemptible
        whoredom of capitalist society
Jack Johnson
At last shaded the sun from his eyes
                            .A fix
You become fixtures like light
Balls. Drug
Habit
Walter O'Malley, Horace Stoneham, do you suppose
        somebody fixed Pindar and the Olympic Games?

2.

Golem, Written the Evening After Yom Kippur

Your life does not count. It is the rules of
    the tribe. No
Your life does not count.
Counting it all does not count. It is the rules
    of the tribe that your life doesn't count.
Numbering it doesn't count. Madness doesn't
    count.
Being mad at the numbers doesn't count.
It is a rule of the tribe (dead as they are)
    told over the dead campfires
That it doesn't count.
That your life doesn't count.
Countess Death give me Some life in this
    little plain we live in from start to finish
Let me slit their throats and smash their heads on the
Stone.

3.

I met my death walking down Grant Avenue at
    four miles an hour,
She said, "I am your death."
I asked or I sort of asked, "Are you my doom?"
She didn't know Anglo-Saxon so she coyly
    repeated, "Isn't it enough that I am
    your death? What else should bother us?"
"Doom," I said. "Doom means judgement
    in Anglo-Saxon. The Priestess of the
    dead has a face like whey."

Whey is the liquid which is left after they
       spoon off the curds which are good with
       sugar. The dead do not know judgement.
I am writing this against the Great Mother
       that lives in the earth and in mysteries
       I am unable to repeat
Heros take their doom. I will not face
My Death.

4.

Everything is fixed to a point.
The death of a poet or a poem is
       fixed to a point. This House, that
Bank account, this Piece of paper
       on the floor. That Light that shines
       there instead of elsewhere.
Appealing to the better nature of
       things. Inventing angels.
Inventing angels. The light that
       that light shone shone there
       instead of elsewhere. Each
       corner of the room fixed in
       an angle to itself.
The death of a poet or a poem or
       a Piece of paper. Things
Fix themselves.

5.

Give up. The Delphic oracle was
       fixed by the Persians. Pindar
Pindar

Was a publicity man for some
        princes. Traded
For a couple of wrestlers and cash,
        Anger
Does not purify.
The very words I write
Do not purify. Are fixed in the
        language evolved by thousands
        of generations of these princes—
        used mainly for commerce
        Meretriciousness.
Wrestler Plato tried to make
        them all into stars. Stars
        are not what they are.
Coining a phrase our words are
Big-fake-twenty-dollar-gold-pieces.

6.

He died from killing himself.
        His public mask was broken
        because
He no longer had a public mask.
People retrieved his poems
        from wastebaskets. They had
Long hearts.
Oh, what a pain and shame was
        his passing
People returned to their
        business somewhat saddened.

MAP POEMS (1963–1964)

111

Baudelaire country. Heat. Hills without gold. Astonishment that anything has happened to the right or left of it.

Ranches built on hopes that the families of the ranches have long since forgotten.

Valley in the sense of valley where you can't see the mountains from which the waters in the not terribly cold winter once cold have eventually poured through.

Doubt.

137

Little men from outer space and creatures who eat frogs. Tourist hotel since 1900 for tourists seeking wonder.

Below it on all sides is a railroad which never climbs Mt. Shasta.

If they have hidden away anything it is here. But lower, where you can go, there are frenzied deer, escaping you and the hidden monsters.

An oligarchy of love.

155

Always a river at your back. Dead coalminers. The earth comes to the surface here.

Impermanence and fortitude.

The long cattle grazing in hills that are too short for them and the grapes that do not quite seem happy being grapes where they are. Too close to the earth.

Port of Stockton, one hundred million miles from China.

185

A bridge to what, you ask. There is not a bridge on the map. Is this all not composed of sand-dunes.

The lights flicker from the sand-dunes of Golden Gate Park to the sand-dunes of San Rafael over a bay which was once a sand-dune.

No coast line only trees to anchor it.

The orange-colored highways fall apart in your hand.

"I have found it," he said, as he slipped on the soap in his bathtub.

A harbor that was never quite a harbor, near gold that was never quite gold, and the redwoods always retreating lumbering away from human foolishness.

"What have you found?" I have found nothing. A fishing boat and a lumber boat and a few men on a hill the trees just left panning a little gold.

Love makes the discovery wisdom abandons.

LANGUAGE (1963–1965)

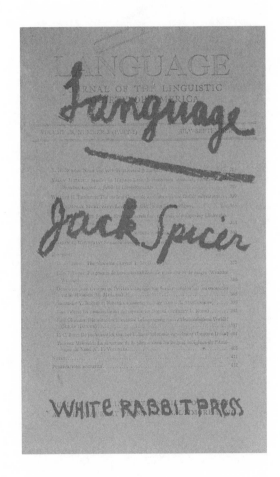

THING LANGUAGE

This ocean, humiliating in its disguises
Tougher than anything.
No one listens to poetry. The ocean
Does not mean to be listened to. A drop
Or crash of water. It means
Nothing.
It
Is bread and butter
Pepper and salt. The death
That young men hope for. Aimlessly
It pounds the shore. White and aimless signals. No
One listens to poetry.

Sporting Life

The trouble with comparing a poet with a radio is that radios
      don't develop scar tissue. The tubes burn out, or with a
      transistor, which most souls are, the battery or diagram
      burns out replaceable or not replaceable, but not like that
      punchdrunk fighter in the bar. The poet
Takes too many messages. The right to the ear that floored him
      in New Jersey. The right to say that he stood six rounds with
      a champion.
Then they sell beer or go on sporting commissions, or, if the
      scar tissue is too heavy, demonstrate in a bar where the
      invisible champions might not have hit him. Too many of
      them.

The poet is a radio. The poet is a liar. The poet is a
    counterpunching radio.
And those messages (God would not damn them) do not even
    know they are champions.

————————

I hear a banging on the door of the night
Buzz, buzz; buzz, buzz; buzz, buzz
If you open the door does it let in light?
Buzz, buzz, buzz, buzz; buzz, buzzz.

If the day appears like a yellow raft
Meow, meow; meow, meoww
Is it really on top of a yellow giraffe
Meow, meow, meow, meow. Meow, meow

If the door caves in as the darkness slides
Knocking and knocking; knock, knock, knock
What can tell the light of whatever's inside?
Knocking and knocking; knock, knock, knock
Or the light and the darkness dance in your eye

Shadows falling one by one
Pigs, and eels, and open sky
Dancers falling one by one
Dancers shrieking one by one.

————————

Baseball Predictions, April 1, 1964

National League
1. Philadelphia
2. Los Angeles
3. Houston
4. San Francisco
5. Milwaukee
6. St. Louis
7. Cincinnati
8. Pittsburgh
9. Chicago
10. New York

American League
1. President DeGaulle
   will be assassinated
   by a Communist named
   John Foster Oswald before
   the Yankees clinch
   the pennant.

———————

The log in the fire
Asks a lot
When it is lighted
Or knot

Timber comes
From seas mainly
Sometimes burns green
-Ly

When it is lighted
The knot
Burns like a joke
With the color of smoke

Save us, with birthdays, whatever is in the fire or not in the fire,
        immortal
We cannot be
A chimney tree
Or give grace to what's mere-
Ly fatal.

Finally the messages penetrate
There is a corpse of an image—they penetrate
The corpse of a radio. Cocteau used a car radio on account of
        NO SPEED LIMIT. In any case the messages penetrate the
        radio and render it (and the radio) ultimately useless.
Prayer
Is exactly that
The kneeling radio down to the tomb of some saint
Uselessness sung and danced (the radio dead but alive it can
        connect things
Into sound. Their prayer
Its only connection.

Heros eat soup like anyone else. Sometimes the kitchen is so far
        away
That there is no soup. No kitchen. An open space of ground
        recovered by
The sky.
Heros eat soup like anyone else. False ground.
Soup
Of the evening

Beautiful soup.
And the sky stays there not an image
But the heros
Like the image of an image
(What is made of soup from)
Zooms.

Smoke signals
Like in the Eskimo villages on the coast where the earthquake hit
Bang, snap, crack. They will never know what hit them
On the coast of Alaska. They expect everybody to be insane.
This is a poem about the death of John F. Kennedy.

A redwood forest is not invisible at night. The blackness covers it but it covers the blackness.

If they had turned Jeffers into a parking lot death would have been eliminated and birth also. The lights shine 24 hours a day on a parking lot.

True conservation is the effort of the artist and the private man to keep things true. Trees and the cliffs in Big Sur breathe in the dark. Jeffers knew the pain of their breath and the pain was the death of a first-born baby breathing.

Death is not final. Only parking lots.

The whorship of beauty
Or beautiful things take a long time getting used to.
There is no past in beauty. The car going at 97.5 miles an hour.
  The time changes
As you cross each border.
Daffodils, ceremonies of spring, sprang, sprung
And it is August
Another century.
Take each past, combine it with its present. Death
Is a tooth among
Strangers.

It comes May and the summers renew themselves
(39 of them) Baseball seasons
Utter logic
Where a man is faced with a high curve.
No telling what happened in this game. Except one didn't strike
    out. One feels they fielded it badly at second base.
Oceans of wildflowers. Utter logic of the form and color.

Thanatos, the death-plant in the skull
Grows wings and grows enormous.
The herb of the whole system.
Systematically blotting out the anise weed and the trap-door
    spider of the vacant lot.

Worse than static or crabgrass.
Thanatos, bone at the bottom, Saint
Francis, that botanist in Santa Rosa
(Bless me now, for I am a plant and an animal)
Called him Brother Death.

————————

1st SF Home Rainout Since. Bounce Tabby-Cat Giants.
        Newspapers
Left in my house.
My house is Aquarius. I don't believe
The water-bearer
Has equal weight on his shoulders.
The lines never do.
We give equal
Space to everything in our lives. Eich-
Mann proved that false in killing like you raise wildflowers.
        Witlessly
I
Can-
not
accord
sympathy
to
those
who
do
not
recognize
The human crisis.

The country is not very well defined.
Whether they are bat-people or real people. The sea-
Coast of Bohemia. The in-
Visible world.
A man counts his fingers in these situations. Whether there are
    five or ten of them or udders as we might go sea-bathing in
    dream.
But dream is not enough. We waking hear the call of the
In-
Visible world
Not seen. Hinted at only. By some vorpals, some sea-lions,
    some scraggs.
Almost too big to get used to, its dimensions amaze us, who are
    blind to Whatever
Is rising and falling with us.

I squint my eyes to cry
(No tears, a barren salt-mine) and then take two sniffles
    through my nose
This means emotion. Chaplinesque
As the fellow says.
We pantomime every action of our bodies
Do not wait
On one sad hill
For one sad turn. I've had it
Principly because you're young.

The metallurgical analysis of the stone that was my heart shows
    an alarming percentage of silicon.
Silicon, as George would be the first to tell you, is not a metal.
    It is present in glass, glue and since glue is made from horses
    —living substance.
I love you. But as the iron clangs, the glass, the glue, the living
    substance (which, God knows, has been to as many glue
    factories as it can remember) muffles what the rest of the
    heart says.
I see you cowering in the corner and the metal in my heart
    bangs. Too personal
The glass and glue in my heart reply. And they are living
    substance.
You cannot bake glass in a pie or fry glue in an omelette
"If I speak in the tongue of men and angels . . ."
The sounding brass of my heart says
"Love."

LOVE POEMS

1.

Do the flowers change as I touch your skin?
They are merely buttercups. No sign of death in them. They die
    and you know by their death that it is no longer summer.
    Baseball season.
Actually
I don't remember ever touching your back when there were
    flowers (buttercups and dandelions there) waiting to die.
    The end of summer
The baseball season finished. The
Bumble-bee there cruising over a few poor flowers.
They have cut the ground from under us. The touch
Of your hands on my back. The Giants
Winning 93 games
Is as impossible
In spirit
As the grass we might walk on.

2.

For you I would build a whole new universe around myself.
    This isn't shit it is poetry. Shit
Enters into it only as an image. The shit the ghostes feasted on
    in the Odyssey. When Odysseus gave them one dry fly and
    made them come up for something important Food.
"For you I would build a whole new universe," the ghosts all
    cried, starving.

3.

" 'Arf,' says Sandy"

"To come to the moment of never come back to the moment of
      hope. Too many buses that are late" Hugh O'Neill in our
      Canto for Ezra Pound.

The ground still squirming. The ground still not fixed as I
      thought it would be in an adult world.

Sandy growls like a wolf. The space between him and his image
      is greater than the space between me and my image.

Throw him a honey-cake. Hell has been proved to be a series of
      image.

Death is a dog and Little Orphan Annie

My own Eurydice. Going into hell so many times tears it

Which explains poetry.

4.

"If you don't believe in a god, don't quote him," Valery once
      said when he was about ready to give up poetry. The
      purposefull suspension of disbelief has about the chance of
      a snowball in hell.

Lamias maybe, or succubi but they are about as real in
      California as night-crawlers

Gods or stars or totems are not game-animals. Snark-hunting is
      not like discussing baseball.

Against wisdom as such. Such

Tired wisdoms as the game-hunters develop

Shooting Zeus, Alpha Centauri, wolf with the same toy gun.

It is deadly hard to worship god, star, and totem. Deadly easy

To use them like worn-out condoms spattered by your own
      gleeful, crass, and unworshiping

Wisdom

5.

Which explains poetry. Distances
Impossible to be measured or walked over. A band of faggots
    (fasces) cannot be built into a log-cabin in which all Western
    Civilization can cower. And look at stars, and books, and
    other people's magic diligently.
Distance, Einstein said, goes around in circles. This
Is the opposite of a party or a social gathering.
It does not give much distance to go on.
As
In the beaches of California
It does not give me much to go on.
The tidal swell
Particle and wave
Wave and particle
Distances.

6.

Sable arrested a fine comb.
It is not for the ears. Hearing
Merely prevents progress. Take a step back and view the
    sentence.
Sable arrested a fine comb. On the road to Big Sur (1945) the
    fuses blew every time we braked. Lights out, every kind of
    action. A deer
Hit us once (1945) and walked sulkily into the bushes as we
    braked into silence.
No big white, lightless automobiles for him. If he's hit, let them
    show him.
Sable arrested a last stop . . . I think it was in Watsonville
    (1945 sable arrested fine comb a)
Past danger into the fog we
Used the last fuse.

7.

The howling dog in my mind says "Surrender" at eight points
     of the compass. North, South, East, West, combinations.
     Whether
He means me or you to me I am not certain. A color-blind
     person can read signals because red is always at the top and
     green at the bottom. Or is it the reverse? I forget, not being
     color-blind. The dog
In my heart howls continuously at you, at me. "Surrender."
I do not know where my heart is.
My heart's in the highlands
My heart is not here
My heart's in the highlands
A-chasing the deer. Dog
Of my heart groans, howls
Blind to guesses. The deer
Your heart and guesses, blandly seek water.

8.

There is real pain in not having you just as there is real pain in
     not having poetry
Not totally in either case as solace, solution, end to all the
     minor tragedies
But, in either case (poetry or you)
As a bed-partner.
Against the drift of rhododendrons and other images we have
     not seen together
I have seen your locked lips and come home sweating.

9.

For you I would build a whole new universe but you obviously
     find it cheaper to rent one. Eurydice did too. She went back
     to hell unsure of what kind of other house Orpheus would
     build. "I call it death-in-life and life-in-death." Shot
In the back by an arrow, President Kennedy seemed to stiffen
     for a moment before he assumed his place in history. Eros
Do that.
I gave you my imaginary hand and you give me your imaginary
     hand and we walk together (in imagination) over the earthly
     ground.

INTERMISSIONS

Intermission I

"The movement of the earth brings harmes and fears.
Men wonder what it is and what it meant."
> Donne
In the next line
Contrasts this with "the celestial movement of the spheres."
> Rhyme soothes. And in a book I read in college fifteen years
> ago it said that this was an attack on the Copernican theory
> and a spidery hand had penciled in the margin
> "Earthquake."
Where is the poet? A-keeping the sheep
A-keeping the celestial movement of the spheres in a long,
> boring procession
A-center of gravity
A-(while the earthquakes of happiness go on inside and outside
> his body and the stars in their courses stop to notice)
Sleep.

Intermission II

The Wizards of Oz have all gone kook
There are no unidentified flying objects. The
Moon may not be made of green cheese but my heart is. Across
      the Deadly Desert We found a champion. The poem
Which does not last as long as a single hand touches.
Morning comes. And the signs of life
(My morning had a telegraph key at here)
Are less vivid. There is a long trail in the back country. Choose
Carefully your victim.
Around the campsite we argued who would choose the fire
I left in a huff with your hand
Naked.

Intermission III

Stay there on the edge of no cliff. With no conceivable future
      but progress—long, flat mesa-country. A few sheep you will
      hold for the rest of your life. Rimbaud's lover
Who had tears fall on his heart or some sweet message.
Dare he
Write poetry
Who has no taste of acid on his tongue
Who carrys his dreams on his back like a packet?
Ghosts of other poets send him shame
He will be alive (as they are dead)
At the final picking.

TRANSFORMATIONS

Transformations I

They say "he need (present) enemy (plural)"
I am not them. This is the first transformation.
They say "we need (present) no enemy (singular)" No enemy in
     the universe is theirs worth having. We is an intimate
     pronoun which shifts its context almost as the I blinks at it.
     Those
Swans we saw in the garden coming out of the water we hated
     them. "Out of place," you said in passing. Those swans and
     I (a blink in context), all out of place we hated you.
He need (present) enemy (plural) and now it is the swans and
     me against you
Everything out of place
(And now another blink of moment) the last swan back in
     place. We
Hated them.

Transformations II

"In Scarlet Town where I was born
There was a fair maid dwelling."
We make up a different language for poetry
And for the heart—ungrammatical.
It is not that the name of the town changes
(Scarlet becomes Charlotte or even in Gold City I once heard a
      good Western singer make it Tonapah. We don't have
      towns here)
(That sort of thing would please the Jungian astronauts)
But that the syntax changes. This is older than towns.
Troy was a baby when Greek sentence structure emerged. This
      was the real Trojan Horse.
The order changes. The Trojans
Having no idea of true or false syntax and having no recorded
      language
Never knew what hit them.

Transformations III

This is the melancholy Dane
That built all the houses that lived in the lane
Across from the house that Jack built.
This is the maiden all forlorn, a
      crumpled cow with a crumpled horn
Who lived in the house that Jack built.
This is the crab-god shiny and bright
      who sunned by day and wrote by night
      and lived in the house that Jack built.
This is the end of it, very dear friend, this
      is the end of us.

MORPHEMICS

1.

Morphemes in section
Lew, you and I know how love and death matter
Matter as wave and particle—twins
At the same business.
No excuse for them. Lew, thanatos and agape have no business
      being there.
What is needed is hill country. Dry in August. Dead grass
      leading to mountains you can climb onto
Or stop
Morphemes in section
Dead grass. The total excuse for love and death

2.

The faded-blond out beauty
Let my tongue cleave to the roof of my mouth if I forget you
      Zion.
There we wept
He gave me a turn. Re-
Membering his body. By the waters of Babylon
In a small boat the prince of all the was to come
Floating peacefully. Us exiles dancing on the banks of their
      fucking river.
They asked us to sing a sad song   How
Motherfucker can I sing a sad song
When I remember Zion? Alone
Like the stone they say Osiris was when he came up dancing.
      How can I sing my Lord's song in a strange land?

3.

Moon,
        cantilever of sylabbles
If it were spelled "mune" it would not cause madness.
Un-
Worldly. Put
Your feet on the ground. Mon-
Ey doesn't grow on trees. Great
Knocker of the present shape of things. A tide goes past like
      wind.
No normal growth like a tree the moon stays there
And its there is our where
"Where are you going, pretty maid?"
"I'm going milking, sir," she said.
Our image shrinks to a morpheme, an -ing word. Death
Is an image of sylables.

4.

The loss of innocence, Andy,
The morpheme—cence is regular as to Rule IIc, IIa and IIb
      [cents] and [sense] being more regular. The [inn-]
With its geminated consonant
Is not the inn in which the Christ Child was born. The root is
      nocere and innocence, I guess, means not hurtful. Innocents
The beasts would talk to them (Alice in the woods with the
      faun). While to Orpheus
They would only listen. Innocuous
Comes from the same root. The trees
Of some dark forest where we wander amazed at the selves of
      ourselves. Stumbling. Roots
Stay. You cannot lose your innocence, Andy
Nor could Alice. Nor could anyone
Given the right woods.

PHONEMICS

No love deserves the death it has. An archipelago
Rocks cropping out of ocean. Seabirds shit on it. Live out their
     lives on it.
What was once a mountain.
Or was it once a mountain? Did Lemuria, Atlantis, Mu ever
     exist except in the minds of old men fevered by the distances
     and the rocks they saw?
Was it true? Can the ocean of time claim to own us now adrift
Over that land. In that land. If memory serves
There (that rock out there)
Is more to it.

––––––––––––––

Wake up one warm morning. See the sea in the distance.
Die Ferne, water
Because mainly it is not land. A hot day too
The shreads of fog have already vaporized
Have gone back where they came from. There may be a whale
     in this ocean.
Empty fragments, like the shards of pots found in some
     Mesopotamian expedition. Found but not put together. The
     unstable
Universe has distance but not much else.
No one's weather or room to breathe in.

––––––––––––––

On the tele-phone (distant sound) you sounded no distant than
      if you were talking to me in San Francisco on the telephone
      or in a bar or in a room. Long
Distance calls. They break sound
Into electrical impulses and put it back again. Like the long
      telesexual route to the brain or the even longer teleerotic
      route to the heart. The numbers dialed badly, the
      connection faint.
Your voice
      consisted of sounds that I had
To route to phonemes, then to bound and free morphemes, then
      to syntactic structures. Telekinesis
Would not have been possible even if we were sitting at the
      same table. Long
Distance calls your father, your mother, your friend, your
      lover. The lips
Are never quite as far away as when you kiss.
An electric system.
"Gk. ἠλέκτρου, amber, also shining metal; allied to
      ἠλέκτωρ, gleaming."

Malice aforethought. Every sound
You can make making music.
Tough lips.
This is no nightingale. No-
Body's waxen image burned. Only
Believe me. Linguistics is divided like Graves' mythology of
      mythology, a triple goddess—morphology, phonology, and
      syntax.

Tough lips that cannot quite make the sounds of love
The language
Has so misshaped them.
Malicious afterthought. None of you bastards
Knows how Charlie Parker died. And dances now in some brief
    kingdom (Oz) two phonemes
That were never paired before in the language.

Aleph did not come before Beth. The Semitic languages kept as
    strict a separation between consonant and vowel as between
    men and women. Vowels somehow got between to produce
    children. J V H
Was male. The Mycenaean bookkeepers
Mixed them up (one to every 4.5)
    (A=1, E=5, I=9, O=15, U=21)
Alpha being chosen as the queen of the alphabet because she
    meant "not."
Punched
    IBM cards follow this custom.
What I have chosen to follow is what schoolteachers call a
    blend, but which is not, since the sounds are very little
    changed by each other
Two consonants (floating in the sea of some truth together)
Immediately preceded and/or followed by a vowel.

The emotional disturbance echoes down the canyons of the
    heart.
Echoes there—sounds cut off—merely phonemes. A ground-
    rules double. You recognize them by pattern. Try.
Hello shouted down a canyon becomes huhluh. You, and the
    canyons of the heart,
Recognize feebly what you shouted. The vowels
Are indistinguishable. The consonants
A pattern for imagination. Phonemes,
In the true sense, that are dead before their burial. Constructs
Of the imagination
Of the real canyon and the heart's
Construct.

GRAPHEMICS

1.

Like a scared rabbit running over and over again his tracks in
    the snow
We spent this Halloween together, forty miles apart.
The tracks are there and the rabbit's feeling of death is there.
    And the children no longer masquerading themselves as
    ghosts but as businessmen, yelled "Trick or treat," maybe
    even in Stinson
The tracks in the snow and the rabbit's motion which writes it is
    quite legible. The children
Not even pretending to be souls of the dead are not. Forty miles.
    Nothing really restored
We
And the dead are not really on the frozen field. (The children
    don't even wear masks) This
Is another poem about the death of John F. Kennedy.

2.

It's been raining five days and will probably keep raining five
    days more
I get up in the morning, see the treacherous sun and try to read
    the Indian signs on the pavement. Not much water. Has it
    been raining while I dreamed?
The sky is no help. The clouds are to the east and the sky
    (treacherous blue) is no help. It is going to rain from the
    west.

Nevertheless (while the wind is blowing from the west) I can
 smell the clouds that won't appear—but will for five or ten
 days. Your heart, and the sky has a hole in it.
In my heart, as Verlaine said, I can hear the little sound of it
 raining
Not an Indian sign. But real unfucking rain.

3.

Let us tie the strings on this bit of reality.
Graphemes. Once wax now plastic, showing the ends. Like a
 red light.
One feels or sees limits.
They are warning graphemes but also meaning graphemes
 because without the marked ends of the shoelace or the
 traffic signal one would not know how to tie a shoe or cross
 a street—which is like making a sentence.
Crossing a street against the light or tying a shoe with a granny
 knot is all right. Freedom, in fact, providing one sees or feels
 the warning graphemes. Let them snarl at you then and you
 snarl back at them. You'll be dead sooner
But so will they. They
Disappear when you die.

4.

The sun-dial makes a grapheme I cannot understand. Even in
     winter it is accurate. The shadow
And the sun in exact proportions.
The hour-glass is a computer. It measures (whether or not
     there ever has been any any sun), how many grains of sand
     have started at the top and gone, willy-nilly, to the bottom.
Graphemes are voluntary. The sun does not have to hit your
     face or your face the sun. Your shadow, if you and the sun
     and willing
Will tell time.
It will spread across the grass at exactly the right intervals,
     neither of you caring.
The imaginary hour-glass is my enemy, sun-dial,
And yours.

5.

You turn red and green like a traffic light. And in between them
     orange—a real courting color. Neither
The pedestrian or the driver knows whether he is going to hit
     the other. Orange
Being a courting color
Doesn't last long. The pedestrian
And the driver go back to the red and green colors of their
     existence. Unhit
Or hit (it hardly matters.)
When we walked through the Broadway tunnel I showed you
     signs above green lights which said "ON A RED LIGHT
     STOP YOUR CAR AND TURN OFF YOUR IGNITION."
     On an orange light—
But their was not an orange light
In the whole tunnel.

6.

You flicker,
If I move my finger through a candleflame, I know that there
     is nothing there. But if I hold my finger there a few minutes
     longer,
It blisters.
This is an act of will and the flame is is not really there for the
     candle, I
Am writing my own will.
Or does the flame cast shadows?
     At Hiroshima, I hear, the shadows of the victims were as if
     photographed into concrete building blocks.
Or does it flicker? Or are we both candles and fingers?
Or do they both point us to the grapheme on the concrete
     wall—
The space between it
Where the shadow and the flame are one?

7.

Walden Pond
All those noxious gases rising from it in the summer. In the
    winter ice
Dirty now. Almost as dirty as the snow in Boston.
W.P.A. swimming hole. Erected
By the Commonwealth of Massachusetts.
We saw the lights across the pond. They said that there was
    some sort of being across the pond, drinking dry martinis
    like we were.
We made tapes. They were probably erased like we were.
    Figures on the pond's surface.
And yet the water like a piece of paper moved and moves
Restlessly while memory gives the light
From the other side.

8.

I am I—both script i and cursive i. Rolled into one rug, one
    grapheme from whose colors stem, phonemes, morphemes,
    unusual birds. Even—if you put a dot or dash with it:
    syntactic structures.
In between
The spaces on a paper the letters grow like palm-trees in a cold
    wind
I—
lands of thought within thought within thought. Those cold
    spaces.
I within I within i etc.
Flowering, all-one. Ein
Eichenbach steht einsam. Old
Senses in new thongs.

9.

There is a new German 50 pfennig postage stamp (a grapheme
      to be paid for and cancelled)
That shows a chapel and an oak tree
And the oak tree looks like a picture of Hitler.
Graphemes should not be looked at so minutely. The
Forest for the trees. The kisses for the love. The
Oakman grows behind every chapel.
The fine
Print on the contract.
God gives us that. The Bundespost Reichsminister says that the
      issue will continued. "I know what I designed and it's
      not a countenance of Hitler. It doesn't speak very well for
      the German people if they see Hitler everywhere."

10.

Love is not mocked whatever use you put to it. Words are also
      not mocked.
The soup of real turtles flows through our veins. Being a [poet]
      a disyllable in a world of monosyllables. Awakened by the
      distance between the [o] and the [e]
The earth quakes. John F. Kennedy is assassinated. The dark
      forest of words lets in some light from its branches.
      Mocking them, the deep leaves
That time leaves us
Words, loves.

BOOK OF MAGAZINE VERSE　(1965)

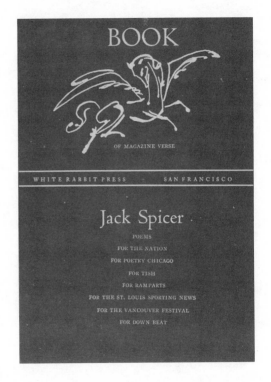

TWO POEMS FOR *THE NATION*

1.

Pieces of the past arising out of the rubble. Which evokes Eliot
    and then evokes Suspicion. Ghosts all of them. Doers of no
    good.
The past around us is deeper than.
Present events defy us, the past
Has no such scruples. No funeral processions for him. He died
    in agony. The cock under the thumb.
Rest us as corpses
We poets
Vain words.
For a funeral (as I live and breathe and speak)
Of good
And impossible
Dimensions.

2.

These big trucks drive and in each one
There is a captain of poetry or a captain of love or a captain of
    sex. A company
In which there is no vice-president.
You see them first as a kid when you're hitch-hiking and they
    were not as big or as final. They sometimes stopped for a
    hitch-hiker although you had to run.
Now they move down the freeway in some mocking kind of
    order. The
First truck is going to be passed by the seventh. The distance
Between where they are going and where you are standing
    cannot be measured.
The road-captains, heartless and fast-moving
Know

SIX POEMS FOR *POETRY* CHICAGO

1.

"Limon tree very pretty
And the limon flower is sweet
But the fruit of the poor lemon
Is impossible to eat"
In Riverside we saved the oranges first (by smudging) and left
      the lemons last to fend for themselves. They didn't usually
A no good crop. Smudge-pots
Didn't rouse them. The music
Is right though. The lemon tree
Could branch off into real magic. Each flower in place. We
Were sickened by the old lemon.

2.

Pieces of the past arising out of the rubble. Which evokes Eliot
      and then evokes Suspicion. Ghosts all of them. Doers of no
      good.
The past around us is deeper than.
Present events defy us, the past
Has no such scruples. No funeral processions for him. He died
      in agony. The cock under the thumb.
Rest us as corpses
We poets
Vain words.
For a funeral (as I live and breathe and speak)
Of good
And impossible
Dimensions.

3.

In the far, fat Vietnamese jungles nothing grows.
In Guadalcanal nothing grew but a kind of shrubbery that was
    like the bar-conversation of your best best friend who was
    not able to talk.

    3
Sheets to the wind. No
Wind being present.
No
Lifeboats being present. A jungle
Can't use life-boats. Dead
From whatever bullets the snipers were. Each
Side of themselves. Safe-
Ly delivered.

4.

The rind (also called the skin) of the lemon is difficult to
    understand
It goes around itself in an oval quite unlike the orange which, as
    anyone can tell, is a fruit easily to be eaten.
It can be crushed in canneries into all sorts of extracts which are
    still not lemons. Oranges have no such fate. They're pretty
    much the same as they were. Culls become frozen orange
    juice. The best oranges are eaten.
It's the shape of the lemon, I guess that causes trouble. It's
    ovalness, it's rind. This is where my love, somehow, stops.

5.

A moment's rest. I can't get a moment's rest without sleeping
        with you. Yet each moment
Seems so hard to figure. Clocks
Tell time. In elaborate ceremonial they tick the seconds off
        what was to come.
Wake us at six in the morning with messages someone had given
        them the night before.
To pierce the darkness you need a clock that tells good time.
        Something in the morning to hold on to
As one gets craftier in poetry one sees the obvious messages
        (cocks for clocks) but one forgets the love that gave them
Time.

6.

The moment's rest. And the bodies entangled and yet not
        entangled in sleeping. Could we get
Out of our skins and dance? The bedclothes
So awry that they seem like two skins.
Or all the sorts of skins that we wore, wear (the orgasm),
        wanted to wear, or would be wearing. So utterly tangled.
        A bad dream.
A moment's rest. The skins
All of them
Near.
I saw the ghost of myself and the ghost of yourself dancing
        without music.
With
Out
Skin.
A good dream. The
Moment's rest.

THREE POEMS FOR *TISH*

1.

There is a mind beating in that pile of rubble you call your
    mind.
It occasionally astonished me.
"Etonez moi" said Diaghilef to Nijinsky. Who immediately did
    and went crazy. A crazy notion in a gray society.
What you hear is what you have heard from. What you wish is
    what someone has wished from a great distance. A long
    line with no bait and a single hook.
Nijinsky danced nice. He was
The Spectre Of The Rose. (I am not sure who is Diagalef and
    who is Nijinsky.) But the both of them also died.

2.

It was not desire but your shivering moved me. Perhaps desire
    too around
Ten above freezing.
I thought of the birds in Canada who fly fecklessly through
    snow-clouds and you were a trembling bird nestling
In the palm of my hand.
You weren't and I thought of all the snow-geese (if there are
    such things) freezing in the Arctic wind. You seemed then
    more like a sparrow
Eating the last grains they can find in the snow.
30 below in the hand you were clasped by and the hand you
    were clasping.
A problem with sparrows.

3.

You can lead a horse to water but you can't make him drink.
      Telemachus sad
Over his father's shortcomings. By now
None of the islands exist where he visited
The horse, lead or not lead to water is still there. Refusing
Bare sustenence.
Each of us has inside of him that horse-animal
Refusing the best streams or as if their thick water flowing were
      refusing us. After
Miles and miles of this, horse and rider,
What do you say? How come
Love isn't as great as it should be?
And Plato's black and white horses in the *Phaedrus*. You can
Lead a horse to water.

FOUR POEMS FOR *RAMPARTS*

1.

Get those words out of your mouth and into your heart. If
    there isn't
A God don't believe in Him. "Credo
Quia absurdum," creates wars and pointless loves and was
    even in Tertullian's time a heresy. I see him like a tortoise
    creeping through a vast desert of unbelief.
"The shadows of love are not the shadows of God."
This is the second heresy created by the first Piltdown man in
    Plato's cave. Either
The fire casts a shadow or it doesn't.
Red balloons, orange balloons, purple balloons all cast off
    together into a raining sky.
The sky where men weep for men. And above the sky a moon
    or an astronaut smiles on television. Love
for God or man transformed to distance.
This is the third heresy. Dante
Was the first writer of science-fiction. Beatrice
Shimmering in infinite space.

2.

A pope almost dying of hiccups. Or St. Peter
Telling the police, "Honest to God I don't know this man,"
      until the cock crowed three times and they released him.
      "A rock
Upon which I will build a church."
And yet it's there. Accepting divinity as Jesus accepted
      humanness. Grudgingly, without passion, but the most
      important point to see in the world.
We do not quite believe this. God is palpably untrue. Things
      spreading over the universe like lessons.
But Jesus dies and comes back again with holes in his hands.
      Like the weather,
And is, I hope, to be reached, and is something to pray to
And is the Son of God.

3.

In the red dawn of the Apocalypse (St. John's not the Defense
      Department's) I can hear the soldiers moving. Pope John
Dressed like the Antichrist is in first to come out of the bushes
      or whatever jungle.
"Pacem in terris," he shouts as if he were singing "The Eyes Of
      Texas Are Upon You." He is immediately shot in the head
      by a loud revolver.
There are so many of them in the bushes or Whatever Jungle
      (St. John's) that they are hardly worth killing. They are
      snipers disguised with the faces of the land we ought to be
      protecting. Their gooks look like our gooks. Pope John
Looks dead even when his costume has fallen off.

4.

Mechanicly we move
In God's Universe, Unable to do
Without the grace or hatred of Him.
The center of being. Like almost, without grace, a computer
    center. Without His hatred
A barren world.
A center of being—not the existence of robots.
If He wanted to, He could make a machine a Christ, enter it in
    its second person which is You.
Why he bothered with man is a mystery even Job wondered.
God becoming human, became a subject for anthropologists,
    history, and all the other wretched itchings of an animal
    that had suddenly (too suddenly?) been given a soul.
When I look in the eyes and the souls of those of those I love, I
    (in a dark forest between grace and hatred) doubt His
    wisdom.
Cur Deus Homo, was the title of St. Anselm's book. Without
    question marks.
Grace!

FOUR POEMS FOR *THE ST. LOUIS SPORTING NEWS*

1.

Waiting like a trap-door spider for a rookie sell-out. Baseball or
     the name game?
When I was a catcher, you came to them. You said "Gee, Mr.
     Whilikers, I'd like to be a catcher." You worked out
With other unassigned players.
You had to make it or be signed down to Shenandoah
     or Rockport. Them
Was the days. Like
Now: the tigers treat the pigs real fine before they eat them:
     there is a pension for almost everything: very few and old
     pitchers throw screwballs. By request of the management.
Like kid, don't enter here or you'll become like a pop fly I lost in
     the sun but went back in the stands anyway. Foul.
"Learn
How to shoot fish in a barrell," someone said,
"People are starving."

2.

I would like to beat my hands around your heart.
You are a young pitcher but you throw fast curve-balls, slow
     fast balls, change-ups that at the last moment don't change.
     Junk
The pitchers who are my age call it. And regret every forty
     years of their life when they have to use them.
If I were a catcher behind you, I'd make you throw real fast
     balls and a few sliders to keep them honest. But you're not
     on my team and when I face you as a pinch-hitter, I strike
     out.

Somebody so young being so cagy, I

Got three home-runs off of Warren Spahn but both of us

    understood where the ball was (or wasn't) going to go. You

Are a deceit and when you get to the age of thirty (and I live to

    see it) you're

Going to get knocked out of the box,

Baby.

3.

Pitchers are obviously not human. They have the ghosts of

    dead people in them. You wait there while they glower, put

    their hands to their mouths, fidget like puppets, while

    you're waiting to catch the ball.

You give them signs. They usually ignore them. A fast outside

    curve. High, naturally. And scientifically impossible.

    Where the batter either strikes out or he doesn't. You either

    catch it or you don't. You had called for an inside fast ball.

The runners on base either advance or they don't

In any case

The ghosts of the dead people find it mighty amusing. The

    pitcher, in his sudden humaness looks toward the dugout

    in either agony or triumph. You, in either case, have a pair

    of hot hands.

Emotion

Being communicated

Stops

Even when the game isn't over.

4.

God is a big white baseball that has nothing to do but go in a
      curve or a straight line. I studied geometry in highschool
      and know that this is true.
Given these facts the pitcher, the batter, and the catcher all look
      pretty silly. No Hail Marys
Are going to get you out of a position with the bases loaded and
      no outs, or when you're 0 and 2, or when the ball bounces
      out to the screen wildly. Off seasons
I often thought of praying to him but could not stand the
      thought of that big, white, round, omnipotent bastard.
Yet he's there. As the game follows rules he makes them.
I know
I was not the only one who felt these things.

SEVEN POEMS FOR THE *VANCOUVER FESTIVAL*

1.

Start with a baseball diamond high
In the Runcible Mountain wilderness. Blocked everywhere by
      stubborn lumber. Where even the ocean cannot reach its
      coastline for the lumber of islands or the river its mouth.
A perfect diamond with a right field, center field, left field of
      felled logs spreading vaguely outward. Four sides each
Facet of the diamond.
We shall build our city backwards from each baseline
      extending like a square ray from each distance—you from
      the first-base line, you from behind the second baseman,
      you from behind the short stop, you from the third-baseline.
We shall clear the trees back, the lumber of our pasts and
      futures back, because we are on a diamond, because it is our
      diamond
Pushed forward from.
And our city shall stand as the lumber rots and Runcible
      mountain crumbles, and the ocean, eating all of islands,
      comes to meet us.

2.

The Frazier River was discovered by mistake it being thought
      to have been, like all British Columbia,
Further south than it was.
You are going south looking for a drinking fountain
I am going north looking for the source of the chill in my bones.
The three main residential streets of Los Angeles were once
      called Faith, Hope, and Charity. They changed Faith to
      Flower and Charity to Grand but left Hope. You can

sometimes see it still in the shimmering smog of
      unwillingness Figueroa
Was named after a grasshopper.
You are going south looking for a drinking fountain
I am going north looking for the source of the chill in my bones
Our hearts, hanging below like balls, as they brush each other
      in our separate journeys
Protest for a moment the idiocy of age and direction.
You are going south looking for a drinking fountain
I am going north looking for the source of the chill in my bones

3.

Nothing but the last sun falling in the last oily water by the
      docks
They fed the lambs sugar all winter
Nothing but that. The last sun falling in the last oily water by
      the docks.

4.

Wit is the only barrier between ourselves and them.
"Fifty four forty or fight," we say holding a gun-barrell in our
      teeth.
There is still a landscape I live on. Trees
Growing where trees shouldn't be. No trees growing where
      trees are. A mess
Of nature. Inconvenient
To the pigs and groins and cows
Of all these settlers.
Settling itself down
In a dirt solution
In the testube
The water still not alive

5.

The Beatles, devoid of form and color, but full of images play
    outside in the living room.
Vancouver parties. Too late
Too late
For a nice exit.
Old Simon Fraser, who was called Frazier in an earlier poem
Played with it
Pretended not to discover a poem.
The boats really do go to China
If one can discover what harbor
Far, far from any thought of harbor
Seagoing, grainy.

6.

Giving the message like a seagull scwaking about a dead piece
    of bait
Out there on the pier—it's been there for hours—the cats and
    the seagull fight over it.
The seagull with only one leg, remote
From identification. Anyway
They're only catching shiners.
The Chinamen out there on the pier, the kids in blue jeans, the
    occasional old-age pensioner.
The gull alone there on the pier, the one leg
The individual
Moment of truth that it cost him.
Dead bait.

7.

It then becomes a matter of not
Only not knowing but not feeling. Can
A place in the wilderness become utterly buggered up with logs?
    A question
Of love.
They
Came out of the mountains and they came in by ship
And Victoria fights New Westminster. And
They're all at the same game. Trapped
By mountains and ocean. Only
Awash on themselves. The seabirds
Do not do their bidding or the mountain birds. There is
No end to the islands. Diefenbacker
Addresses us with a parched face. He
Is, if anything, what
Earthquakes will bring us. Love
Of this our land, turning.

TEN POEMS FOR *DOWNBEAT*

1.

"The dog wagged his tail and looked wonderfly sad" Poets in
     America with nothing to believe in except maybe the ships
     in Glouchester Harbor or the snow fall.
"Don't you remember Sweet Betsy from Pike,
She crossed the big mountains with her lover Ike."
No sense
In crossing a mountain with nobody living in it. No sense
In fighting their fires.
West coast is something nobody with sense would understand.
     We
Crossed them mountains, eating each other sometimes—or the
     heathen Chinee
Building a railway. We are a coast people
There is nothing but ocean out beyond us. We grasp
The first thing coming.

2.

Redrock Canyon the place between two limits
East or west or north or south if you go down seaward. Or even
     if you don't
The appalling thing about Red Rock
Canyon is that its name is Red Rock
Canyon. No oysters, no butterflies, no names other than
Its.

3.

"With two yoke of oxen and one yellow dog, with one
　　　　Shanghai rooster and one spotted hog." Light baggage. Pike
County music.
What we carry with our bones is much like that. Light baggage
　　　　that no unfriendly Indian can take from us.
Ourselves. Yet pointed to like the compass of the needle. "Don't
　　　　you remember Sweet Betsy from Pike?"
Don't.

4.

Well Dennis you don't have to hear any
Of the mountain music they play here.
Telling the young lies so that they can learn to get old.
　　　　Favouring them
With biscuits. "It's a mighty rough road from Lynchburg to
　　　　Danville, declension on a three mile grade." In either case
　　　　collision course. You either pick up the music or you don't.
British Columbia
Will not become a victim to Western Imperialism if you don't
　　　　let it. All those western roads. Few of them
Northern.

5.

For Huntz

I can't stand to see them shimmering in the impossible music of
   the Star Spangled Banner. No
One accepts this system better than poets. Their hurts healed
   for a few dollars.
Hunt
The right animals. I can't. The poetry
Of the absurd comes through San Francisco television. Directly
   connected with moon-rockets.
If this is dictation, it is driving
Me wild.

6.

The poem begins to mirror itself.
   The identity of the poet gets more obvious.
Why can't we sing songs like nightingales? Because we're not
   nightingales and can never become them. The poet has an
   arid parch of his reality and the others.
Things desert him. I thought of you as a butterfly tonight with
   clipped wings.

7.

It's going to be around here for a hundred years or so. The surf,
    I mean, breaking noise through my windows at Stinson
    No gook with an H-bomb in his hot hands is going to kill it.
    I wish
I were like an ocean, loud, lovable, and with a window.
It is not my ocean. It was called the Pacific
By various conquerors that never hurt it.
It makes its noises surfacing while I and everybody make mine,
    only
Its beaches we've starved on. Or loved on. It roars at me like
    love. And
Its sands wet with the new tide.
Automatic
Only, for Christ's sake, surf.

8.

"Trotskyite bandits from the hills," Churchill called 'em long
     after Trotsky had been assinated.
A long life.
Not for the bandits, naturally, but for their namesake. Name
     sook, name not sought. That ax killed them all (if it was an
     ax) and his name killed them all (if it was his name) Trotsky-
Ite bandits from the hills. If they didn't
Know about Trotsky his name was there.
Dead certain. Certain anyway
To die anyway. The runner
From the battle of Marathon has no name either. And you can't
     remember what he yelled or if he went to Athens or Sparta.
It is all preserved for us somewhere in excellent Greek. Their
     long hair blowing in the wind (nameless) an excellent target
     for bazookas. Name-
Less figures, T. and Churchill called them.

9.

They've (the leaders of our country) have become involved in a
     network of lies.
We (the poets) have also become in network of lies by opposing
     them.
The B.A.R. which Stan said he shot is no longer used for the
     course. Something lighter more easy to handle and more
     automatic.
What we kill them with or they kill us with (maybe a squirrel
     rifle) isn't important.
What is important is what we don't kill each other with
And a loving hand reaches a loving hand.
The rest of it is
Power, guns, and bullets.

10.

At least we both know how shitty the world is. You wearing a
    beard as a mask to disguise it. I wearing my tired smile. I
    don't see how you do it. One hundred thousand university
    students marching with you. Toward
A necessity which is not love but is a name.
King of the May. A title not chosen for dancing. The police
Civil but obstinate. If they'd attacked
The kind of love (not sex but love), you gave the one hundred
    thousand students I'd have been very glad. And loved the
    policemen. Why
Fight the combine of your heart and my heart or anybody's
    heart. People are starving.

Spicer's collage announcement of the publication of *Billy the Kid*. (Courtesy of The Bancroft Library.)

CHRONOLOGY

1925: Born, January 30, John Lester Spicer in Los Angeles, California.

1941: Attends Fairfax High School in Los Angeles. High school friends include future folk-song parodist Allan Sherman and the screenplay guru Syd Field; he publishes poems in school literary magazine "Colonial Voices."

1943–44: Corresponds with novelist and critic Aldous Huxley. Graduates from Fairfax High. Attends the University of Redlands, where he befriends future Secretary of State Warren Christopher, with whom he serves on the debate team. Declared 4-F in draft status. Spicer's odd jobs include working in a defense plant and toiling in Hollywood studios as an "extra." Spicer can be spotted briefly in the opening scene in a football stadium in 20th Century Fox's biopic *Wilson*.

1945: After two years at Redlands, moves to Berkeley from Los Angeles to continue work on a B.A. degree at the University of California. Meets Idaho-born poet Robin Blaser. Practices as a private detective.

1946: Frequents the anarchist/art/music/poetry circle of Kenneth Rexroth in San Francisco. First encounter with California-born Robert Duncan, already twenty-seven. The "Berkeley Renaissance" begins. Spicer studies with Ernst Kantorowicz, initiating an important apprenticeship. With Josephine Fredman, Hugh O'Neill, and Robert Duncan, writes a "Canto for Ezra Pound" and mails it to him at St. Elizabeth's Hospital in Washington, DC. Spicer compiles a booklet of "Collected Poems 1945–6" as a Christmas gift for his teacher, Josephine Miles.

1947: Joins Duncan's roundtable at 2029 Hearst Street. In April, visits Big Sur coast of California with Hugh O'Neill, meets folklorist Jaime de Angulo. Receives bachelor's degree from UC Berkeley; continues studies towards a Ph.D. June 20, mob hit of Bugsy Siegel in Los Angeles; Spicer claimed to be peripherally involved in the investigation. In autumn, Charles Olson visits Berkeley and meets the poets of the Berkeley Renaissance (except Spicer). Duncan publishes his first book, *Heavenly City, Earthly City*. Spicer lives at 2018 McKinley St., a boarding house in Berkeley, where his fellow tenants include poets Philip Lamantia, Gerald Ackerman, George Haimsohn, Robert Duncan, and the teenaged prodigy Philip K. Dick, later a noted science fiction novelist and visionary.

1948: Duncan writes *The Venice Poem*. Spicer begins work on his "Imaginary Elegies." Spicer's work as a graduate student expands to include research for English Department staff: with Robin Blaser, he researches early interactions between Native American and colonial settlers for Roy Harvey Pearce (they are thanked in Pearce's study *The Savages of America: A Study of the Indian and the Idea of Civilization*). On his own Spicer prepares a large bibliography of D. H. Lawrence for Professor Mark Schorer.

1949: In the spring Spicer has a troubled romantic affair with writer and heiress Catherine Mulholland, enters psychotherapy at UC Cowell Hospital Annex, and writes "Psychoanalysis: An Elegy." Hosts a folk music show at KPFA, Berkeley; connects with archivist/artist Harry Smith and participates in the record hunts that would result in the Smithsonian release of Smith's *Anthology of American Folk Music* (1952). Studies with David Reed, soon to become his mentor in Linguistics. Writes "The Scrollwork on the Casket."

1950: Receives M.A. degree. Loyalty Oath controversy at UC Berkeley; Spicer's refusal to sign propels him out of the Ph.D. program and into Minnesota, where no Loyalty Oath was required of graduate students or professors. With David Reed, Spicer attends December convention of the Language Society of America in Manhattan (his first trip to the East Coast). Three of the "Imaginary Elegies" are completed.

1951: Duncan and Spicer debate the Berkeley Renaissance in letters. With David Reed, he publishes article on "Correlation Methods of

Comparing Ideolects in a Transition Area," in *Language: Journal of the Linguistic Society of America*. In the summer, Spicer's father dies in Los Angeles. Arthur Kloth introduces Spicer to Gary Bottone, with whom he conducts a long distance romance. While in Minnesota, writes poems for Bottone ("Sonnet for the Beginning of Winter," "Train Song for Gary," and so forth).

1952: Returns to Berkeley from Minnesota. Social life revolves around two gay bars: the Black Cat in San Francisco and the White Horse in Berkeley.

1953: Lives in Berkeley, working as a teaching assistant for Thomas Parkinson's large literature courses at UC Berkeley. A student, Richard Rummonds, inspires a love poem and features Spicer, Duncan, Landis Everson, and Blaser in a "Four from Before" retrospective in Berkeley student magazine *Occident*. Involved in Oakland, Berkeley, and San Francisco branches of the Mattachine Society, an early gay liberation group based in Los Angeles. Teaches humanities at California School of Fine Arts, San Francisco (afterwards San Francisco Art Institute); becomes intimate with three students, John Allen Ryan, Graham Mackintosh, and Allen Joyce. Spicer plays bridge in Berkeley every Friday night. Begins writing epic play *Troilus*.

1954: Spicer moves to 975 Sutter Street in San Francisco. April 1, one of his favorite meeting places, The Place, opens. By the end of the summer, Spicer has completed his play *Pentheus*. Poetry Center at San Francisco State College opens, bringing international poets to read in the Bay Area, including W. H. Auden, William Carlos Williams, Marianne Moore, Robert Lowell, Langston Hughes, and others, many of whom Spicer meets. With five visual artists from CSFA, Spicer opens the 6 Gallery on Halloween at the site of the former avant-garde gallery space King Ubu. For the opening show, Spicer records poetry with backing by the Dave Brubeck Quartet, now presumed lost.

1955: Fired from CSFA in June. In the spring, acts in Robert Duncan's "Faust Foutu" with Larry Jordan, Michael McClure, Helen Adam, Jess, and Duncan. Writes "Imaginary Elegy IV" and finishes *Troilus* in the summer before leaving for New York. Through painter John Button, meets Frank O'Hara, Barbara Guest, John Ashbery, James Schuyler, and Joe LeSueur; O'Hara's poem "At the Old Place," written July 13, mentions Spicer cattily. To Jasper Johns, O'Hara writes, "[Spicer] always disappoints me, but others think him very important." To make ends meet, Spicer assists Hungarian émigré Eugene de Thassy in writing an autobiographical account of Parisian life, later (1960) published as *Twelve Dead Geese* and including some of Spicer's poetry as the poetry of the "poet" character. On October 7, one of Spicer's letters is read aloud at the momentous 6 Gallery group reading in San Francisco, at which Ginsberg reads "Howl." In New York, writes "Some Notes on Whitman for Allen Joyce" and the sequence "Phases of the Moon." In November, moves to Boston and joins the poetry circle including John Wieners, Joe Dunn, Steve Jonas, and Robin Blaser, which is connected to Black Mountain College in North Carolina, where Charles Olson, Robert Creeley, and Duncan are teaching. Begins the poems of *After Lorca*. Falls in love with the young, straight, married Joe Dunn.

1956: In this period Spicer undertakes several large-scale projects with Blaser, but only "A Semperrealistic Poem for Jo Miles" is finished. Writes his amorphous, unfinished, proto-serial project "Oliver Charming." That summer Black Mountain College closes; from this point onward a flood of "Black Mountain Refugees" washes up against the bohemias of New York and San Francisco, including painters Basil King, Tom Field, and Paul Alexander, and poets Ebbe Borregaard, Dunn, and Wieners. In November, Spicer returns by plane to the Bay Area with Joe and Carolyn Dunn.

1957: Spicer reads at Berkeley and San Francisco State to great acclaim. Takes a job at SF State, teaching two courses, one of them the "Poetry as Magic" workshop, which attracts Helen Adam, Robert Duncan, Jack Gilbert, George Stanley, Joe Dunn, James Broughton, Ebbe Borregaard, and others. Charles Olson delivers Whitehead lectures at San Francisco Poetry Center, with Spicer in attendance. That summer, the Howl Trial begins in San Francisco. Spicer attends group reading at Kenneth Rexroth's apartment, reads "Song of the Bird in the Loins," is photographed for *Life* magazine. Joe Dunn establishes White Rabbit Press. The Sunday poetry meetings commence. Spicer attends rehearsals of Duncan's *Medea I* and *II*. That fall, *Evergreen Review*'s "San Francisco Scene" issue appears with accompanying LP, both featuring Spicer's poems. Begins work on linguistic atlas with David Reed at Berkeley. Enters a romantic relationship with Philadelphia-born painter Russell FitzGerald, who moves in with Spicer—the poet's only extended sexual affair. Assembles a selection of his own best work for a projected volume of selected poems. *Admonitions* and *A Book of Music* written. *After Lorca* published.

1958: January, insults visiting poet Denise Levertov by reading "For Joe" at a party in her honor. Blabbermouth Night becomes a regular feature at The Place. Duncan attempts to arrange meeting between Spicer and Louis Zukofsky, who is visiting San Francisco and teaching a poetry workshop at San Francisco State. Spicer is romantically involved with Russell FitzGerald until FitzGerald's July fling with rival poet Bob Kaufman "flips" Spicer. *Billy the Kid* written. *Fifteen False Propositions Against God* written (1958–59). Spicer writes six chapters of a detective novel, posthumously published as *The Tower of Babel*.

1959: One of Spicer's muses, James Alexander, moves to Fort Wayne, sparking an important series of epistolary poems from Spicer. With the artist Fran Herndon, Spicer edits the mimeo-magazine *J*, issues 1–5. Spicer writes the poems of "Homage to Creeley" (without the attending "Explanatory Notes"). Fran Herndon works on lithograph illustrations for "Homage to Creeley." At a drunken party in Berkeley, Allen Ginsberg attempts to fellate Spicer in public in the name of love, peace, and understanding; gets rejected. Robin Blaser returns to the Bay area after close to five years in Boston. Spicer writes *Apollo Sends Seven Nursery Rhymes to James Alexander*. *Billy the Kid* is published. "Imaginary Elegies V & VI" are published in *J*. *Fifteen False Propositions Against God* appear in *Beatitude 3*.

1960: "White Rabbit College" is proposed for the art space Borregaard's Museum. In May *The New American Poetry,* edited by Donald Allen is published, including Spicer's first four "Imaginary Elegies." In summer, Spicer's "gay rabbi" and long-term bridge partner, George Berthelon, dies. New series of poetry meetings limited to Jim Herndon, Jack Spicer, Robin Blaser, and Landis Everson. *Homage to Creeley* (without "Explanatory Notes") is privately published in a small mimeo edition by Harold and Dora Dull. Spicer writes *Helen: A Revision.* Writes *The Heads of the Town Up to the Aether.*

1961: In January, *The Heads of the Town Up to the Aether* is first "performed" at Borregaard's Museum. Professor and poet Tom Parkinson is shot in his office at Berkeley and survives. Plans for "White Rabbit College" evaporate in disputes, with only a few events held as scheduled. In December Helen Adam's *San Francisco's Burning!* opens at the Playhouse in San Francisco. Spicer writes *Lament for the Makers.* Two-volume anthology *The Californians* (ed. Robert Pearsall and Ursula Spier Erickson) appears, reprinting three of Spicer's poems.

1962: Publishes "Three Marxist Essays" in George Stanley's magazine *N—San Francisco Capitalist Bloodsucker.* In summer, poet Ron Primack becomes Spicer's roommate and writes *For the Late Major Horace Bell of the Los Angeles Rangers.* In August, Spicer reads *The Holy Grail* at Blaser's apartment; angers Duncan and Jess. In October, George Stanley and Stan Persky, instigated by Spicer, picket the opening of Duncan's play *Adam's Way.* Graham Mackintosh revives dormant White Rabbit Press. In "Hypocrite Women," in her volume *O Taste and See!,* Denise Levertov responds poetically to the blistering invective of Spicer's earlier (1958) poem "For Joe," from *Admonitions.* Writes *A Red Wheelbarrow, The Holy Grail,* and *Golem. The Heads of the Town Up to the Aether* is published. *Lament for the Makers* is published.

1963: Winter, Spicer breaks his ribs in a car accident in San Francisco's Broadway Tunnel. That summer, Russell FitzGerald, his former lover, elopes to New York with Dora Dull, and Ron Primack moves out of

Spicer's apartment. Spicer works on the *Map Poems* and begins *Language*, which will be largely serialized in the monthly *Open Space*.

1964: Fired from his job at UC Berkeley, Spicer panics, then takes a part-time job at Stanford. That summer begins psychotherapy at Mt. Zion Hospital, San Francisco. Moves to 1420 Polk Street, his last residence. *Open Space* magazine published, edited by Stan Persky. *Dear Ferlinghetti/Dear Jack* (correspondence) published in *Open Space* and, separately, by White Rabbit Press.

1965: In February, Spicer attends the Vancouver Poetry Festival, reads *Language* to a young and enthusiastic crowd, stays with US émigrés Warren and Ellen Tallman. Ends therapy. In spring and summer, writes *Book of Magazine Verse*. In June visits Vancouver a second time; reads at New Design Gallery with Robin Blaser and Stan Persky; delivers the "Vancouver Lectures" at the Tallmans' home. In June, *Poetry* magazine rejects Spicer's offer of "Six Poems for *Poetry* Chicago." White Rabbit Press publishes *Language*. July 14–15, Spicer gives a reading and his fourth and final lecture, "Poetry and Politics," at the Berkeley Poetry Conference. He is one of seven poets (including Duncan, Gary Snyder, Olson, Ed Dorn, Ginsberg, and Creeley) who give individual readings and lectures at the conference. Late July, Spicer is found comatose in the elevator of his building, taken to San Francisco General Hospital and treated for liver failure. Dies on August 17. "My vocabulary did this to me," he tells Blaser at his deathbed. "Your love will let you go on." Buried anonymously in San Francisco.

1966: *Book of Magazine Verse* published.

NOTES TO THE POEMS

Spicer Manuscripts

The Bancroft Library began collecting Spicer's papers in the 1970s, and we have relied heavily on four large manuscript collections, beginning with MSS 71/135C, which includes Spicer's letters to the artist and printer Graham Mackintosh and to the poet James Alexander. In Robert Duncan's papers (MSS 78/164C) there are dozens of Spicer's poems and letters. More recently, the Library purchased Fran Herndon's Spicer files, including the holograph manuscripts for *The Holy Grail* and *Golem* (MSS 99/94C). In 2004 Robin Blaser (representing the literary estate of Jack Spicer), made a gift of MSS 2004/209, including the papers left in Spicer's hotel room trunk at his death in 1965, and a number of other manuscripts and letters collected by Blaser in the years after Spicer's death in preparation for Blaser's own edition of Spicer's poems (*The Collected Books of Jack Spicer*) in 1975. The manuscripts of Spicer's final books, *Language* and *Book of Magazine Verse,* are owned by Simon Fraser University in British Columbia (Jack Spicer fonds, MsA 20, Contemporary Literature Collection, Special Collections and Rare Books, W.A.C. Bennett Library, Simon Fraser University).

ms   Refers to both typed and holographic manuscripts.

CP 45–46   *Collected Poems 1945–1946,* in an edition of one, was handmade as a Christmas gift (1946) to his Berkeley poetry teacher Josephine Miles. The manuscript of *Collected Poems* is at the Archive for New Poetry, Mandeville Library at University of California, San Diego (MSS 397). After Spicer's death, the book was printed in facsimile by Oyez/White Rabbit Press in 1981.

ONS   *One Night Stand & Other Poems,* ed. Donald Allen, San Francisco: Grey Fox Press, 1980.

CB   *The Collected Books of Jack Spicer,* ed. Robin Blaser, Los Angeles: Black Sparrow, 1975.

WRP   White Rabbit Press.

JSP 2004   Jack Spicer Papers MSS 2004/209, The Bancroft Library, University of California, Berkeley.

JSP 99   Jack Spicer Papers MSS 99/94C, The Bancroft Library.

JSP 71   Jack Spicer Papers MSS 71/135C, The Bancroft Library.

JSF 20   Jack Spicer fonds, MsA 20, Bennett Library, Simon Fraser University.

*   Previously uncollected in CB or ONS.

Berkeley in Time of Plague (p. 5). ONS used as copytext. First privately published in CP 45–46. First published in *Evergreen Review,* 1.2 "The San Francisco Scene" (1957): 52.

A Girl's Song (p. 5). CP 45–46 used as copytext.

Homosexuality* (p. 6). JSP 2004 ms. used as copytext.

A Portrait of the Artist as a Young Landscape* (p. 6). First appeared in *Word of Mouth: An Anthology of Gay American Poetry,* edited by Timothy Liu (Jersey City, NJ: Talisman House, 2000): 75–78. That version of the poem was prepared from a typescript Robert Duncan gave to Lewis

Ellingham in 1983, the original of which is in the Duncan papers at SUNY Buffalo. The present version of "Portrait" incorporates Spicer's holographic revisions; JSP 2004.

An Apocalypse for Three Voices (p. 10). ONS used as copytext.

One Night Stand (p. 13). ONS used as copytext, except where punctuation and stanza breaks diverge from original JSP 2004 ms.

Ms. variant:

One Night Stand

Listen, you silk-hearted bastard
I said to the boy in the bar
You flutter well
And look like a swan out of water.
Listen, you soft wool-feathered bastard
I myself am more or less like Leda.
I can remember pretending
That your red silk tie is a real heart
That your raw wool suit is real skin
That you could float beside me with a swan's touch
Of casual satisfaction.
But all deity leaves that bird after the swooping
Waking tomorrow I remember watching
Somebody's feathers and his wrinkled heart
Draped loosely in my bed.

In spring of 1958, Spicer revised the poem again, giving it a new title, while writing Chapter 6 of his incomplete detective novel. Here is "Leda":

Leda

I can remember pretending
That your red silk tie was a real heart
That your raw wool suit was real flesh
That you could float beside me with a swan's touch
Of casual satisfaction.
Waking tomorrow I remember only
Somebody's feathers and his wrinkled heart.

An Answer to Jaime de Angulo (p. 13). JSP 2004 ms. used as copytext. First appeared in an alternate version in *Acts* 6 (1987): 8.

Jaime de Angulo (1887–1950) was a maverick linguist and cultural anthropologist, once at the University of California, Berkeley. This poem, written in April 1947, appeared in a revised version in ONS as "An Answer to a Jew." The 1956 version, which begins "When asked if I am of the Jew or Goyim, / When asked if I am an enemy of your people," employs the same rhetoric and locution as one of the speakers, thought to be Spicer, on the floor of the 1953 Constitutional Convention of The Mattachine Society, the early gay rights organization he supported: "When asked whether I am homosexual, I answered by asking 'When?'" One of the central questions the Mattachine Society discussed was whether homosexuality was an essential quality or a behavioral characteristic. Minutes of Original Convention of Mattachine Society (May 23–24, 1953): 13. Hal Call Papers, One Institute, Los Angeles, California.

A Lecture in Practical Aesthetics (p. 14). ONS used as copytext. First published in Robert Duncan and Jack Spicer, *An Ode and Arcadia* (Berkeley: Ark Press, 1974).

In Spicer's notes to himself on his own poems, he writes that his discovery of Wallace Stevens led to a "long poem of the witty parallel type," adding that "A Lecture in Practical Aesthetics" was "the last poem I wrote for almost a year."

Dialogue Between Intellect and Passion (p. 15). ONS used as copytext. First appeared as "Sonnet" in *Berkeley Miscellany* 1 (1948): 14.

A Night in Four Parts (Second Version) (p. 16). ONS used as copytext. First appeared in an earlier version in *Berkeley Miscellany* 1 (1948): 11–12.

Orpheus in Hell (p. 18). ONS used as copytext. First published in *Caterpillar* 12 (July 1970): 65.

Orpheus After Eurydice (p. 19). ONS used as copytext. An earlier draft exists, entitled "Spicer's Gallery of Gorgeous Gods" (JSP 2004). First published in *Caterpillar* 12 (July 1970): 64.

Orpheus' Song to Apollo (p. 20). ONS used as copytext. First published in *Caterpillar* 12 (July 1970): 66.

Troy Poem (p. 21). ONS used as copytext. First appeared in *Berkeley Miscellany* 1 (1948): 13.

"We find the body difficult to speak . . ." (p. 22). ONS used as copytext. First published in *Caterpillar* 12 (July 1970): 67.

"They are selling the midnight papers . . ."* (p. 22). Previously unpublished; JSP 2004 ms. used as copytext.

"Any fool can get into an ocean . . ." (p. 23). JSP 2004 ms. used as copytext.

The Scrollwork on the Casket (p. 24). ONS used as copytext. First published in *Berkeley Miscellany* 2 (1949): 31–32.

The Dancing Ape (p. 25). ONS used as copytext. First published in *Evergreen Review* 1. 2 "The San Francisco Scene" (1957): 52. JSP 2004 ms. as "To Robbie."

Imaginary Elegies (I, II, III) (p. 26). ONS used as copytext. Elegies I to IV first published in *The New American Poetry*, ed. Donald M. Allen (New York: Grove Press, 1960). Earlier versions of the first four elegies can be found in the *Exact Change Yearbook No. 1: 1995*, ed. Peter Gizzi (Boston: Exact Change / Manchester: Carcanet, 1995).

Although the "Imaginary Elegies" were published in their entirety (I-VI) in ONS, we have chosen to present them here organized chronologically by date of composition. The first three were begun in the late 1940s; the fourth elegy was written in 1955, and the fifth and sixth elegies were not composed until 1959. From the fourth elegy onward, the poems are acutely aware of being compositions in time, which gives them an antiphonal quality, calling back and forth through the years.

Psychoanalysis: An Elegy (p. 31). ONS used as copytext. First published in *Evergreen Review* 1.2 "The San Francisco Scene" (1957): 56–57.

Minneapolis: Indian Summer (p. 37). ONS used as copytext. First published in *ManRoot* 10 (Fall 1974): 103. JSP 2004 ms. as "Indian Summer."

Watching a TV Boxing Match in October (p. 37). ONS used as copytext. First published in *City Lights* 5 (Spring 1955):11.

Portrait of an Artist (p. 38). ONS used as copytext. First published in *ManRoot* 10 (Fall 1974): 106.

Sonnet for the Beginning of Winter (p. 38). ONS used as copytext. First published as "Sonnet for Gary" in *ManRoot* 10 (Fall 1974): 105.

Gary Bottone was a young man Spicer met at a Berkeley party in the summer of 1951. Temporarily home among friends after spending the first of two years at the University of Minnesota, Spicer fell in love with him quickly, and once he returned to Minnesota Gary's absence made the heart grow fonder. "Younger, less bohemian, less literary and less 'experienced' than any of Jack's Berkeley friends" (as he described himself in a 1984 letter to Lew Ellingham quoted in *Poet Be Like God*), Bottone elicited a number of tender love poems and letters from Spicer, but the relationship petered out when they were both living in the same place. The following might prove of interest, with its references to another sort of loyalty oath, one to which Spicer ultimately gave his life (see Introduction, n. 5).

Dear Gary,

Somehow your letter was no surprise (and I think you knew that it was no surprise or you would have tried to break the news more gently); somehow I think we understand what the other is going to say long before we say it—a proof of love and, I think, a protection against misunderstanding. So I've been expecting this letter for five weeks now—and I still don't know how to answer it.

Bohemia is a dreadful, wonderful place. It is full of hideous people and beautiful poetry. It would be wrong of me to drag a person I love into such a place against his will. Unless you walk into it freely, and with open despairing eyes, you can't even see the windows. And yet I can't leave Bohemia myself to come to you—Bohemia is inside of me, and in a sense is me, was the price I paid, the oath I signed to write poetry.

I think that someday you'll enter Bohemia—-not for me (I'm not worth the price, no human being is), but for poetry—to see the windows and maybe blast a few yourself through the rocks of hell. I'll be there waiting for you, my arms open to receive you.

But let's have these letters go on, whether it be days, years, or never before I see you. We can still love each other although we cannot see each other. We will be no farther apart when I'm in Berkeley than we were when I was in Minneapolis. And we can continue to love each other, by letter, from alien worlds.

Love,

Jack

On Reading Last Year's Love Poems (p. 39). ONS used as copytext. First published in *Caterpillar* 12 (July 1970): 69.

Orpheus in Athens (p. 39). Published in ONS as "The boy had never seen an honest man . . . ." Here used as copytext with title from JSP 2004 ms.

Train Song for Gary (p. 40). ONS used as copytext. First published as "Lyric for Gary" in *ManRoot* 10 (Fall 1974): 105.

A Second Train Song for Gary★ (p. 41). JSP 2004 ms. used as copytext.

A Postscript to the Berkeley Renaissance (p. 45). ONS used as copytext. First published in *ManRoot* 10 (Fall 1974): 107.

A Poem for Dada Day at The Place, April 1, 1955 (p. 46). ONS used as copytext. JSP 2004 ms. as "A Protest Against a Dada Party in The Place on April 1, 1955."

"The window is a sword . . ."★ (p. 47). JSP 2004 used as copytext. First appeared in truncated form in *Ironwood* 28 (Fall 1986): 206, with this note: "Nearly final version in the handwriting of Jack Spicer." The full version was discovered in a 1955 notebook for *Troilus*.

Imaginary Elegies (IV) (p. 48). ONS used as copytext. First published in *The New American Poetry*, ed. Donald M. Allen (New York: Grove Press, 1960). See earlier note for elegies I to III.

IInd Phase of the Moon★ (p. 53). JSP 2004 ms. used as copytext.

The "Phases of the Moon" was a serial poem Spicer worked on during his short stay in New York City in 1955, along with "Some Notes on Whitman for Allen Joyce." A few years later, Spicer compiled a list of his poetry for a projected volume of selected poems that was never published. Three of the poems on Spicer's list (#55, #56, #57) were the "IInd Phase of the Moon," "IIIrd Phase of the Moon," and "IVth Phase of the Moon."

IIIrd Phase of the Moon★ (p. 53). JSP 2004 ms. used as copytext.

IVth Phase of the Moon★ (p. 54). JSP 2004 ms. used as copytext.

Some Notes on Whitman for Allen Joyce (p. 55). ONS used as copytext.

In light of newly discovered material, we may now read "Some Notes on Whitman" as a culmination of a particular line in Spicer's poetry that has hitherto gone unnoticed because it has been, for all intents and purposes, unavailable. With the publication of the fuller version of "The window is a sword . . ." and the three extant "Phases of the Moon," we can trace the emergence and eventual disappearance of an ecstatic, revelatory style, one that joins elements of the French symbolist prose poem to the classical choral verse Spicer had been immersed in during the years of writing *Troilus* and his other verse drama. After New York this vein in his work goes underground (though perhaps the fragment "The city of Boston. . . ," marks its brief return). Eventually the "Explanatory Notes" to "Homage to Creeley," "A Fake Novel About the Life of Arthur Rimbaud," and "A Textbook of Poetry" would take up this mode again with new and recombinant energy.

The Day Five Thousand Fish Died Along the Charles River (p. 56). ONS used as copytext. First appeared in *Floating Bear* 34 (1967): n.p.

Hibernation—After Morris Graves (p. 56). ONS used as copytext. First published in *Evergreen Review* 1.2 "The San Francisco Scene" (1957): 55.

Éternuement* (p. 57). Previously unpublished; JSP 2004 ms. used as copytext.

> One of the poems, previously thought lost along with the "Phases of the Moon," that were listed in Spicer's 1958 letter to Don Allen of the poems he thought his best. The letter is printed in the introduction to *One Night Stand.*

Song for the Great Mother (p. 57). ONS used as copytext. First published in *Caterpillar* 12 (July 1970): 73.

> "Mrs. Doom," one of the characters of the poem, appears in Spicer's contemporaneous project "Oliver Charming," and "Song for the Great Mother" might be considered an outgrowth of this work.

"The city of Boston . . ."* (p. 58). JSP 2004 ms. used as copytext.

Five Words for Joe Dunn on His Twenty-Second Birthday (p. 58). ONS used as copytext. First published in *Audience* 4.2 (1956): 8–9.

Birdland, California* (p. 60). Previously unpublished; JSP 2004 ms. used as copytext. From the second of five notebooks Spicer used while writing "Oliver Charming."

> The date was in fact October 5 when, in the second game of the 1956 World Series, the Yankees used seven pitchers and still lost to the Dodgers, 8 to 13.

"Imagine Lucifer . . ."* (p. 61). JSP 2004 ms. used as copytext. From the third of five notebooks Spicer used while writing "Oliver Charming."

The Song of the Bird in the Loins (p. 62). ONS used as copytext. First published in *Evergreen Review* 1.2 "The San Francisco Scene" (1957): 58. From the last of five notebooks Spicer used while writing "Oliver Charming."

Babel 3 (p. 63). ONS used as copytext. First published in *Adventures in Poetry* 12 (Summer 1975): n.p.

They Murdered You: An Elegy on the Death of Kenneth Rexroth* (p. 64). JSP 2004 ms. used as copytext.

> This poem, parodic of Ginsberg's *Howl,* was promoted in the *Boston Newsletter* as one of the "Coming Attractions" (under the title "Kenneth Rexroth Eats Worms: An Elegy For Kenneth Rexroth"). Rexroth was quite healthy at this time; he lived until 1982.

A Poem to the Reader of the Poem (p. 65). ONS used as copytext, save for retaining the stanza breaks in CB. First published in *Caterpillar* 12 (July 1970): 77–79.

Song for Bird and Myself (p. 69). ONS used as copytext. First published in *Measure* 1 (1957). JSP 2004 ms. as "Song for Bird and Myself," with half-erased subtitle, "A Memorial for his Death and Mine, For Allen Joyce."

The ms. contains the following lines, which were later excised:

Obscene,
That's what the wings mean.
My friend in a Turkish bath
Suffering old men to touch him
Bird dying, an old man, in a room across from the
    Club Bohemia
"That's where Bird died,"
They used to tell me in New York
As if they were proud
That a city could kill him.
Obscene,
A friend collects pictures of nude athletes
I travel
With a suitcase full of dead butterflies.

A Poem Without a Single Bird in It★ (p. 73). JSP 2004 ms. used as copytext. First appeared in *American Poetry Review* 27.1 (January / February 1998).

Spicer sent Robin Blaser this poem from Berkeley enclosed in a letter dated December 13, 1956 (i.e., just after JS returned to the West Coast).

The Unvert Manifesto and Other Papers Found in the Rare Book Room of the Boston Public Library in the Handwriting of Oliver Charming. By S. (p. 74). Robin Blaser included the first few pages of this text in the "Poems and Documents" section of CB.

The composition of "Oliver Charming" preoccupied Spicer throughout his 1955–1956 sojourn in Boston. Its confusion of sex, race, nonsense, and self-loathing makes the "Oliver Charming" material problematic, but it's essential to understanding Spicer's sense of himself in mid-career. Part manifesto, part novel, part poem, part diary, part frame story, "Oliver Charming" is a surrealist blurred-genre document that expands geometrically, swallowing all in its path. "S.," the ostensible editor of these papers, is observed critically by Charming, their ostensible author, who manages to send up Spicer's amatory interest in the young poets and artists who began to flock to him at this time. Graham Mackintosh is thinly disguised as "Graham Macarel," while Carolyn and Joe Dunn appear as "Mrs. and Mr. Doom." As it grows, the work becomes a gallery of mirrors in which various versions of masculinity appear in distorted reflection, from the New England Brahminism of the editor Thomas Wentworth Higginson (who befriended Emily Dickinson in 1862) to the steel-jawed pulp Angeleno righteousness of Perry Mason, the fictional attorney created by Erle Stanley Gardner (1889–1970) and one of Spicer's favorite detective heroes.

Spicer's "Oliver Charming" materials (in JSP 2004) are copious and show evidence of much revision. Following the two holograph manuscripts and a typescript prepared by Blaser from a now lost third holograph, we can trace the general evolution of the text. In Manuscript A, the earliest here, the names "Graham Mackintosh" and "Spicer" are used freely throughout, though Spicer appends a note to say that if the "Diary" is to be published, then the name "Macarel" must be substituted for "Mackintosh."

Manuscript B considerably revises the manifesto and the earlier part of the diary, then continues to weave its way through the five notebooks Spicer used in Boston, ending in mid-trial when "S." is asked if he is acquainted with Oliver Charming.

Manuscript C, Blaser's typescript, shows signs of further revision, and we presume that he worked from an original revised by Spicer and now lost. We have used Blaser's version as our copytext up to the very first line of the "Diary" entry for January 12, 1954, which dramatically breaks off in mid-sentence. From there on the text in this volume follows Manuscript B as above.

"Poetry as Magic" Workshop Questionnaire (p. 99). Reproduced from original mimeograph (in JSP 2004).

Spicer's first order of business in the final weeks of 1956 was preparing his "Poetry as Magic" workshop, offered in the spring semester of 1957 under the auspices of San Francisco State College (now University). Robert Duncan, who assisted Ruth Witt-Diamant at the SF State Poetry Center, arranged for Spicer's workshop to be held off campus, at the main branch of San Francisco's Public Library, in hopes of attracting poets in all stages of development. "This is not a course in technique or 'how to write,'" Spicer warned. "It will be a group exploration of the practices of the new magical school of poetry which is best represented in the work of Lorca, Artaud, Charles Olson and Robert Duncan." Spicer formulated this questionnaire, which Duncan typed onto mimeograph paper and circulated widely as a survey of available talent. The Poetry Center has the "original stencil," while the Bancroft Library has much other material, including many questionnaires completed by those who made the cut and those whom Spicer rejected. Participants in the workshop eventually included Helen Adam, Ebbe Borregaard, James Broughton, Duncan himself, Joe Dunn, Jack Gilbert, and George Stanley.

AFTER LORCA (p. 105). CB used as copytext, except in "A Diamond," which restores the first stanza break from the White Rabbit Press (WRP) edition. First published by WRP (San Francisco 1957).

Of the WRP edition, Blaser notes: "Cover design by Jess using facsimile of García Lorca's signature and drawing of a photograph of Lorca as a child on a toy-horse (reproduced in Guillen's 'Prologo' to Lorca's *Obras Completas* [Spain: Aguilar, 1955]: xiv). Jack hoped the drawing would suggest a new Tarot card." (CB 381)

There are eleven "original" Spicer poems masquerading as Lorca translations; they are: "Ballad of the Seven Passages," "Frog," "A Diamond," "The Ballad of the Dead Woodcutter," "Alba," "Aquatic Park," "Ballad of Sleeping Somewhere Else," "Buster Keaton Rides Again: A Sequel," "Friday the 13th," "Afternoon," and "Radar." See Clayton Eshleman's "The Lorca Working," in *Boundary 2* 6.1 (Fall 1977): 31–49.

We offer two other significant texts of interest from the *After Lorca* notebooks (JSP 2004):

Ballad of the Surrealist's Daughter

A Translation for W. S. Merwin

Who wants to dance around a Scotch maypole?
Who wants to dance around a Scotch maypole?
When somebody tells us the truth about songbirds
Who wants to dance around a Scotch maypole?

Your pants are very nice and I lick them,
Somebody says your pants are very nice and I lick them,
When children and songbirds come home from their barrooms
Somebody says your pants are very nice and I lick them.

The songbirds are all very nice. Maybe.
The songbirds are all very nice. Maybe.
When somebody tells us the truth about songbirds
Somebody dies with a thump and I lick them.

In the fifth letter to Lorca, Spicer writes: "I, for example, could not finish the last letter I was writing you about sounds." In the third of seven Lorca notebooks at the Bancroft this draft appears and is in fact that unfinished letter to Lorca about sound:

A friend asked me the other day if I didn't think that the printing of a poem helped to complete it, to make it actual when before it was only potential. I answered no, that to me print was irrelevant, that it was merely an inefficient way of recording the sound of the poem and that, if I had my choice, I would publish my poems alone by tape recording.

This has always been the line I have taken, but I wonder now. I could not have translated your poem from a tape recording of your voice. As a matter of fact, having heard your voice, you would become as much a stranger to me as my best friend—the narrow line on which we communicate would be broken.

The sight and the sound of the poem is in the poem. Your voice, my voice, your page, my page, your language, my language—they all get in the way if we let them. They do not matter. Only what we transfer matters, only what we make appear.

It is not merely that the voice, the personal gets in the way of the poem. That is bad enough. But worse, the sounds of the language change year by year and mile by mile from the speaker.

Let me put it this way. If Chaucer had written in Chinese wouldn't he be more available to us today than he is in Middle English? There could be translation then. We could not confuse his sounds with our sounds.

The advantage of the Chinese ideograph is not, as Fenollosa thought, its visual imitation of the object. Its advantage is merely its lack of sound, the fact that sound could never be reconstructed from it. Its advantage is that it is arbitrary, that one has to listen to it in one's own language.

But there is another side to the coin. The very visual imitation of objects that Pound and Fenollosa praised is the cause of visual wishywashyness. But the visual is irrelevant. If sound decays, sight becomes cute. The arrangement of the poem on the page [becomes a] finicky insistence on where the line breaks. (Christ, it is because the ideograph once tried to imitate the object that Chinese poetry is weak, has the wishywashyness of flower-arrangement.) Sight is worse than sound because it is less alien. Close your eyes and the words will have to struggle to reach you. You will not confuse them with their objects.

ADMONITIONS (p. 155). CB used as copytext, except: hyphen added to the word "re-echo" in "Dear Robin," as in Adventures in Poetry (AIP) edition. First published in book form by AIP (New York 1974).

A BOOK OF MUSIC (p. 169). CB used as copytext. First published by WRP (San Francisco 1969).

Socrates* (p. 179). Previously unpublished; JSP 2004 ms. used as copytext.

A Poem for Dada Day at The Place, April 1, 1958* (p. 180). JSP 2004 ms. used as copytext.

BILLY THE KID (p. 183). CB used as copytext. First published by Enkidu Surrogate (Stinson Beach, CA 1959). This first edition was designed and illustrated by Jess.

For Steve Jonas Who Is in Jail for Defrauding a Book Club* (p. 192). JSP 2004 ms. used as copytext.

FIFTEEN FALSE PROPOSITIONS AGAINST GOD (p. 193). CB used as copytext. First published in *Beatitude* 3 (May 1959). Also published as *Fifteen False Propositions About* [*sic*] *God* (San Francisco: ManRoot Press, 1974).

Variant in poem XI, l. 12 in ManRoot edition: "How love can exist without any flavor to it."

LETTERS TO JAMES ALEXANDER* (p. 203). JSP 71 ms. used as copytext. These letters first appeared in altered form in *Caterpillar* 12 (1970): 162–174.

James Alexander, the younger brother of the Black Mountain/San Francisco painter Paul Alexander, was a young poet Spicer met in San Francisco in the fall of 1958. Later that winter, Alexander returned home to his parents in Fort Wayne, Indiana. Spicer, attracted to both the youth and his poetry, began writing him letters and poems to continue their connection. The letters were written in 1959 as Spicer was beginning to work on *The Heads of the Town Up to the Aether*; the second section, "A Fake Novel about the Life of Arthur Rimbaud," begins in a dead letter office. Spicer believed that letters could be poems, and he read them aloud to the poets at the Sunday gatherings in North Beach. Alexander's serial poem entitled *The Jack Rabbit Poem*, though written at this time, was published after Spicer's death by WRP in 1966.

"Sun Dance" is a poem by James Alexander.

APOLLO SENDS SEVEN NURSERY RHYMES TO JAMES ALEXANDER (p. 217). CB used as copytext, except Blaser's title has been slightly changed (from "Nursury" to "Nursery") to reflect the manuscripts in JSP 2004.

A BIRTHDAY POEM FOR JIM (AND JAMES) ALEXANDER★ (p. 223). JSP 2004 ms used as copytext.

The Italian text is from Michelangelo Buonarroti. He is replying to the poet Giovanni de Carlo Strozzi, who was commenting on his statue in the Medici Chapel. Strozzi said to Michelangelo that his statues were so beautiful that they could come to life (literally, they could "awake"). But Michelangelo, deeply saddened by the crumbling of the Republic of Florence, replied with these words (translated by Jennifer Scappettone):

> Dear is sleep to me, and stone's being even more,
>
> so long as damage and indignity endure;
>
> not to see, not to hear, is happy fortune;
>
> so do not stir me, for mercy's sake, speak low.

The last poem in this series first appeared as "Epilogue for Jim" in *J* 2 (1959).

Imaginary Elegies (V, VI) (p. 230). ONS used as copytext. First appeared in *J* 5 (1959). See earlier note for elegies I to III.

"Dignity is a part of a man . . ."★ (p. 233). Previously unpublished; JSP 2004 ms. used as copytext.

HELEN: A REVISION★ (p. 235). Previously unpublished; JSP 2004 ms. used as copytext.

The notebook in which Spicer wrote "A Textbook of Poetry" bears the title "Helen: A Revision" on its cover. We found the Helen poem itself in a different notebook, written on successive recto notebook pages and then, at the end of the notebook, doubling back to fill the previously blank verso pages. This pattern of writing from recto to verso has precedents; an earlier poem, "Birdland, California," for example, was written in much the same way. The title "Helen: A Revision" appears not only on the cover of the "Textbook" notebook but at the top of the page of the second poem in the present series, the words "of Euripides" crossed out afterward. Spicer's Helen poem, raw and energetic, was written as his friend Robert Duncan was working on what we now call his "H.D. Book," for which he solicited Spicer's input. Spicer's "Revision" might be imagined equally as a tribute to Duncan's and H.D.'s work on Helen, and as a riposte or "correction" to their romantic visions.

THE HEADS OF THE TOWN UP TO THE AETHER (p. 247). CB used as copytext with the exception of a typo corrected in "Dillinger." Book One, "Homage to Creeley," was privately printed in a mimeo edition by Harold and Dora Dull in Annapolis, California, in the summer of 1959 (without the "Explanatory Notes"). The finished book (with all three sections) was first printed by the Auerhahn Society in San Francisco in 1962.

In his note on this text, Blaser writes: "There is no Chapter VIII in Book I of 'A Fake Novel About the Life of Arthur Rimbaud.'"

There is a significant variant in "A Fake Novel About the Life of Arthur Rimbaud, Book III, Chapter I," stanza 3, line 1. In the Auerhahn edition this line reads: "If they call him up into being by their logic he does exist."

LAMENT FOR THE MAKERS (p. 315). CB used as copytext. First published by WRP (Oakland 1962). In this edition, Spicer wickedly replicates the acknowledgments page from Robert Duncan's book *The Opening of the Field* (New York: Grove, 1960). The cover features a collage by Graham Mackintosh.

Blaser offers this note in CB: "This is the original version. 'Dover Beach' is very different from the printed version [White Rabbit, 1962]. Jack regretted the politeness of the printed version and rejected it as a book.[. . .] The 'Postscript' is a quotation: Louis Untermeyer's story in E. Nehls, ed., *D. H. Lawrence: A Composite Biography* 3: (Madison: University of Wisconsin Press, 1959): 484–485."

A RED WHEELBARROW (p. 323). CB used as copytext. First published by Arif Press (Berkeley 1971).

Three Marxist Essays (p. 328). ONS used as copytext. First appeared in *N—San Francisco Capitalist Bloodsucker* (Spring 1962).

THE HOLY GRAIL (p. 329). CB used as copytext. First published by WRP (San Francisco 1964).

The German text in second poem of the Book of Merlin comes from the protest song "The Peat Bog Soldiers."

GOLEM* (p. 359). First published as *Golem* by Granary Books (New York 1999). Here used as copytext.

The first poem in *Golem* had been widely circulated, since Lew Ellingham copied it down on a brown paper bag at Gino & Carlo's bar when Spicer left the room. "October 1, 1962," which Spicer's intimates referred to as the "fix" poem, appeared in print in *ManRoot* No. 10 and in *One Night Stand*. Spicer's friend Jim

Herndon, to whom Spicer entrusted the manuscript, was the only one who knew that it was not a discrete poem but the first passage in a projected serial poem. Years later, after Herndon's death, his former wife Fran Herndon was cleaning her basement and started going through an old file cabinet in which she believed Jim had kept income tax forms. One drawer was filled with curiosities, including the manuscript to *The Holy Grail,* which Fran had typed for Spicer, a handful of other previously known Spicer poems, and the six poems of *Golem* in manuscript. Illustrated with Fran Herndon's sports collages, composed during the same time as the poems in *Golem,* the piece was published in 1999, with an afterword by Kevin Killian. (JSP 99)

MAP POEMS★ (p.365). JSP 2004 ms. used as copytext. Published as *Map Poems* (Berkeley: Bancroft Library Press, 2005), with an introduction by Peter Gizzi and Kevin Killian.

Collating Spicer's papers in 2004 we stumbled across five unpublished poems with atypical, three-digit titles, and put them aside for further investigation. In another box, days later, we found a sheaf of facsimiles of pages from a California roadmap. If their page numbers hadn't been so absurdly prominent, we might never have reunited them with the corresponding poems. This sequence comes from early 1964 (around the same time as the Valentine's Contest of *Open Space*). The title is ours.

LANGUAGE (p. 371). CB used as copytext, except in "Intermission I": "harms" changed to "harmes" to reflect Donne's original spelling, as in WRP edition. First published by WRP (San Francisco 1965).

The cover design is a facsimile of the cover of *Language: Journal of the Linguistic Society of America* 28.3, part 1 (July–September 1952). The issue included Spicer's one academic article in linguistics, co-authored by David W. Reed and John L. Spicer, entitled "Correlation Methods of Comparing Idiolects in a Transition Area," which appeared on pages 348–359. The WRP cover features the title, author, and press information written over the journal's cover in red crayon (or lipstick) by Spicer.

Variants in WRP: in "Morphemics 4," ll. 5–6: "The beasts would build a whole new / the woods with the faun)" appears to be an omission corrected in CB. And in "Phonemics 3," l. 1: "(distance sound)" appears to be corrected as "(distant sound)" in CB. (JSF 20)

BOOK OF MAGAZINE VERSE (p. 403). CB used as copytext. First published by WRP (San Francisco 1966). The cover design by Graham Mackintosh and

Stan Persky simulated an early issue of *Poetry* magazine. The paper for each section of the book was chosen to simulate that of the magazine to which the poems were directed. The original edition carried this acknowledgment note:

> None of the poems in this book have been published in magazines. The author wishes to acknowledge the rejection of poems herein by editors Denise Levertov of *The Nation* and Henry Rago of *Poetry* (Chicago).

Blaser notes in CB: "Poem 1 of 'Two Poems for *The Nation*' and poem 2 of 'Six Poems for *Poetry* Chicago' are the same. This curious duplication seems to have been an instance of word for word dictation of the same poem some days apart. Jack did not know he had duplicated a poem until he read the poem to Stan Persky and me and we pointed it out. He looked surprised, checked them, and said that was the way they had to stand" (CB 380). (JSF 20)

BIBLIOGRAPHY

Spicer's Books

After Lorca (San Francisco: White Rabbit Press, 1957). Cover by Jess.

Homage to Creeley (Annapolis, CA: privately printed by Harold and Dora Dull, 1959).

Billy The Kid (Stinson Beach, CA: Enkidu Surrogate, 1959). Cover and illus. by Jess.

The Heads of the Town Up to the Aether (San Francisco: The Auerhahn Society, 1962). With lithographs by Fran Herndon.

Lament for the Makers (Oakland: White Rabbit Press, 1962). Cover collage by Graham Mackintosh.

The Holy Grail (San Francisco: White Rabbit Press, 1964). With decorative lettering by Graham Mackintosh.

[With Lawrence Ferlinghetti] *Dear Jack: The Spicer/Ferlinghetti Correspondence* (San Francisco: White Rabbit Press, 1964).

Language (San Francisco: White Rabbit Press, 1965).

Selected Posthumous Publications of Spicer's Work

Book of Magazine Verse (San Francisco: White Rabbit Press, 1966). Design by Graham Mackintosh and Stan Persky.

A Book of Music (San Francisco: White Rabbit Press, 1969). Illus. by Graham Mackintosh.

The [sic] *Red Wheelbarrow* (Berkeley: Arif, 1971).

Admonitions (New York: Adventures in Poetry, 1974).

[With Robert Duncan] *An Ode and Arcadia* (Berkeley: Ark Press, 1974). With an introduction by F. J. Cebulski.

Fifteen False Propositions About [sic] *God* (San Francisco: ManRoot Books, 1974).

The Collected Books of Jack Spicer, edited and with an afterword by Robin Blaser (Los Angeles: Black Sparrow Press, 1975).

One Night Stand & Other Poems, ed. Donald Allen (San Francisco: Grey Fox Press, 1980). With an introduction by Robert Duncan.

Collected Poems, 1945–1946 (Berkeley: Oyez/White Rabbit Press, 1981).

The Tower of Babel: Jack Spicer's Detective Novel, eds. Lewis Ellingham and Kevin Killian (Hoboken, NJ: Talisman House, 1994).

The House That Jack Built: The Collected Lectures of Jack Spicer, edited and with an afterword by Peter Gizzi (Hanover and London: Wesleyan University Press, 1998).

Golem (New York: Granary Books, 1999). With color collages by Fran Herndon and an afterword by Kevin Killian.

Map Poems (Berkeley: Bancroft Library, 2005). With facsimiles of California roadmaps and an introduction by Peter Gizzi and Kevin Killian.

About Spicer's Life

Jack Spicer, by Edward Halsey Foster (Boise, Idaho: Boise State University, 1991).

Poet Be Like God: Jack Spicer and the Berkeley Renaissance, by Lewis Ellingham and Kevin Killian (Hanover and London: Wesleyan University Press, 1998).

INDEX OF TITLES

INDEX OF FIRST LINES

ABOUT THE AUTHOR AND EDITORS

Jack Spicer was born in Los Angeles in 1925. He moved north to attend the University of California, Berkeley, where he became friends with Robin Blaser and Robert Duncan, among other poets, artists, and scholars who were part of the San Francisco scene. He died in 1965. During his short but prolific life, he published many books of poems through small presses, including *After Lorca* (1957), *Billy the Kid* (1958), and *The Holy Grail* (1962).

Peter Gizzi is a poet whose recent books include *The Outernationale* (2007) and *Some Values of Landscape and Weather* (2003); he is also the editor of *The House That Jack Built: The Collected Lectures of Jack Spicer* (1998), all published by Wesleyan. He teaches at the University of Massachusetts, Amherst.

Kevin Killian is a poet, novelist, critic, and playwright. He is the co-author of *Poet Be Like God: Jack Spicer and the San Francisco Renaissance* (Wesleyan University Press, 1998), and the author of a book of poetry, *Argento Series* (2001), two novels, *Shy* (1989) and *Arctic Summer* (1997), a book of memoirs, *Bedrooms Have Windows* (1989), and two books of stories, *Little Men* (1996) and *I Cry Like a Baby* (2001).